# RENT CONTROL:
## A SOURCE BOOK

# RENT CONTROL:
# A SOURCE BOOK

## John Gilderbloom
## and friends

FOUNDATION FOR NATIONAL PROGRESS
HOUSING INFORMATION CENTER

**RENT CONTROL: A SOURCE BOOK**
**By John Gilderbloom and friends**

Third Edition copyright 1981 by John Ingram Gilderbloom. All rights reserved.

**ISBN 0-938806-01-7**

**Library of Congress Catalogue Card Number: 80-70624**

**Foundation for National Progress,**
**Housing Information Center**
**P.O. Box 3396**
**Santa Barbara, California 93105**

for
my Dad
and Ron Atlas

# Acknowledgments

I would like to thank a number of people and organizations who were instrumental in putting together this book: Derek Shearer came up with the idea of putting together this book. Grants from the Shalan Foundation, W.H. Ferry and Seed Fund over the past 4 years provided the financial assistance needed to do the research and write up the results; the grants also gave me the assistance needed to collect and edit the other articles in this reader. I would also like to thank Stanley Sheinbaum, Mary Ann Mott, Sunflower Foundation, W.H. Ferry and my father who graciously supplied the funds necessary to typeset, design, proofread, print and distribute this book. Ann Olson of Swede Press and Wendy Thermos of the University of California, Santa Barbara, publications department were responsible for book production and design. Karen Shapiro designed the cover of the book. The articles were proofread by Rebecca Levy, Don Combs, Jason Strum, Neal Linson, David Engel and Patricia Fowler. Grace Fong Tam, Robert Rosenthal, Noel Young, Maureen Harrington De Vivas, Steven Mustafa Skelly, Louise Kollenbaum, Dian-Aziza Ooka, Chester Hartman, Peter Dreier, Dan Poynter, Tim Siegel and Patricia Fowler made important suggestions as to the style and content of the book. Both Robin Evans and Elizabeth Goldstein of the Foundation for National Progress provided crucial technical assistance. Thanks also to Mark Dowie for opening many doors. And lastly I would like to warmly thank Patricia Fowler who gave me lots of support, encouragement and feedback in the overall production of this book.

John Gilderbloom

# Introduction

A renters revolt has swept across the nation. Close to 120 municipalities have enacted some form of rent control during the past decade. Approximately 100 other cities are now considering some form of rent control to put the brakes on runaway housing costs. As the housing crisis gets worse, rent control is becoming one of the big issues of the 80's. It will rival the Civil Rights movement of the 60's in both scope and intensity. The battle will be one of human rights versus property rights.

Rent control is a viable step toward solving the rental housing crisis. It means an end to exorbitant rent increases, better maintenance and code enforcement, and protection against unfair evictions. Rent control is needed because the private market has worked to *create* rather than *solve* the housing crisis. The housing crisis can be solved only by government intervention that *challenges* rather than *accommodates* the special interests of powerful bankers, landlords, and developers. Rent control does just this.

This book is for the individual who wants to know the ABC's of rent control — how to write a model rent control law, how to get it passed, how to administer it and how it will affect the housing stock. The reader also explains the economics of income property, reasons for the rental housing crisis and innovative housing programs beyond rent control. In addition, a bibliography of essential books, newsletters, legal and tenant organizations is provided.

The need for an authoritative book on rent control is great. Tenant leaders and government officials have no manual on the nuts and bolts of rent control. This book attempts to fulfill this need.

## Section I

If we are to understand the housing crisis it is imperative that we understand the dimensions of the rental housing crisis. According to a recent study by the Comptroller General, close to one half of the nation's tenants are paying an excessive amount of their incomes on rent. Moreover, the report finds that in certain cities there exists no *affordable housing for low to moderate income persons.* As a result, many tenants are forced to choose between paying for decent food, clothing and health care, or paying rent. The high cost of renting can, therefore, be a cause of tenant impoverishment. But this need not be the case.

## Section II

So what are the causes of this rental housing crisis? Rents are not going up simply because the vacancy rate is low. It's much more complex than that. Rents are high because of collusion among landlords, interest rates increases by banks, and speculation in the market. Competition in the private rental market is almost dead. The reader argues that in certain cases management companies or apartment associations controlling a large proportion of the community's housing stock will set "bottom line" rent increases. The cost of housing increases dramatically when banks raise interest rates on mortgages. When interest rates are raised just 1% (from 8 ½ % to 9 ½ %) on a $40,000 thirty year mortgage, an additional $11,000 in interest payments results. Put another way, that same mortgage in 1965 at 5% entails monthly payments of $215; in 1970 at 10% the same mortgage would cost $350; in 1979 at 14% the monthly mortgage would be almost $500. When a housing unit is sold and is refinanced under higher interest payments terms, the cost of renting that unit soars. And since landlords charge what the "market will bear", an increase in rents can have a "ripple effect" of pulling rents up in neighboring units. This problem is especially acute when speculators are operating in the market, continually turning over property.

## Section III

Rent control is needed to correct the private market's failure to provide affordable and decent housing. Rent control means greater equity between landlord and tenant. With the passage of rent control legislation, no longer can a small percentage of the population (landlords) determine rent levels. Instead, tenants, landlords, and homeowners comprising a community rent control board will determine rent levels. Under most rent control systems rents are not frozen, but are allowed to rise to cover increases in operating costs and guarantee a landlord a fair and reasonable return on investment. These "moderate" rent control systems provide tenants with protection against exorbitant rent increases. In addition, tenants are protected against poor maintenance and code violations as rent control boards have the power to tie allowable rent increases to the quality of housing. Tenants are also given protection against arbitrary evictions from their rental units. Without rent control, tenants do not have these protections; landlords are virtually free to do as they please to their "second class citizens."

## Section IV

The types of rent control laws are as varied as the kinds of cars on the road — some work, some don't. In certain cases rent control laws have caused maintenance and housing starts to fall dramatically. Still in other cases, tenants have written rent control laws that have later been thrown out by the courts. This section is designed to avoid these problems. Several different types of rent control laws are explained including the pros and cons of each. Rent control can be designed just to limit increases, or it can be a comprehensive housing program of speculation controls, condominium controls, just-cause eviction protection, maintenance and capital improvement incentives, as well as public and cooperative housing programs. This section also addresses the question: Who should be exempt from controls? How much should rents be allowed to increase? How is rent control administered? These questions are discussed from a variety of viewpoints. It is safe to say that there exists no single rent control law fit for every city; rent regulations differ because of each municipality's unique political and historical situation. Compromises of one kind or another often have to be made in order to get the kind of support necessary to enact rent ceilings. What's acceptable in Santa Monica might be completely unacceptable in neighboring Los Angeles. In the end, citizens must decide how to write a rent control law that is both workable and politically feasible.

## Section V

Writing a workable rent control law is one thing; getting it passed is another story. Some argue that rent control can only pass when the majority of voters are tenants. While having lots of tenants who are voters certainly helps, it is not necessarily the case that rent control won't pass if tenants are a minority. In fact, a number of east coast cities have passed rent control even though tenants make up less than 10% of the municipalities' population. The key to getting rent control passed is a good campaign strategy. Peter Dreier and Cary Lowe give an overview of the national movement for rent control — its victories, its defeats. A case study is then made of the recent rent control referendum victories in Baltimore and Santa Monica, focusing specifically on the kind of campaign propaganda used by both sides. It is shown that tenants can be outspent 10 to 1 by real estate interests and still come out with a campaign victory.

## Section VI

Once rent control is law, what other workable programs can be introduced by housing activists? This section attempts to give a brief inventory of workable programs that can be enacted on national, state, and local levels. Tenants must be educated to know that fighting for controls on interest rates, speculation, condominium conversion and demolitions can be just as significant as battling for rent ceilings. Moreover, beyond just legislation aimed at giving the renter more rights, we must also look to programs that provide tenants with the opportunity of owning his/her own house. Limited equity cooperative housing is one such viable and workable program that needs to be pushed on a massive scale. The appendix lists important books, newsletters, organizations and legal organizations that might be of assistance in organizing for decent and affordable housing.

But before anything will happen, tenants must organize politically. Rent control is an issue around which tenants are organizing into a growing political force. From New York to California, from Texas to Michigan, tenants are asserting their right to safe, decent and affordable housing, by calling for "less rent, more control."

# Contents

*XI*

# Section IV: How To Write A Rent Control Law...........................**107**

*XIV*

# SECTION I

# UNDERSTANDING THE RENTAL HOUSING CRISIS

# Lamenting the Rent

## PETER BARNES

Like some 25 million other heads of households in the United States, I must pay monthly tribute to an absentee landlord for the privilege of having a roof over my head. That tribute is no trifling sum: it amounts to about one quarter of my income. Part of it covers the legitimate cost of constructing and maintaining the building I live in, and I have no complaint about that. But a good-sized portion is profit for banks, insurance companies, real estate agents and present and past landlords.

My fellow renters are disproportionately poor, young and dark-skinned. In 1969, according to the US Census, the median household income for renters was $6300; for homeowners it was $9700. Three out of four married couples under 25 years of age are renters, as are nearly 60 percent of non-whites (compared to 35 percent of whites all ages). The renters' handicap is that they haven't inherited or amassed enough capital to lift themselves out of the status of tenancy. For this they are doubly punished: their housing is generally older and of poorer quality than that of nonrenters, and they must disproportionately subsidize the income of landlords, bankers, brokers and insurers — those whom I call real estate parasites.

By contrast to the renter, the homeowner is able to cut down his losses to the parasites. True, he generally pays for his house twice over, once for the property itself and again for the money to buy the property. In this sense banks are really landlords to us all: everyone must pay a tithe to the money-lenders for a roof over his head. The homeowner is also absurdly socked by title insurance companies, which collect several hundred dollars for reinsuring the same title they verified for a string of previous owners. But the homeowner gets some breaks that the renter doesn't. He can deduct from his federal and state income taxes the tithe paid to money-lenders. And he can recoup a good part of the tithe when he sells his house later, just as the

16

person who buys from him can recoup from the next buyer, and so on until and even after the building crumbles.

The people who fare best of all are not those who own their homes, but those who own the homes of others. They too must pay a tithe to the money-lenders, but unlike the homeowner they are able to recoup the entire amount of the tithe — and then some — not at some future date but every month when the rent checks come in. Typically about 40 percent of a tenant's rent goes to pay the landlord's financing costs. Another one-fifth to one-fourth goes for property taxes, and about one-third covers upkeep, management and other costs. The rest is the landlord's monthly profit, which is not to be confused with the gain he collects when he sells or refinances the building, or with the tax shelter benefits he receives from depreciation and interest write-offs. If inflation starts to gallop it doesn't hurt the landlord: he can raise rents and cut back services while his financing costs remain constant, and he reaps a larger capital gain in the end.

The renters' burden is increased when buildings are resold or refinanced. For reasons that will be explained in a moment, landlords generally don't like to hold a property for too long; they prefer to sell old holdings and acquire others. Each time a new landlord buys a building, he borrows money to pay off the previous landlord. Since the price of the building will have risen, and interest rates most likely will have risen too, the financing costs of the new landlord will be higher than those of the old landlord. Each sale also means a six or seven percent commission for a real estate agent and another round of closing costs and title insurance fees. All these added costs are no problem for the new landlord: he raises rents, which accounts for the seemingly illogical fact that rents in old buildings don't decrease after construction costs are paid off. Rents increase because the same old building can be resold a dozen times, providing succor for generation after generation of parasites.

Much the same result comes about when a landlord refinances rather than sells a building. Refinancing works like this. Suppose a landlord buys a building for $100,000 with $20,000 down and an $80,000 loan. After several years the building is worth $120,000 and the principal outstanding on the loan has been reduced to $60,000 thanks to the tenants' monthly rent checks. The landlord then refinances the building by taking out a new mortgage, say, for $100,000. He pays off the $60,000 still left on the old loan and pockets the $40,000, in effect cashing in the equity his tenants built up for him, plus part of the gain from the building's rise in value. Wondrously, he pays no capital gains tax on the $40,000 because it is in the form of a loan rather than the proceeds from a sale. And because he still owns the building, he continues to receive his month-to-month profits and retains title to future appreciations in value. The only problem is that he must make higher payments on his new, larger loan, but again this is easily solved by raising rents.

The government adds injury to insult through its lopsided tax laws. Consider first the local property tax, which is largely passed on to renters by landlords. A family paying $200 a month to its landlord is probably paying $40 or more in property taxes. So the actual rent is $160, with a "sales tax" of $40, or 25 percent, tacked on. No other commodity sold in the United States, with the possible exception of cigarettes, liquor and gasoline, carries such a heavy tax add-on. It's regressive since low-income people spend a higher proportion of their incomes on housing than the well-to-do. Several states have tried to lessen the regressivity of the property tax as it affects homeowners by granting partial exemptions or "circuit-breaker" relief in the form of income tax reduction or rebates. But only California, Michigan and Vermont give similar property tax relief to non-elderly renters, and even in these states the renters' relief is small compared to homeowners.

The federal income tax discriminates against tenants by allowing homeowners, but not renters, to deduct that portion of their housing costs attributable to mortgage interest and local property taxes. This is an enormous subsidy and increases with the owner's income. According to the Tax Reform Group, the average $7000-a-year homeowner in 1972 saved $20 thanks to these deductions; the average $100,000-a-year homeowner saved $2500.

Another tax subsidy for owners is the low rent at which profits from the sale of housing are taxed. Landlords pay the capital gains rate — half that at which renters' wages are taxed. Homeowners pay no capital gains tax if they buy a new house within one year. The renter's effective income tax rate is several percentage points higher because of these preferences to owners.

Perhaps the juiciest break for absentee landlords is the deductibility of depreciation on properties that increase in value over time because the land beneath them rises, as does the cost of constructing new housing. The tax laws nevertheless permit landlords to deduct from taxable income a fictitious and, in the early years of ownership, substantial amount of depreciation. What's more, a non-depreciating property can be depreciated not just once but several times, with each successive landlord getting his chance to play the game. This is one reason real estate is such an attractive tax shelter for the wealthy. It's also a major cause of housing resales, and thus of rising rents.

Consider what happens after Landlord A buys a large apartment house and enjoys its hefty depreciation and interest deductions for several years. (Like depreciation deductions, interest deductions are concentrated in the early years of ownership because loan repayments contain more interest than principal at first.) When Landlord A's tax deductions drop too low, he sells the building for a capital gain to Landlord B, who begins his own top-heavy sequence of depreciation and interest deductions. Landlord A in turn uses his profits to buy another building on which he can get those juicy front-end deductions once again, and both landlords raise rents to cover the higher financing costs of their new loans. About half the annual investment in real estate goes into buying or refinancing existing buildings, rather than into putting up new ones. If resale and refinancing were discouraged instead of encouraged by the tax laws, there'd be more new housing built, and rents would be lower.

The federal government has made several efforts to aid renters. Loan guarantee programs of the Federal Housing Administration and the Veterans Administration have reduced the amount of savings needed to escape from tenancy. Low-rent public housing and publicly subsidized private housing have provided shelter for many, and direct rent subsidies have helped others to live in landlord-owned units that they otherwise could not afford. But contrast these federal approaches with housing policy in Scandinavia and other western European countries. There, the effort has been to reduce the subsidies renters pay to real estate parasites, rather than to subsidize those subsidies with government handouts. It has been done by rent control, municipal ownership of land; cooperative nonprofit ownership of housing, and so-called index loans in which financing costs, instead of being fixed for the entire term of a mortgage, are low initially and rise only at the rate of the cost of living or other price indices.

For the moment, however, true co-ops — not to be confused with condominiums — are a rarity, as are rent control, index loans and other arrangements that might reduce the profits made by landlords

forking over those maddening monthly tributes. We may join tenant
unions and otherwise protest, but the laws of the market and the state
are stacked against us.

# Rental Housing: A National Problem That Needs Immediate Attention

## COMPTROLLER GENERAL
## (GENERAL ACCOUNTING OFFICE)

### LOWER INCOME FAMILIES SEVERELY AFFECTED BY LACK OF AFFORDABLE RENTAL UNITS

Lower income families are finding it increasingly difficult to locate affordable rental housing. The national rental vacancy rate has been declining since 1974. The March 31, 1979 rental vacancy rate of 4.8 percent was the lowest rate since the Bureau of the Census began collecting the information. Families needing larger units are finding it more difficult to locate suitable housing because the national vacancy rate is 3.8 percent for housing units with 5 rooms and 2.8 percent for those with 6 or more rooms. In addition to the low vacancy rates, many renters are paying excessive portions of their incomes for rents. For example, in 1977, 7.4 million renters were paying more than 35 percent of their income for rent. About 86 percent of these renters had annual incomes of less than $7,000.

A number of factors have combined to adversely affect renters in general and lower income renters in particular. For a number of years, renter incomes have not kept pace with rent increases; operating costs for rental housing have increased significantly in recent years; fewer new private rental units have been built in recent years; and abandonments and conversions of rental units to condominiums have further limited the number of affordable rental units. At the same time, rapidly increasing cost of homeownership has meant that more families must depend on rental housing in the future. Each of these factors will be addressed in this report.

## LOW VACANCY RATE IN RENTAL HOUSING

National rental housing vacancy rates during 1978 were about 5 percent and declined to 4.8 percent during the first quarter of 1979, according to the Bureau of the Census. The rate has been declining since 1974, and the 1978 rate is the lowest annual rate since the Census began the vacancy survey in 1956. HUD has acknowledged that the vacancy rate of 5 percent is dangerously low because it interferes with the Nation's mobility possibilities.

The March 31, 1979, national rental housing vacancy rate was 4.8 percent but varied from region to region.

| Region | Percentage vacancy rate |
|---|---|
| Northeast | 4.0 |
| West | 4.5 |
| North Central | 5.0 |
| South | 5.5 |

As shown above, renters in the Northeast and West are likely to have more difficulty finding suitable rental units.

At the time of our review, the rental market in metropolitan Minneapolis-St. Paul was said by HUD officials to be quite tight with a vacancy rate of about 3 percent. The shortage of units affordable by lower income renters was particularly acute, however, with vacancy rates estimated to be about 1 percent. Metropolitan Atlanta was also experiencing a low rental vacancy rate of about 2.3 percent.

The vacancy rate in the Seattle metropolitan area dipped below 2 percent in 1977 and remained near the 2-percent level during 1978. We were informed by several knowledgeable officials that lower income families are most adversely affected by the area's tight rental market.

Another indication of the tight supply is the rate at which newly constructed rental units are rented. According to Bureau of the Census statistics, 80 percent of the privately financed apartments completed during 1977 were rented within 3 months. Apartments on the market for 6 months were 94 percent rented.

The 3- and 6- month rented rates tend to be higher for lower rent units than for higher rent units. This indicates that the supply of units affordable by lower income households is extremely tight and, consequently, they are rented more quickly.

## LOWER INCOME FAMILIES ARE MOST AFFECTED BY CURRENT RENTAL SITUATION

Lower income households are finding it increasingly difficult to locate affordable rental units. A combination of factors is rapidly creating a crisis situation for lower income households. First, the rapidly increasing cost of homeownership means that fewer lower income families will become homeowners and thus must depend on rental housing. Second, while median rents have increased by an average of 9.6 percent annually (1973-77), renter income has only increased 5.6 percent annually.

### Limited potential for many renters to be homeowners

Renters, by and large, have lower incomes than homeowners. Although the annual median incomes of all housing occupants have increased since 1973, the increase for renters has been much less than the increase for homeowners. The following graph, based on Annual Housing Survey data, illustrates this trend.

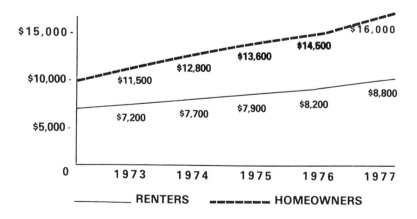

As shown, while the median income of renters rose from $7,200 to $8,800 (an average annual increase of 5.6 percent), the median income of homeowners increased from $11,500 to $16,000 (an average incease of 9.8 percent per year). More significantly, the median income of renters in 1977 ($8,800) was 55 percent that of homeowners ($16,000).

According to Annual Housing Survey data for Atlanta, Minneapolis-St. Paul, and Seattle, annual median incomes of renters were $9,000 (versus $17,500 for homeowners), $7,900 (versus $16,100 for homeowners), and $9,100 (versus $18,000 for home-owners), respectively.

The lower income characteristic of renters is further reflected by the table below:

| Annual income | Number of homeowners (000 omitted) | Percent | Number of renters (000 omitted) | Percent |
|---|---|---|---|---|
| Less than $7,000 | 9,469 | 19.4 | 10,723 | 40.4 |
| $7,000 to $9,999 | 4,797 | 9.8 | 4,232 | 16.0 |
| $10,000 to $14,999 | 8,571 | 17.6 | 5,328 | 20.1 |
| $15,000 or more | 25,929 | 53.2 | 6,232 | 23.5 |
| Total | **48,766** | 100.0 | **26,515** | 100.0 |

According to the table, about 30 percent of the homeowners in 1977 had annual incomes of less than $10,000, while approximately 56 percent of renters had similar incomes. Further analysis of related data showed that of the homeowners with annual incomes of less than $10,000, about 64 percent owned their homes free and clear and thus were relieved of mortgage payments.

Given their low incomes, renters are also negatively affected by the rising cost of homeownership, which forces them to rely primarily on the rental market for housing. For example, homeownership costs by 1976 had reached the point that a monthly expenditure of $465 was required to amortize the mortgage principal and pay the mortgage interest, insurance premiums, property taxes, utility costs, and repair and maintenance expenses on a median price new house which sold for about $44,300. The annual median income for the homebuyers was $21,600 compared to the annual median income for renters of $8,800. In 1976 families with incomes of less than $10,000 accounted for only 4 percent of the single-family housing purchases. Renters' opportunity to become homeowners has been reduced even more since the median sales price of new houses rose to $62,900 in May 1979 — a 42-percent increase since 1976. Likewise, the median sales price of existing homes has increased rapidly to $57,400 in April 1979 — a 13.5-percent increase since April 1978.

The dramatic rise in the selling price and related homeownership costs is putting an increasing number of American families out of the new housing market. Second- and third-time buyers can afford substantial downpayments and prefer large houses with many amenities but new houses are less affordable for younger, middle-income families and first-time buyers. For more information on the cost of housing and homeownership see our report, "Why Are New House Prices So High, How Are They Influenced By Government Regulations, and Can Prices Be Reduced?" (CED-78-101, May 11, 1978).

### The increasing burden of rents

In 1977 about 49 percent of all renters paid 25 percent or more of their income for rent. About 30 percent of all the renters paid 35 percent or more of their income for rent. Since 1970, renters' rent to income ratio has steadily increased. During the period 1970-77, median gross rent as a percentage of income has increased from 20 to 25 percent. The generally accepted rule of thumb is that rent should not be more than 25 percent of a family's income. The following schedule shows the increased number of renters paying 25 percent of their annual income for rent in 1977 compared to 1973.

| | 1 9 7 3 | | 1 9 7 7 | |
|---|---|---|---|---|
| **Number of renters for which data was computed** | 22,438,000 | | 24,365,000 | |
| **Gross Rent as percentage of income** | **Number renters (millions)** | **Percent** | **Number renters (millions)** | **Percent** |
| 25 to 34 percent | 3.7 | 16.5 | 4.5 | 18.4 |
| 35 percent or more | 5.5 | 24.4 | 7.4 | 30.3 |
| Total | **9.2** | 40.9 | **11.9** | 48.7 |

The number of renters paying 35 percent or more of their income for rent has increased by about 1.9 million (or 35 percent) during the 1973-77 period. Of the 7.4 million renters paying 35 percent or more of their income for rent, 4.2 million (or about 57 percent) paid more than 50 percent of their income for rent. Of the 7.4 million renters paying 35 percent or more, about 86 percent had annual incomes of less than $7,000.

The latest data available for Atlanta, Minneapolis-St. Paul, and Seattle indicates rent-to-income ratios similar to the national statistics. In terms of the percentage of renters paying 25 percent or more of income for rent, 42 percent (1975 data) of Atlanta renters, 50 percent (1974 data) of Minneapolis - St. Paul renters, and 44 percent (1976 data) of Seattle renters fall into this category.

According to HUD, these statistics are clear indications of the increasing burden of rents on renter hosueholds. Also, although homeownership costs are also increasing, they are partially offset by favorable tax provisions and by equity appreciation from inflation. With none of these benefits, renters are faced with allocating more of their income for rents.

During our field work, we obtained various reports and other documentation attesting to the severe effect of the rental housing situation on lower income renters.

The Seattle Emergency Housing Service's March 1978 report entitled "Survey of Affordable Rental Housing for Low Income Families" disclosed the following:

— There are virtually no suitable private market apartment units for low and moderate-income families in Seattle.

— Low-income families are forced to reside in substandard, neglected dwellings. Unable to compete in the standard rental and homeowner market, this is all that is available to them.

In its May 1978 report entitled "Emergency Housing in King County" (Seattle), the Emergency Housing Task Force stated that:

— Both low-income working families and public assistance families face increasing difficulty renting in the commercial market due to the disparity between their income and rental rates and the increasing bias against renting to families with children.

— The severe shortage of low-cost housing makes it extremely difficult for a low-income person or family to locate affordable housing.

In Minneapolis, a Rental Housing Task Force concluded in its July 1976 report, "The Crisis in Rental Housing," that "The average tenant in Minneapolis is already paying too much for rental housing and cannot afford any increases, even if justified, and the situation is worsening." In March 1978, HUD's Minneapolis-St. Paul area office estimated that 57,459 lower income renter households needed housing assistance.

The city of Atlanta estimated in January 1979 that 63,376 renter households were in need of housing assistance. Of these households, 62 percent were spending more than a quarter of their income for rent, 29 percent were living in substandard housing, and 9 percent were living in overcrowded conditions.

A large number of American families are facing serious problems in finding affordable rental housing. We believe that the rental housing situation, particularly in terms of low vacancy rates and escalating operating costs, will grow more severe and will create problems for a growing number of American families.

## FEWER AFFORDABLE RENTAL UNITS FOR LOWER IN-COME FAMILIES

There is little privately financed, multifamily rental housing being constructed nationwide for lower income families. According to an official of Citicorp Real Estate, Inc., starts of unsubsidized rental units during 1978 were the second lowest (1975 was lower) in 20 years. At the same time, increased operating and maintenance costs in rental housing contributed to a rising trend toward abandonment, foreclosure, and conversions to condominiums . According to HUD's Tenth Annual Report on the National Housing Goals (February 1979), during the period 1973-76, about 1.1 million renter-occupied housing units were removed from the inventory.

Various reasons are cited for the declining private rental housing market, including high costs of construction, land, financing, and insufficient rents. When discussing the situation, nearly every official contacted told us that at the current market rent level, privately financed rental units were not profitable. HUD's Task Force on Housing Costs commented on the problem in its May 1978 final report, stating that "in many areas both new and rehabilitated rental housing are becoming commercially infeasible without subsidies."

## FEW UNSUBSIDIZED RENTAL UNITS ARE BEING CONSTRUCTED FOR THE LOWER INCOME

Officials we contacted unanimously stated that costs have increased dramatically during the past few years, particularly in the areas of financing, building materials, labor, and land. These cost increases, coupled with lagging rents and rapidly escalating operating costs, have created a situation where privately financed, multifamily rental housing is no longer considered a viable investment. Although rents have increased, the increases have not kept pace with the increased cost of constructing, financing, and operating rental housing. Most officials told us that they had diverted their efforts to more profitable ventures, such as condominiums, single-family homes, commercial properties, and warehouses. According to a Joint Economic Committee report of November 1978 entitled "Multifamily Housing Demand: 1975-2000,"

> "sophisticated investors view the multifamily structure,
> except under unique circumstances and unique locations,
> as a relatively riskful, noninflation proof investment."

The lagging rents were mostly attributed to the overbuilding of rental units that occurred in the early 1970s, which resulted in high vacancy rates and owner's reluctance to raise rents because of the risk of losing tenants. The Brookings Institution's 1978 report entitled "Public Policy and the Rising Cost of Housing" stated that "rents have not gone up fast enough to keep up with the cost of ownership." The study also concluded that rental housing owners have been precluded from raising rents, despite soaring operating costs, because of the significant number of rental units on the market from 1970-73.

According to a January 1979 HUD analysis of the Minneapolis-St. Paul housing market, the striking decline in multifamily production is due to a number of factors and the "current high interest rates and costs of production and management also make many rental projects economically unfeasible."

Our discussions with knowledgeable officials disclosed that the majority of the multifamily housing units current being built are either

**Unfurnished Units Completed by Rent Class: 1970-77 (note a)**

Units by monthly rent

| Year | Units completed | Less than $200 | $200 to $245 | $250 or more | Median rent |
|---|---|---|---|---|---|
| 1970 | 322,700 | 199,300 | 78,700 | 44,700 | $188 |
| 1971 | 333,200 | 211,900 | 82,900 | 38,400 | 187 |
| 1972 | 498,000 | 293,000 | 133,500 | 71,500 | 191 |
| 1973 | 531,700 | 313,100 | 138,800 | 79,800 | 191 |
| 1974 | 405,700 | 216,900 | 111,400 | 77,400 | 197 |
| 1975 | 222,900 | 97,000 | 63,800 | 62,100 | 211 |
| 1976 | 157,000 | 56,200 | 56,900 | 43,900 | 219 |
| 1977 | 194,400 | 51,100 | 72,000 | 71,300 | 232 |
| 1978 | 227,900 | 42,000 | 71,400 | 114,500 | 250 |

a/Units are located in buildings with 5 units or more and are privately financed and unsubsidized.

(1) subsidized (2) high-rent, or (3) condominiums.

The high-rent characteristic of the new units is supported by the preceding Bureau of the Census table showing the units completed by rent levels during the period 1970-77.

As shown the median monthly rent for units completed in 1970 was $188 compared to $250 for 1978. In 1978, only 42,000 units (or 18 percent of the total completed) were at rent levels of $199 per month or less. Given the accepted rent to income ratio of 25 percent, these units would be affordable by families with annual incomes of about $9,500.

As mentioned earlier, median renter income in 1977 was $8,800, and about 46 percent of all renters earned less than $10,000.

A comparison of the Department of Labor's Bureau of Labor Statistics Consumer Price Index for 1973-77 supports the housing officials' concern over lagging rents. During that period, housing costs (shelter, household furnishings and operation, and fuel and utilities) increased an average of 8 percent per year, while rent increase averaged only 4.7 percent.

We measured the trend of rents in the Seattle area by comparing the area's residential rent index with the construction cost index and the market value index of a single-family for the periods 1979-78.

**According to various officials, market rents would have to increase about 25 percent above current levels in order to stimulate new investment in the private multifamily rental market.** Research by Goldman-Sachs (an investment banking firm) concluded that before it considered multifamily housing an approporiate investment for its clients, a 20- to 25-percent increase in rents would need to be established. Several officials cautioned, however, that such an increase in rents could result in a loss of tenants (and income) and the potential imposition of rent controls. From a tenant's point of view, such an increase in rents would act as an additional hardship on those households that are already paying an excessive portion of their income for rent.

We found that apartment owners in Atlanta are taking advantage of the tight rental occupancy conditions to boost rents between 10 and 20 percent annually and/or transfer utilities from owner-paid to tenant-paid. Rents in Minneapolis-St. Paul have risen about 8 to 10 percent per year since 1976. According to the local HUD area offices, landlords are being cautious about raising rents significantly; however, the current shortage of units has enabled landlords to become increasingly more selective in renting. For

30

example, many landlords are renting only to adult households with no children.

Officials mentioned other factors that discouraged construction of new rental units, such as (1) the threat of future rent controls, (2) tenant and community activism, (3) increasing land costs and real estate taxes, (4) new and costly codes and regulations, and (5) the existence of other, more profitable investment opportunities...

## CONDOMINIUM CONVERSIONS

We found few sources of national data regarding the extent of apartments being converted to condominiums. Unlike other national housing indicators which are followed closely, condominium conversions have not been adequately measured. During 1978 about 100,000 rental units were estimated to be converted to condominiums and for 1979 another 130,000 units are expected to be converted.

Condominium conversion has become popular in Minneapolis-St. Paul since 1976, with about 5,000 rental units already converted and up to an estimated 3,000 units in the process of being converted as of December 1978. HUD's Minneapolis-St. Paul area office attributes the area's shortage of rental units to limited rental construction and to condominium conversions. HUD also recognized that condominium apartments may continue to be initiated as rental apartments because of the greater availability of government financing under existing market rental rate programs. HUD realizes that many of these rental apartments are intended for conversion to condominium units shortly upon completion of construction. Further, if this trend continues, HUD believes that annual losses of rental units through conversions will outstrip units being added through private construction.

One developer in Minneapolis told us that he has stopped building new rental housing and is now purchasing apartment buildings to be converted into condominiums. At the time of our review, he had already converted 844 units and was in the process of converting an additional 250 units.

During 1977 and 1978, the metropolitan Seattle area experienced a significant increase in the number of rental units being converted to condominium units — about 6,574 rental units were converted. Although these lost units represented only a small portion of the rental housing inventory, many of them had previously served lower income families. To determine the effect of condominium conversions on low-and moderate-income households, the city of Seattle studied all condominium conversions that had taken place in the city up to July 1, 1978. The study showed that condominium conversions were beginning to affect the housing supply available to low-and moderate-income households in Seattle. This finding was based on the fact that of 672 units converted in 1977-78 with prior rent data, a minimum of 56 percent had been rental units affordable by low-and moderate-income households. After conversion, about 88 percent of the units were no longer affordable for such households.

Although no reliable quantitative data regarding condominium conversions was obtained concerning metropolitan Atlanta, indications were that conversions have not been extensive in the past.

An April 1979 special release of "U.S Housing Markets" discussed the trend of conversions. The number of conversions in 1977 and 1978 was estimated to be 50,000 and 100,000, respectively, with 130,000 projected for 1979. Although three-quarters of the conversions occurred in seven major housing markets, the trend is supposedly broadening and becoming more significant elsewhere.

U.S. Housing Markets attributes the trend to (1) the increasing demand for homeownership, with its tax benefits and inflation hedge and (2) the fact that returns from rental ownership have been low — rent increases have not been able to keep pace with costs of operation — even in markets with very high occupancy. Also, the low return is even more evident in markets with rent control or the fear of it. It is reported that most apartment buildings are worth twice as much after conversion compared to continuing as rentals. The low return on rentals and the strength of the conversion market are seen as responsible for the fact that

> "many, perhaps most, new rentals are designed — and some even financed — as condos, with the goal of converting as soon as they have used up their tax shelter."

Low rates of return and rent control (or the threat thereof) were the primary reasons behind B.F. Saul Real Estate Investment Trust's recent decision to begin selling and converting its approximately 6,400 middle-income rental apartments to condominiums. We were told by a Trust official that annual rent increases of 20 to 25 percent for 3 consecutive years and annual pass-throughs of increased operating costs thereafter would be necessary to make the apartments attractive investments. Given the current rental market, however, such rent increases would be unreasonable and uncompetitive and would have resulted in tenant turnovers. The Trust official believes that their situation is not atypical and that other real estate investment trusts with apartment holdings are experiencing similar low returns. An Atlanta developer told us that as long as rents are held back, apartment owners would find conversions to be more lucrative.

The Joint Economic committee report of November 1978 views the increasing trend of conversions as an indication that private rental operators are reluctant to continue operations despite preferential tax legislation.

## ABANDONMENTS AND DEMOLITIONS

We found that accurate and reliable information regarding the extent and impact of abandonments and demolitions was not generally available. We cited this information in our report on housing abandonment (CED-78-126, Aug. 10, 1978) after sending questionnaires to the 201 largest U.S. cities to assess the significance of the abandonment problem. The report noted that available evidence indicates that housing abandonment is becoming a more serious problem across the nation. According to the report, 113 of the 149 cities responding to the questionnaire reported having housing abandonment problems to some degree. Of the cities included in our review, St. Paul considered the problem to be substantial, while Minneapolis considered the problem to be small. Atlanta and Seattle did not respond to our questionnaire.

A January 1979 report on a HUD-commissioned survey of abandonment in 230 declining U.S. cities reported observable levels of abandonment in 150 of the cities during 1978. A total of 259,505 dwelling units were reported to be abandoned in the 150 cities of which about 186,000 (or 71.7 percent) were multifamily units. Of these areas included in our review, HUD's survey found that 3,600 multifamily units were abandoned in Atlanta, 631 in Minneapolis-St. Paul, and 100 in Seattle.

Information gathered in Minneapolis-St. Paul and Seattle did not indicate that abandonment or demolitions were significant problems. During the period 1974-78, the city of Atlanta, however, lost about 6,600 housing units — about 2,030 through abandonment and approximately 4,570 through demolition. In addition, a city-sponsored study found that about 38,700 (or 32 percent) of Atlanta's renter-occupied housing units in 1977 were in some form of deterioration with about 4,100 of the units actually in a dilapidated condition.

*Excerpt reprinted from Comptroller General of the General Accounting Office, "Rental Housing: A National Problem that Needs Immediate Attention," November 8, 1979.*

# Consumer Price Index Rent Increases

## JOHN INGRAM GILDERBLOOM
## AND MIKE JACOB

The suggestion of rent increases matching increases in the "cost of living" has been thrown around frequently. Both statewide and local apartment owner groups have recommended to their members that rents be raised with the "cost of living", as measured by the Consumer Price Index (CPI) for all items.

In August, 1979, real estate interests groups launched an initiative drive in California requiring all rent control laws to allow landlords to raise rents annually according to the yearly percentage increase in the Consumer Price Index for all items.

To tenants, a CPI rent increase policy may seem attractive and further, may seem to be relief from a currently exploitative situation where some tenants are suffering 50%, 75%, 100% or greater rent increases.

Rent increases in line with the CPI seem, at first glance, a reasonable approach. The Consumer Price Indexes, after all, are measures of "inflation" in the costs of goods and services — so it seems that raising rents along with the costs of other items should be fair to everyone. If the "cost of living " goes up 12%, isn't it "fair" that rents also go up 12%? NO! A closer look at CPI rent increases reveals that such a policy can mean rent increases *far greater* than actual landlord cost increases. The reason is that ⅓ to ½ or more of landlords' costs are unaffected by inflation (Santa Monica Rent Control Board, 1979;2:Gilderbloom 1978; 14 Jacob, 1979;2).

With the exception of refinancing costs, mortgage payments are generally fixed, and therefore unaffected by increases in the "cost of living". Three studies (Sternlieb, 1974; 1975: Santa Monica Rent Control Board: 1979) examining the operating expenses of landlords show that increases in total costs are normally ½ of the CPI or less. This is particularly true in California, where under Proposition 13, property taxes are also unaffected by increases in the "cost of living". Property taxes increase at a rate of only 2% per year until a building is sold.

Data in a study done for the real estate industry by George Sternlieb (1974) illustrate that costs do not increase faster than ½ CPI. Sternlieb (1974:33) examined the operating expenses of 3893 non-rent controlled units in the greater Boston area. Total operating costs — including mortgage payments — rose approximately 6.85% between 1971 and 1973, an average of 3.43% per year. Meanwhile, the Consumer Price Index for all items in the Northeast rose 12.9% between 1971 and 1973, an average of 6.45% per year (Bureau of the Census, 1978:492). While landlords' costs were increasing an average of 3.43% a year the CPI for all items increased an average of 6.45% a year.

These findings are replicated in another study by Sternlieb (1975:III-4) examining rent-controlled apartments in Fort Lee, New Jersey. In this study, Sternlieb examined the operating expenses of 2,769 apartment units between 1972 and 1974. Total operating costs, including mortgage payments, increased approximately 10.92% over the two year period, or approximately 5.89% per year. The Consumer Price Index for all items during the same period increased about 11.65% a year. The figures show the increases in landlords' costs to be about ½ the CPI.

Using figures supplied by the Institute of Real Estate Management, the Santa Monica Rent Control Board estimated that landlords' costs in 1978 went up 4.68% over a 12-month period. But because of "recent increases in energy costs in Santa Monica", the Rent Control Board allowed a 5.25% rent increase for the year. This is in contrast to the 10.5% increase in the CPI between April 1978, and April 1979, in the Los Angeles/Long Beach/Anaheim area (Bureau of Labor Statistics, 1979:63). Moreover taking savings from Proposition 13 into consideration, the study showed total operating costs actually decreased over the 12-month period (Santa Monica Rent Control Board, 1979:3).

In essence, the data indicate that full CPI rent increases are excessive. The data show that rent increases of one-half CPI are sufficient to cover general cost increases of rental units.

It is no wonder real estate interests have proposed a

constitutional amendment in California which would force local rent controls to allow full CPI rent increases. This is especially significant since there is evidence that rents over the past ten years have lagged behind general consumer price increases (Bureau of the Census, 1978: 490-499). In the United States, the CPI for all items increased from a base of 100% in 1967 to 193.2% in May of 1978, while residential rents during the same period increased only to 162.2%. The implications of a landlord policy to raise rents according to the full CPI may mean even higher rent increases for many tenants than they have been experiencing.

### Notes

1. The question arises, what is the impact on cash-flow profits when rents are increased with the full CPI? The following illustrations are meant to display cost increases involved in landlording and the impact of CPI rent increases on cash flow (income taken in from rents, etc., versus expenses paid out). In no way should the illustration be construed to deal with actual profits in real estate. The major profits involved, which are not dealt with here, are appreciation (growth in value of the property over time), and depreciation tax savings.

A 24-unit building was listed for sale in the May, 1979, **Multiple Listing Service**, published by the Santa Barbara Board of Realtors. The price listed was $540,000. Under financing arrangements normal in early May, 1979 (20% downpayment, 10% interest, 30-year term), the monthly mortgage payments would be $3,781. (With current Federal Reserve policies, rates are currently much higher, and almost any interest-rate example is obsolete between calculation and final publication. However, the example serves adequately.)

Property taxes, under California's Proposition 13, will amount to 1% of reported purchase price, or $450 a month. The taxes will increase at a rate of 2% per year until the building is sold.

All other expenses - maintenance and repair, insurance, utilities, etc. - are listed in the MLS at $16,296 a year, or $1,358 a month.

The total monthly expenses at purchase are as follows:

### Total Monthly Expenses

| | |
|---|---|
| Mortgage | $3,791 |
| Taxes | 450 |
| Other | 1,358 |
| | |
| Total | $5,599 |

If the CPI increases over the next five years after purchase at 7%, 10%, 12% and 8%, and 9% and "other" expenses increase at these rates, while the mortgage remains fixed and taxes increase at a rate of 2% per year, the total monthly cost increases will be as follows (Year 0 is the year of purchase):

| Year | CPI Increase | Monthly Costs | %Increase from Previous Year |
|------|-------------|---------------|------------------------------|
| 0 | -- | $5,599 | -- |
| 1 | 7% | $5,703 | 1.85% |
| 2 | 10% | $5,957 | 2.70% |
| 3 | 12% | $6,058 | 3.43% |
| 4 | 8% | $6,211 | 2.52% |
| 5 | 9% | $6,395 | 2.96% |

Total costs are increased at a rate of about 1/3 CPI. If rents are charged that will just cover costs, the average rents will start at $233 a month, in the 24 unit building (rounded to the nearest dollar), and will increase by $33, or 14.16% over the five-year period. This can be compared with rent increases at the full CPI:

| Year | CPI Increase | Rents Covering Costs | Rents Raised with CPI |
|------|-------------|---------------------|----------------------|
| 0 | -- | $233 | $233 |
| 1 | 7% | $238 | $249 |
| 2 | 10 | $244 | $274 |
| 3 | 12% | $252 | $307 |
| 4 | 8% | $259 | $332 |
| 5 | 9% | $266 | $362 |

The tenant forced to live with full CPI rent increases suffers $125 in rent increases over the 5 years, or 53.64%; the tenant paying increased costs has $33 rent increases, 14.16%.

The cash-flow profit for the landlord raising rents with CPI can be calculated by subtracting the total costs, listed above, from the total income. The figure is then annualized.

## Yearly Cash Flow Profits

| Year | Cash Flow Profit | % Increase from Previous Year |
|------|------------------|-------------------------------|
| 0 | -- | -- |
| 1 | $3,276 | (not calculable) |
| 2 | $8,628 | 163% |
| 3 | $15,720 | 82% |
| 4 | $21,084 | 34% |
| 5 | $27,516 | 31% |

By the fifth year of ownership, the cash flow rate of return on initial downpayment investment ($108,000), including compounding of cash profits from previous years, is 18%. The average cash flow return on initial investment during the period is $15,173, or 14%. Raising rents with the CPI allows for far greater returns in cash flow than can be obtained from most souces. And it need be remembered that the cash flow is *not even the major profit involved*. If, for example, the building appreciates in sales value along with the CPI, after five years it will have grown in value from $540,000 to $838,000, for a before-tax profit of $298,000. This is after the initial investment of $108,000, with the tenants paying all costs thereafter.

Lastly, it should be noted that this building, taken from the Multiple Listing Service, illustrates the *highest percentage* operating costs (24% "Other expenses") the authors could find in the publication. The higher the percentage of the operating costs, the greater the increase in total costs per year will be - since the operating costs go up with the CPI, while the mortage and taxes are either fixed or increase slowly. *The illustration then, is meant to show a generous estimate of increasing costs to owners.* Other examples were readily found in the MLS where the owner paid virtually no operating expenses except for the insurance. Calculated yearly cost increases in these cases amount to absurdly low figures - in the range of .5% per year. In these cases, any rent increases to cover costs are suspect.

2. In his Boston Study, Sternlieb (1974:33) found that operating expenses went up 13.7% in his non-controlled sample. But Sternlieb's estimation of percentage increases in rents and costs prove upon investigation to be erroneous and deceptive. The major problem is the failure to include mortgage payments in total expenses - payments

which comprise about ⅓ to ½ of the landlords' costs. The mortgage is generally fixed and unaffected by increases in the "cost of living" Including mortgage payments in total costs significantly reduces the alleged percentage increase in total expenses. If Sternlieb had included mortgage payments in computing total increases in expenses, he would have found that expenses in the non-rent controlled sample of Boston increased approximately 6.8% - a figure parallel to allowable rent increases in controlled areas.

3. Sternlieb repeats this error in the Fort Lee Study (1975: III-4), where he incorrectly calculated total expenses to be increasing by 22%. Including mortgage payments into total costs and cost increases, the figure would have been 11% instead of 22%.

4. The Santa Monica Rent Control Board granted an increase of 6.24% for the period between April 10, 1978, and August 10, 1979. For purposes of comparison with the CPI, this figure was interpolated to a 12-month period.

**Essay completed 1980.**

# SECTION II

# WHY RENTS ARE GOING UP

# Why Rents Rise: A Reconsideration

## JOHN INGRAM GILDERBLOOM
## AND RICHARD P. APPELBAUM

The rising cost of rental housing has become a serious problem throughout the United States. The Department of Housing and Urban Development, which recommends that no more than 25% of family income go into housing, has found that over two-fifths of the nation's renters now pay greater than that amount on rent. The problem is even more acute for inner city residents where over 80% pay more than the recommended 25%. As rising rents continue to outstrip wage increases, tenants have less and less money to spend on essentials such as health care, food, transportation, and clothing. For some, even the 25% guideline may be too high: urban economist Michael Stone (1975:23) employing Bureau of Labor Statistics standards, has found that a family of four earning under $7,500 needs that amount alone to cover all non-housing necessities. For a family of four earning $8,000, only eight percent remains for housing if other basic necessities such as food, health care, transportation and clothing are to be met first. For many low income people the high cost of housing can contribute significantly to their impoverishment.

The rising cost of home ownership has all but priced low and moderate income persons out of the housing market. For example, with homes currently averaging over $100,000 in Southern California, it is extremely difficult for young working people, the elderly, and members of traditionally disadvantaged minorities in that area to gain access to the private housing market. According to the California Department of Housing and Community Development, as far back as 1973 86% of all renters could not afford to buy their own homes. And the situation in California is not atypical.

As a result of these conditions, the past decade has witnessed the creation of a potentially significant category of tenants — "lifers": those individuals who failed to acquire a home prior to the current inflationary period, and who therefore can reasonably expect to spend their lives as renters. Their condition has been adversely affected by the removal of a proportion of rental housing from the market in the past few years, through condominium conversion and gentrification. For example, it is estimated that fully one-seventh of Washington's population will be displaced by these processes over the next four years. In California, the State Department of Housing and Community Development estimates a shortage of 536,000 housing units for low and moderate income persons at rents they can afford.

Any viable strategy aimed at containing rents must at some point consider the reasons why rents have risen so rapidly in recent years. Unfortunately, there is a great deal of confusion on this account, reflecting a conventional wisdom held by renters and owners alike. This view holds, quite simply, that the current housing crisis is largely a result of an inadequate supply of housing. Similar views are held by government officials (Department of Housing and Community Development, 1977:34-36; Congressional Research, 1978) and a host of real estate organizations (California Housing Council, 1977; Coalition for Housing, 1977; Gruen and Gruen, 1977). The latter typically blames "growth controls" for the inadequate supply. To the extent that this view is incorrect, it misdirects attention away from the real causes of the rising costs of housing in general, and rent gouging in particular. It also divides tenants' groups and advocates of low income housing against those who would otherwise be their natural allies--individuals and groups who oppose untrammeled development and unlimited urban growth.

In a preliminary attempt to explore the influence of scarcity on rental levels in light of other possible influences, we sampled different size categories of California cities.[2] Table I compares the effects of city size and vacancy (our measure of scarcity)[3] on median rent levels in 1970. Several features of this table are worth noting. First, across all categories of cities, size effects are clearly more pronounced than scarcity effects: the difference between the smallest and largest places amounts to some 56%, while the difference between high vacancy and low vacancy places is only 12%. Second, when one controls for size, the effects of vacancy appear to be most pronounced among medium-sized places: neither small nor large cities show significant rental differences by vacancy category. Third, the principle rent

**Table 1**

**Effects of City Size and Rental Vacancy Rate 1970 on Median Rent Levels: California Cities, 1970, U.S. Census**

| Size of City: | Scarcity: vacancy rate | | |
|---|---|---|---|
| | low vacancy rate (under 5%) | high vacancy rate (over 5%) | means |
| Small (2500-10,000) (n50) | $78 | $82 | $81 |
| Medium (10,000-50,000) (n50) | $124 | $103 | $116 |
| Large (over 50,000) (n50) | $125 | $126 | $126 |
| Means * | $111 | $99 | $105 |

(Means* are weighted averages which correct for the effects of sampling within city-size categories.)

44

difference is between the very smallest places and larger ones: medium-size cities have 43% higher rents than small cities, while the difference between medium and large cities is only 9%. This suggests that the smallest places are experiencing a different housing dynamic than other cities.[4] If we examine only medium and large cities, an interesting pattern emerges: rents are comparable in three of the four size/vacancy categories, showing a significant difference only in medium-sized high vacancy cities, where rents are close to one-fifth lower ($103, vs. $124). We will speculate on some possible reasons for this momentarily; for the present, we simply note that the effect of scarcity on rents is not so simple and straightforward as it might otherwise appear: size effects are in general more pronounced, while the interaction of size and scarcity seems to be determinant for all but the smallest places.

This is not meant to suggest that housing scarcity has no effect on rental levels in a given locale — obviously a tight rental housing market can be exploited more easily than a slack one — but it does suggest that there are other factors which intervene in determining rents whose relative importance is presently unknown. While such obvious supply-related costs as land, labor materials, fuel, and maintenance expenditures are generally understood by consumers of rental housing, other determinants of rent may not be so obvious. Principal among these we would include the following:

(1) Locational advantages that accrue to rental property, including access to facilities, area amenities, and other externalities (Harvey, 1973:57-60). This is perhaps one reason for the pronounced size effect on rental levels noted in Table 1 (see also Appelbaum, 1978:34-37), particularly in slack housing markets. Larger places may confer a higher aggregate level of such positive externalities than smaller ones. The same may also be true of faster-growing places, as the recent work of one of the present authors suggests. Looking at all medium sized urban areas in the United States which were geographically self-contained, Appelbaum (1978:34-37); (see also Appelbaum et. al., 1978:19-40) found that size and growth rate accounted for almost two-fifths of the variance in median monthly rent in 1970. Even when the effects of associated factors were taken into account,[6] size and growth continued to be significant, with the difference between slower-growing places (under ten percent decennially) and rapidly-growing places (over twenty-five percent decennially) amounting to about ten percent. This suggests that

contrary to the claims of the housing industry, urban growth may not "solve" the housing crisis through new construction, but rather may exacerbate it through creating a boomtown atmosphere, an increase in locational advantages that result from larger size and such growth-related factors as redevelopment, and possibly also from the price-leading effects of a large volume of new construction. The most profitable housing to build is not low-cost housing, but rather construction tied in with other forms of urban redevelopment that may price low and moderate income persons out of an area completely. Table 2 provides some suggestive evidence on this latter point. This table divides cities into two categories: those with a high intercensal increase in the number of rental units (over 60%), and those with a low increase (under 60%). Three size categories are used as a control, as in the previous table. Interestingly, rents are greater in high increase cities than in low increase cities, amounting to 27% in the smallest and largest places, and 9% in medium sized ones. Furthermore, comparing only medium and large cities, we see that there is no difference in median rents for those places which experienced a low volume of intercensal increase in the number of rental units. This is not what we would expect under the scarcity hypothesis, which would predict rising rents in places which experienced the smallest increase in rental housing supply. If we assume that the increase in the number of units is an index of the volume of new construction during the decade, these data indicate instead the possibility of a price-leading effect: newly-built apartments, priced above existing units, may be pushing overall rent levels up in places where the relative volume of new construction is high. Moreover, its plausible that these newly constructed units, which are generally priced for high income tenants are replacing housing units occupied formerly by low income persons (Gilderbloom, 1979). Unfortunately, no firm conclusions are possible on the basis of these data alone; but the above hypotheses are worthy of being tested on data gathered for that explicit purpose.

(2) The absence of laws designed to inhibit the rapid turnover of properties has caused rents to increase substantially. According to interviews with brokers and realtors, both federal tax policies (for example, accelerated depreciation allowances as enacted between 1954 and 1976) and the logic of pyramiding one's property holdings (also known as speculation) makes it optimal to sell one's property every five to nine years (Jacob, 1978:11-15). As a result, when resale is coupled with rapidly rising interest rates, the cost of refinancing can

**Table 2**

**Effects of City Size In Increase In Rental Housing Stock 1960-1970 on Median Rent Levels: California Cities, 1970, U.S. Census**

| Size of City: | % increase in number of rental units, 1960-1970 | | |
|---|---|---|---|
| | low (under 60%) | high (over 60%) | means |
| Small (25,00-10,000) (n50) | $75 | $95 | $81 |
| Medium (10,000-50,000) (n50) | $111 | $121 | $116 |
| Large (over 50,000) (n50) | $107 | $136 | $126 |
| means * | $93 | $119 | $105 |

(Means* are weighted averages which correct for the effects of sampling within city-size categories.)

drive rents up astronomically. Mortgage payments have increased more than any other landlord costs during the ten year period 1965-1975 (Stone, 1975:23-37), as average interest rates rose from 5.62% to 9.75%--an increase of almost three-quarters.[7] This is especially significant since mortgages typically constitute between one — and two-thirds of a landlord's total expenses. For example, a $40,000 thirty year mortgage at 5% entails monthly payments of $215; at 10%, the same mortgage would cost $350, an increase of two-thirds; at today's 14% interest rate the cost would be almost $500. If payments on such a mortgage were to comprise one-half of a landlord's total costs, a "reasonable" rental increase of one-third would be necessary merely to cover the higher interest payments on the loan. In some areas, including many cities in Southern California, the combined effects of general inflation, favorable tax laws, and rising interest rates have played havoc with the housing market, producing rapid property turnover and consequently routine rent increases of substantial proportions. The solutions to these problems are clearly non-local, although anti-speculation taxes might provide a stopgap measure.[8] In the long run, however, a combination of tax reform and alternative methods of low-cost financing are necessary, along with municipal land-banking and other innovations which remove rental housing from the market place altogether. It is highly unlikely, in the absence of a strong national tenants' movement, that the necessary policies and programs would even be seriously considered as viable options.

(3) Landlord cartels and other forms of association may play a major role in rent increase and one that is scarcely recognized by tenants and public officials. Landlords are organized both statewide and locally. In California, for example, there are the major statewide apartment associations--the Apartment Owners' Association of California (AOAC) and the California Housing Council (CHC). These groups have successfully lobbied for legislation in their interest, and two years ago nearly succeeded in getting the state to pre-empt cities from enacting rent controls. The California Housing Council has played a leading role in defeating local rent control measures by underwriting expensive and highly effective advertising campaigns; it is further tied in at the national level with organizations such as the National Rental Council. This permits a degree of coordination among landlords presently unthinkable among tenants. Both the AOAC and the CHC have recently proposed to their memberships "moderate rent increase policies" where landlords hold themselves to annual increases pegged

to the consumer price index or some other formula as a form of "self restraint".[9] An annual rent increase is thereby guaranteed. Such policies are promulgated in statewide meetings and in real estate house organs. For example, in a recent issue of *Real Estate Review* Richard Garrigon (1978:40-41) discussed the necessity for raising rents an annual 15% through the year 1982.

While statewide organizations may provide guidance for rent increases, it is the local real estate associations that are ultimately responsible for implementation. This is accomplished through their association newspapers and local apartment owners' meetings. A recent article in the *Santa Barbara News Press* (December 3, 1978:F-1), for example, states that landlords at such a meeting were told "when, where, how, and by what dollar amount to raise rents." The coordinating efforts of such associations are greatly facilitated by income property management companies, which often operate apartments on behalf of landlords who do not wish to be involved in the daily problems of landlording. As with apartment owners' associations, the larger the percentage of rental housing stock controlled by management companies in a city, the greater the opportunity for setting "bottom line rent increases". Since management companies have far closer contact with the realities of income property, their role in determining rents can be critical: *often landlords do not tell the companies how much rent to charge, but rather the companies tell landlords how much they can get.* The companies have a direct stake in increasing rents, since they customarily take from six to ten percent off the gross rent receipts as their fee. One example will suffice. In Isla Vista, California--a largely student and youth community of some 15,000 adjacent to the University of California (Santa Barbara)--five management firms control fully three-quarters of all apartments having ten or more units. These firms make an annual listing of all their rentals, suggesting proposed rent increases for each; the lists are then circulated, to enable all the companies to coordinate their annual rent increases. A recent study by the Center for Housing Research, reported in the student newspaper (*Nexus,* March 8, 1979) found that despite considerable Proposition 13 tax savings in Isla Vista, 98% of the rental units controlled by the management companies showed a rent increase. In the period following the passage of the tax cut measure, property taxes in the community dropped by almost three-quarters of a million dollars; rental income on nine-month leases during the same period rose by about one-half million dollars.[10]

The significance of efforts by landlords to set rents cannot be underestimated; to the extent that landlords are successful in such efforts, it is clear that eliminating scarcity through new construction will hardly serve to offset rising rents. Moreover, the existence of collusion is extremely difficult to document, impeding tenants' strategies aimed at breaking up monopoly control over the rental housing market. Nor is it clear how one might effectively research the extent and effect of such collusion, although one project is currently underway in connection with the Attorney General's office for the State of California. The lesson, however, is clear enough: rising rents are subject *to political as well as economic forces,* and must be combatted through political means.

Landlord and real estate groups have recognized that action at the national level can affect the outcome of local initiatives. The housing movement for the most part remains locally based (only seven states have a statewide organization) though a number of progressive federal measures would make life easier for local activists: lower interest rates, more funds for rehabilitation and housing cooperatives, perhaps even an agency to protect the rights of tenants' unions. Also the federal government should put on the agenda job-creating programs to build and rehabilitate energy-efficient, affordable housing. But such programs will require a well-organized and well-informed constituency to challenge private interests in housing.

We do not claim that rent control itself will in any way solve the housing crisis.[11] On the contrary, we recognize that rent control--particularly in its moderate form, which pegs rents to a 'reasonable return' formula rather than to renters' abilities to pay--may instead have the consequence of rationalizing the housing market, reducing disparities in rent levels while diverting attention away from the key issue of affordable housing. Rent control does not question the legitimacy of the private market as a means to providing a basic necessity, at a time when the market appears most ill-equipped to provide that necessity at a price most people can afford. In Marcuse's words (1978:29), "It assumes the existence of that private market. It simply tries to smoothen out that market, to make it function more effectively, to make it more 'orderly.' " But at the same time rent control has substantial potential as an organizing issue. It deals with an issue that is vital and immediate to large numbers of people--and one that likely will become of central concern to growing numbers of renters. It has the potential for building bridges between low and moderate income tenants, who share a common interest as market economics drive the price of housing out of reach for all but the wealthiest. And, most importantly, it focuses attention on the market itself, creating a forum for exposing its limitations and raising the issue of non-market alternatives. Like any reformist issue, the significance of rent control as an organizing strategy will depend on the political savvy of its proponents--on their ability to link it with a wider analysis in the minds of tenants, and on their ability to forge coalitions that cross-cut divisions of class, race, sex, and age. Because renters themselves cross-cut such divisions, the potential is there. The immediate task lies in creating tenants' organizations that go beyond purely local issues: the creation of statewide and even a national tenants' movement to counter the growing organization of the housing industry.

Apart from fighting for rent controls, tenants' organizations should pursue legislation at the state level which would provide a more secure context for organizing. Possible avenues would include "just cause" legislation aimed at curbing arbitrary and sometimes retaliatory evictions, and controls over condominium conversions. But the bulk of efforts must go into creating a strong and widespread tenants' movement. The conditions may be ripe: the phenomenon of "lifers", coupled with the highly revealing failure of property tax cut measures to produce tax relief, has angered tenants and given new life to their organizations. Nor are conditions likely to improve in the near future. It remains to be seen whether the issues can be removed from the narrow arena of economic debate where they have so far been confined, to the larger political one where the sources of the housing crisis are in reality to be found.

---

[1]Special thanks to Dennis Keating, Ed Kirshner, Peter Marcuse, and Myron Moskovitz, for their comments and help on this paper; needless to say, responsibility for its current form lies entirely with the authors. Thanks to John Richardson, Karrie Hindley and Gale Schlesinger who provided valuable research asistance in compiling the data for Tables 1 and 2. Partial support comes from a grant made by the Shalan Foundation of San Francisco. Diane Tilden did the excellent typing.

This comes from a much longer article to be published under the title "Rising Rents and Rent Control: Issues in Urban Reform" to be published in the forthcoming book: "Urban and Regional Planning in an Age of Austerity by Pierre Clavel, John Forester and William Goldsmith. The book was published in 1980 by Pergamon Press. The other part of the article which was written by Peter Drier is published in another part of this reader.

[2] Cities were divided into three size categories: small (2500-10,000 persons), medium (10,000-50,000), and large (over 50,000). Within each category, a random sample of 50 cities was selected to assure adequate representation of size. The analysis which follows must be regarded as purely suggestive of hypotheses; given the sampling procedures (e.g., no attempt was made to isolate cities which lie within larger metropolitan areas from those which are relatively isolated; nor cities which lie within the same metropolitan area and therefore presumably share similar housing characterisitics), stronger inference is not warranted by the data.

[3] The difficulty with using vacancy as a measure of scarcity is treated in Marcuse (1979:103-111). Following conventional treatment, we regard low-vacancy cities as those with lower than 5%, and high vacancy cities as those with higher rates. Presumably, market dynamics differ between these two conditions, the former reflecting a "tight" housing market and the latter a relatively competitive one. As we have previously noted, most contemporary rent control ordinances are written so as to go into effect only when vacancy rates drop below 5%.

[4] For the most part these cities are located in rural areas.

[5] The analysis looked at *all* urbanized areas in the contiguous 48 states that (a) contain only one central city of from 50,000 to 400,000 inhabitants and (b) are at least twenty miles from the closest neighboring urbanized area. These criteria effectively exclude suburbs and cities that are part of large metropolitan agglomerations, thereby standardizing the cities studied.

[6] A multi-variate analysis was performed in which the effects of region, central-city age, percentage of housing in single-family dwellings, and median family income were controlled.

[7] Rates at the time of this writing (June 1979) are running as high as 11.75%.

[8] The voters in Santa Cruz California recently approved such a measure; it was quickly overturned by the courts on the grounds that it

was confiscatory of private property. The decision is currently under appeal.

[9] See Mike Jacob's (1979) "Consumer Price Index Rent Increases: Are They Such A Good Deal?", Oakland, California; California Housing Action and Information Network (page 1) and "Report to Donald E. Burns, Secretary, Business and Transportation Agency on the Validity of the Legislative Findings of AB3799 and the Economic Impact of Rent Control" (1976), Sacramento, Calif.; California Department of Housing and Community Development (page VI-20).

[10] The study found that while total operating costs for apartments fell an average of 8% because of Proposition 13, rent increased approximately 12%.

[11] For a far more extended treatment of this issue, which situates contemporary rent control both theoretically and historically, cross-nationally, see Marcuse (1978).

*Adapted from Dreier, Peter, John Gilderbloom and Richard Appelbaum, 1980, Rising Rents and Rent Control: Issues in Urban Reform in Pierre Clavel, John Forester and William W. Goldsmith, Urban and Regional Planning in an Age of Austerity. Pergamon Press, New York.*

# The Housing Problem

## EMILY PARADISE ACHTENBERG
## AND MICHAEL STONE

*Reprinted from:* **Hostage!** *Housing and the Massachusetts Fiscal Crisis, Boston Community School, Boston, Mass., 1977*

In any society, housing costs a lot to build. Large quantities of materials and many different kinds of labor skills are needed to put a house together. Each building must be located on a unique plot of land and must be connected to utilities. Various sizes and types of houses are needed to accommodate different family needs, climates, and terrains. Despite increasing mechanization, housing is far too complex ever to become a fully-standardized, relatively cheap, assembly-line product like cars.

Under our economic system, housing is even more expensive because the materials and industry used to produce it are privately owned. So the cost of building a house or apartment building also includes the profits made by private developers, builders, and materials producers. In addition, the land underneath houses is privately owned, so housing production costs also include the profits made by land owners and speculators.

Because of the tremendous production cost, builders and developers generally borrow most of the money they need to put up new housing. About 75% of all the money used to finance new housing production in the U.S. is borrowed. And since the sources of money for housing are privately owned and/or controlled, the cost of borrowing money — interest on construction loans — is another part of the cost of producing housing.

In addition, since most housing is privately owned, once a new home is completed it is generally sold to a private buyer. Even a new apartment building will eventually be sold by the developer to a new owner. But few buyers are willing or able to put up the large sum needed to purchase a house or apartment building. So they generally borrow most of the cash needed to buy the finished house — again, from a private lending source.

Finally, since houses and apartment buildings last for a long time, a lot of used buildings are bought and sold over and over again. Houses are sold on the average once every six years. With each sales transaction, the new buyer must borrow the money from a private lender.

Thus the housing industry and the housing market in this country are very dependent on borrowed money — on credit. The major sources of mortgage credit for financing both existing and new housing are banks and other large financial institutions. These institutions have a great deal of control over the supply of housing — how much, if any, gets built — and over the cost of housing — who can afford to live in it — as explained in the next two sections.

## Housing Credit and Housing Supply

Traditionally most of the money for housing has been provided by various types of local thrift institutions — savings banks, savings and loan associations, and cooperative banks. These institutions get most of the money they lend for housing from deposits by local people in savings accounts. But over the years these traditional institutions and savings accounts have become less and less adequate for meeting the credit needs of the housing sector.

First of all, even though some kinds of thrift institutions are legally required to make most of their funds available for housing, this has never been enough to provide all the credit needed by housing. The housing sector has therefore always had to depend to some extent on other sources of money, primarily commercial banks and life insurance companies. But since these particular institutions are not legally required to commit their funds to housing, when other investments are more profitable they have little interest in providing housing credit.

For example, at the peak of economic booms, when expanding industries compete for credit and interest rates are rising, commercial banks cut way back on housing loans. For these banks, tying up money in housing loans for, say, 20 years at a fixed rate of interest is simply less profitable than making short-term loans at rising interest rates. In addition, at such times the banks can get higher interest rates on loans to other kinds of borrowers, like big corporations and government, which can more easily pass their costs on to consumers and taxpayers. The result is a periodic credit "crunch," or shortage of money for housing.

These same ups and downs in the economy affect the availability of mortgage credit from the thrift institutions as well. Even though the thrifts have steadfastly invested most of their money in housing, they can only invest money if they have it. For a long time, they received fairly steady and continuous savings deposits which were used to make housing loans. But over the past 10 years, with increasing inflation and rising interest rates throughout the economy, savings accounts have become less profitable than other forms of investment.

The reason for the thrifts' special problems is that most of their income comes from mortgage loans. This income is used to pay interest on savings accounts. But a large portion of a savings bank's funds are usually tied up in old mortgages which bring in perhaps only 5-6%. This means that the bank cannot easily or quickly raise the interest rates it pays to depositors.

In response, people with fairly large savings accounts of, say, $10,000-20,000 or more, periodically withdraw their money from local savings accounts when they can invest it in more profitable things like government or corporate bonds. Thrift institutions then have to cut back on the amount of credit they provide for housing — because they simply don't have the money to lend.

Finally, a large proportion of the funds which mortgage lenders do have available for housing goes into the sale or refinancing of existing homes and apartment buildings, rather than being used to build new housing. Since lenders seek to protect and increase the value of their existing investments, in most neighborhoods they are eager to make loans which permit the older houses to be bought and sold at higher and higher prices. In fact, since massive new construction could pose a threat to the values of these older buildings, mortgage lenders have a direct financial stake in restricting the flow of credit for new housing.

In some older city neighborhoods where residents' limited incomes are not high enough to pay for the inflated mortgage costs of existing houses, banks may prefer to write off their old investments rather than make any new, risky mortgage loans. This practice, called "redlining," guarantees that property values will decline and generally leads to neighborhood deterioration and destruction. But rather than providing funds for new housing construction, this process simply makes more credit available for the resale and refinancing of homes in higher income communities.

As a result of all these problems, the supply of housing in this country has never been adequate to meet people's housing needs. In the Housing and Urban Development Act of 1968, Congress set a 10-year housing goal of 26 million new and rehabilitated units, or an annual average production rate of 2.6 million homes and apartments. This goal has not been met in a single year. After eight years, only a little more than half the goal — 13.5 million units — have actually been started.

In recent years, the housing shortage has intensified as construction has declined. In 1975, only 1.1 million new units were started nationally. Apartment construction has now dropped to a 30-year low of 200,000 units.

The worsening housing shortage does not result from lack of technical capacity in our economy. The relatively high rates of housing production in 1972 and 1973 (2.3 million units each year) show that much more housing could be built. Rather, the shortage results directly from the dependence of housing on private, profit-oriented mortgage lenders, and from the inability of our economy and financial institutions to meet the growing credit needs of the housing sector.

## Housing Credit and Housing Cost

The housing credit system and the financial institutions which provide housing credit have a great deal of control over the cost of housing, and over who can afford to live in it. For both tenants and homeowners, monthly mortgage payments are the biggest part of housing costs — usually from 30-50% of the total cost of occupying the housing. This includes both the monthly repayment on the owner's mortgage loan (principal) and the cost of borrowing the money (interest).

Monthly mortgage costs are high for several reasons. In the first place, mortgage payments on a new house or apartment reflect the rapidly rising cost of housing production, including the cost of labor, land, and materials as well as interest on the construction loan. The cost of interest on housing construction loans has been the most rapidly rising element of housing production costs — up 148% between 1970 and 1974. Construction interest now amounts to about 10% of the sale price of a new house. (See Table 2)

The most important factor effecting monthly mortgage payments, though, is the rising cost of interest on the long-term loans used to buy homes or apartment houses. As interest rates have risen generally in the past 10 years, thrift institutions and other private lenders have charged higher and higher interest rates on their mortgage loans. Since 1965, average mortgage interest rates have increased from 5.62% to 9.75%, or almost 75% (see Table 1).

Rising interest rates have had an ever greater impact on the monthly cost of owning or living in a house, because the cost of a typical single-family house has also doubled since 1965. For example, if you had bought a $20,000 house in 1965 with a 25% down payment ($5000), your monthly mortgage payments at 5.6% interest would have been about $93.

---

## Table 1.
## Monthly Cost of living in a
## Typical Single Family House (1965 vs. 1975)

|  | 1965 | 1975 |
|---|---|---|
| 1. Average sales price - single family house | $20,000 | $40,000 |
| 2. Mortgage interest rate | 5.62% | 9.74% |
| 3. Monthly mortgage payment | $93 | $267 |
| 4. Monthly property taxes (Boston) | $96 | $164 |
| 5. Total monthly cost - mortgage and taxes | $189 | $431 |
| 6. Minimum annual income needed | $9072 | $20,688 |

Notes
1. National Association of Home Builders, Boston Globe, October 14, 1975.
2. Secondary market yields on FHA mortgages, December averages, Wall St. Journal, October 20, 1975.
3. 25% down payment, 25 year term.
4. 1965 · tax rate = $115.20 per $1000 of assessed valuation. Assumes
   assessed value = ½ market value.
   1970 · tax rate = $196.70 per $1000 of assessed valuation. Assumes
   assessed value = ¼ market value.
5. Line 3 + line 4.
6. Line 6 x 4 x 12. Assumes family should pay no more than 25% of annual income for mortgage payments and property tax.

---

But if you bought the same house today for $40,000 with 25% down ($10,000), the mortgage payments alone would cost you $267

Table 2
Changes in Share of Major Cost Items
for a Typical Single Family House

|  | Fourth Quarter 1970 | | Fourth Quarter 1974 | | Percent Change 1970-74 |
|---|---|---|---|---|---|
|  | Cost | Percent Distribution | Cost | Percent Distribution | |
| 1. Hard Cost | $13,188 | 54.3% | $18,040 | 48.4% | 38.8% |
| Labor | 4,198 | 17.3 | 3,820 | 15.6 | 38.6 |
| Material | 8,990 | 37.0 | 12,220 | 32.8 | 35.9 |
| 2. Land | 4,925 | 20.2 | 7,958 | 21.3 | 61.6 |
| 3. Financing | 1,580 | 6.5 | 3,917 | 10.5 | 147.9 |
| 4. Overhead and Profit | 2,940 | 12.1 | 4,513 | 12.1 | 53.5 |
| 5. Other Cost | 1,667 | 6.9 | 2,872 | 7.7 | 72.3 |
| Sales Price | $24,300 | 100.0% | $37,300 | 100.0% | 53.5% |

Source: National Association of Home Builders

Table 3
How Much It Costs to Live in Boston (Fall 1975, Family of 4, lower budget)

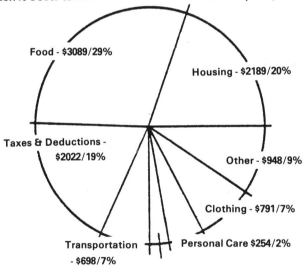

Food - $3089/29%
Housing - $2189/20%
Taxes & Deductions - $2022/19%
Other - $948/9%
Clothing - $791/7%
Personal Care $254/2%
Transportation - $698/7%

Total - $10,777/100%

59

per month. This represents an increase of nearly 200% in addition to a 100% increase in the required down-payment!

With the rising cost of housing and credit, families need more and more money just to pay for the same house or apartment. According to the federal government's standard, the average family should pay no more than one-quarter of its annual income for shelter, whether they rent or own. Based on the above example, in 1965 you would have needed an income of about $9000 to afford the monthly cost of mortgage payments and property taxes alone on a typical single family house in Boston (see Table 1). But in 1975, you would need to earn more than $20,000 to buy the same house!

If you were a tenant in the house instead of the owner, these same higher mortgage and property tax payments would be passed on in the form of higher rents, so you'd still need to earn more than $20,000 to afford to live there.

## Housing Credit, Housing Cost and Income

There has always been a sizeable fraction of the population too poor to be able to repay the mortgage loans needed to produce or buy privately-owned housing — even at the low interest rates which existed 20-30 years ago. In recent years, as housing costs and interest rates have sky-rocketed, the problem has grown even worse. In the U.S. today, only 15% of the population can afford the mortgage payments on a typical, new, single-family home now costing over $40,000. In high-cost areas like Boston, the situation is even worse — mostly due to rising mortgage interest costs.

The high and rising cost of housing and mortgage credit forces many families to pay more than they can reasonably afford for shelter, whether they buy or rent. According to one official estimate, at least 6.7 million renter households in the U.S. were paying unreasonably high rents in 1970. This figure is really an understatement — since it excludes all homeowners as well as families with incomes greater than $10,000. And it generally accepts the standard that 25% of income is a reasonable proportion to spend on housing.

Actually, this arbitrary government standard ignores the real living costs faced by most poor and working class households. How much a family can afford to spend for housing depends on how much they have left over after paying for food, clothing, medical care, and other necessities. This partly depends on the family situation — for example, how many children, their ages, and the number and age of

**60**

adults in the family. A household of two adults and five school-age children obviously has to spend quite a lot for food, clothing, and other "non-shelter" costs, leaving a relatively small proportion of the family budget for housing. By comparison, a single, elderly person generally has lower non-housing costs and could probably afford to spend more for housing.

The single most important factor, though, in determining how much a family can afford for housing is its annual income. Two identical families, say with two adults and two children of the same age, will have to pay relatively similar amounts for food, clothing, other non-housing items. But what's left over for housing will be a relatively large amount if the family earns $15,000 a year — and little, if any, if the family's annual income is only $5,000. For the higher income family, 25% of their income might be a reasonable amount to pay for housing — but for the lower income family, even 5% might be too much.

Just how much can families at different income levels afford to pay for housing, and still have enough left over for food, clothing, and other necessities? According to the U.S. Bureau of Labor Statistics, in 1975 a typical four-person household in the Boston area needed an annual income of $10,777 just to maintain the minimum adequate living standard (Boston has the highest living cost in the continental U.S.) At this income level, a family can afford to spend about $3089 a year for housing, or $182 per month — about 20% of its total budget. Another 29% goes for food and 19% goes for income and social security taxes (see Table 3).

Table 4 shows the maximum amount that a 4-person family can afford to spend for housing if they earn anywhere from 0-$12,000, assuming that they have the same non-housing expenses identified in the BLS "lower budget." It shows that in Boston today, for a typical family of 4 with an income of less than about $12,000 a year, 25% is too much to pay for housing. Indeed, for a family of 4 earning $7,000 or less *any* amount for housing is more than they can afford!

These figures reveal the inadequacy of the official government standard for measuring the housing cost problem. Actually, more than 16 million households — 8 million tenant households and 8 million homeowner households — were paying more for housing than they could afford in 1970, based on the more accurate measure that considers real family budget costs and family income (see Table 5). This represents more than 25% of all households in the U.S. — and more than 40% of all households earning under $10,000 a year. More than one out of 3 tenant families — and nearly one out of 2 tenant families earning less than $10,000 a year — are paying too much of their incomes for rent according to this definition.

Since 1970, prices have risen even faster than the incomes of most families. So even these figures understate the extent of the housing cost problem in our society!

---

**Table 4**
**Maximum Affordable Housing Costs,**
**4-Person Family, Boston (Fall 1975)**

|  | Maximum Amount Available for Housing* | | |
|---|---|---|---|
| Income $ per year | $ per year | $ per month | % of Income |
| $ 7000 or less | 0 | 0 | 0 |
| $ 8000 | $ 389 | $ 32 | 4.9% |
| $ 9000 | $1103 | $ 92 | 12.4% |
| $10,000 | $1802 | $150 | 18.0% |
| $11,000 | $2499 | $208 | 22.7% |
| $12,000 | $3202 | $267 | 26.7% |

*Derived from U.S. Bureau of Labor Statistics, "Autumn 1975 Urban Family Budgets and Comparative Indexes for Selected Urban Areas," 1976. Total non-housing expenses provided by the BLS "lower budget" for a 4-person household in Boston were subtracted from income, as well as personal income and social security taxes corresponding to each income level. The resulting figure is the amount each family can afford to spend on housing while still having enough income to maintain the minimum adequate standard of living, according to BLS standards.

---

## Housing Credit and the Economy

Over the past 30 years, housing has been by far the biggest user of borrowed money — of credit — in the entire economy. Housing has borrowed more money than the federal government, more money than private industry, more money than state and local governments, more money than consumers have borrowed for all items like cars and refrigerators. We are now over $500 billion in debt on our housing; that's nearly $2500 in debt for each and every person in the country. And this debt has accumulated almost entirely in the last 30 years.

The need for such immense amounts of borrowed money for housing and the cost of this money — interest rates — have been causing rapidly increasing problems for the housing sector and for the

**Table 5**
**Households Paying More Than They Can**
**Afford for Shelter (U.S., 1970)**

| Annual Income | Number of Households (in millions) | | |
|---|---|---|---|
| | Owners | Renters | Total |
| Under $2000 | 3.8 | 3.9 | 7.7 |
| $2,000 - $2,999 | 1.4 | 1.2 | 2.6 |
| $3,000 - $3,999 | 1.1 | 1.1 | 2.2 |
| $4,000 - $4,999 | 0.5 | 0.6 | 1.2 |
| $5,000 - $5,999 | 0.7 | 0.7 | 1.3 |
| $6,000 - $6,999 | 0.4 | 0.3 | 0.8 |
| $7,000 - $7,999 | 0.4 | 0.2 | 0.6 |
| Total | 8.3 | 8.0 | 16.3 |
| % of All Households | 21 % | 34 % | 26 % |
| % of Households Earning Less than $10,000 | 40 % | 46 % | 43 % |

Derived from U.S. Bureau of Labor Statistics, "Autumn 1975 Urban Family Budgets and Comparative Indexes for Selected Urban Areas," 1976, and U.S. Bureau of the Census, Census of Housing, 1970, HC (2)-1, Tables A-1, 2, 3. The figures show the number of households paying more for housing than the amount available after taking into account all necessary non-housing consumption expenditures, plus personal income and social security taxes corresponding to each income level and family size.

economy as a whole. These problems are extremely serious. They have developed because the government has tried to find ways to prop up the housing industry and to use housing to prop up the economy as a whole without confronting the basic inadequacies of our economic system.

Our type of economy has a built-in problem. On the one hand, businesses and corporations that employ people want to maximize their profits. So wages have to be kept at the lowest possible level, while the price of housing and other things people need remains high. Credit provides a way of selling things at high prices without having to give people higher incomes. Instead of taking the money from the rich and using it to give everyone a good standard of living, our economic system forces people to borrow the money they need, and pay it back — with interest.

This growing credit system, though, only creates further problems. "Buy now, pay later" is profitable for those who have the money to lend only if there is a "later." The credit system hocks the future. It makes claims on the income the borrowers expect to receive in the future. That is, in order for the credit system to survive, in order for the lender to make a profitable business out of lending, in order for producers to be sure they can sell things profitably, the economy has to grow and grow and grow without end. The system must grow in order to be able to pay off past debts; but in order to grow it has to create more debt. And so the pressure to grow builds up more and more.

During the Great Depression of the 1930's, the whole economy collapsed with the downfall of the credit system. Without credit to finance the selling of things, producers wouldn't produce. Lenders had to write off many of their debts as uncollectable. Many banks went out of business, people lost their houses, and the amount of debt was reduced. Eventually the whole process began again, when a war came along to restart production.

Today we face many problems similar to the 1930's, except that the amount of debt in the economy is much greater, and housing is a much more significant part of the total debt. For example, in 1920 the per capita (per person) mortgage debt on housing amounted to about 13% of the per capita annual after-tax income of the population. By 1950, even though the economy had grown tremendously, debt had grown much faster; per capita housing mortgage debt was up to 27% of per capita after-tax income. Over the past 25 years, mortgage debt has continued to grow twice as fast as income, so that per capita mortgage debt is now about 55% of per capita income. As explained later in this booklet, the growing problems of debt in the economy are a major part of the current crisis, both nationally and in Massachusetts.

Summary

The traditional suppliers of housing credit in our economy have been less and less able to finance the necessary production to meet housing needs. As a result, we are faced with a growing housing shortage. At the same time, the high and rising cost of housing credit has meant that fewer and fewer people can afford to live in new housing. And a growing number of families — at least 16 million households, 60 million people nationally — are forced to pay more than they can afford for housing, leaving less for other necessities like food and clothing. Finally, the tremendous growth in housing credit poses increasing problems for the economy as a whole, as our housing debt grows faster than people's ability to pay for it.

# A View From Industry

## MICHAEL BRENNEMAN

**Stentzel:** In a panel discussion a couple of weeks ago, you referred to the ''enormous changes'' going on in the D.C. housing market. Could you explain those changes and some of the factors involved?

**Brenneman:** Let's look at the factors first, the changing demographic factors. We now have a tremendously high percentage of one — and two — person households. I suspect that more than 60 percent of the households in Washington fit in that category. These households, especially two-income households, are also more affluent than ever before. One of the major changes here is because of women's lib and things associated with that. Women have higher incomes today, and lenders are required to recognize that income. We have some condominiums where nearly 50 percent of the purchasers are women. That's astounding in a fairly large building.

We also have the phenomenon of a generation of children, essentially raised in the suburbs, who are coming back to the city, or who are renting in the city and decide to stay rather than go back to the suburbs. It's almost a rebellion against the sterility of the suburban atmosphere.

**Stentzel:** To what extent are these changes national and not peculiar to D.C.?

**Brenneman:** I think you're seeing the same thing in Boston and Philadelphia and Chicago and other cities, but perhaps with not quite as much force as here. It's beginning to happen, though. All these forces are really national in nature. When the fuel crisis hit in 1974, we started getting a pretty heavy number of phone calls from people living way out in Virginia and Maryland. They just flat out said, ''We're coming back''. This is still happening across the country.

In the early '70s there were tremendous housing bargains in D.C. For $30-40,000 you could have a hell of a place, instead of putting a lot more into a suburban house and having to drive 40 minutes to work. Individuals beat the speculators to these places for awhile. The speculators had not yet seen the turn.

**Stentzel:** But that's changed now.

**Brenneman:** The speculators didn't lose much time picking up steam. Now it's a neck-to-neck thing between young couples and the speculators. But the speculator usually gets there first, simply because he has an army of people out there shopping for him. By the time a couple gets it today, a house has usually passed through one or two hands.

**Stentzel:** What role do speculators play in boosting prices quicker or higher?

**Brenneman:** Perhaps quicker, but not higher. The market of home buyers in the final analysis determines what the price is going to be on that property. I think the speculator has his place. The speculator in some cases facilitates the sale to the final user; he is used to dealing with a variety of sellers; he has developed systems to expedite the transfer of property. Of course, that's not favorable in everybody's eyes, because of the displacement issue and so forth.

**Stentzel:** We are interested not only in the economic forces but in some of the social consequences. You mentioned the displacement issue. We see largely white, affluent people moving into one-or two-person dwellings that used to house considerably larger, poor, black families. What kinds of problems does that present to you as a developer?

**Brenneman:** I wouldn't say that it presents a problem. It presents opportunities, and perhaps challenges. I think the biggest problem is in nearby counties which are getting the spillover of low- and moderate-income large families, primarily black. They are being pushed out of the District of Columbia.

This is part of an historical tide that takes place in any city over a long period of rejuvenation and deterioration. I don't believe it's possible to stop that tide. The city council has tried to slow the tide and has not been able to do so. Nor do I think it can — constitutionally at least.

Some people say there is an appalling housing crisis in the District in terms of availablity of housing. But there appears to be no real shortage of housing per se. There may be a shortage of money to afford housing on the part of some people. But that doesn't mean that the housing stock isn't there. They just haven't got the money to pay for it.

**Stentzel:** Houses that were $30,000 in 1970 are now selling for $100,000 or more. A city official estimated that houses on the average are appreciating $1,000 every eight weeks; he added that the skyrocketing prices have simply knocked low-income people out of the market. Near our neighborhood, a speculator bought two pieces of property for $70,000, sold them the next month for $270,000 and now they're on the market for $350,000. The street is full of low-rent places whose occupants, all black, feel their days are numbered...

**Brenneman:** Let's not kid ourselves. There is no way, short of massive government intervention in the form of subsidies, that low-income families can remain in areas undergoing renovation. It can't happen. When people target a block and the renovation process starts, the tax assessor alone, if no other force, will insure that those low-income families have to leave.

**Stentzel:** What likelihood is there of massive government intervention?

**Brenneman:** Very little. The ability to pay isn't there; the ability of the taxpayer to pay isn't there. Proposition 13-type thinking is abroad in the land, and I for one am somewhat glad. I honestly don't see a huge government program coming into play.

**Stentzel:** There was a meeting last week at HUD (Department of Housing and Urban Development) where Assistant Secretary (Geno) Baroni talked about the human benefits and human costs of revitalization and rejuvenation of our cities. He said that the heaviest costs were being borne by the poor and the elderly. What is your reaction to Baroni's statement?

**Brenneman:** My reaction is: Where the hell has he been the last 20 years? Certainly our cities are going to be revitalized; that's been an announced common goal for a number of years. And certainly if there's going to be that revitalization, it's going to be accompanied by an influx of taxpaying citizens. And they had better pay a lot of taxes if the city's going to carry itself. Productive people, if you will. Those who are nonproductive or less productive — the infirm, the aged, the welfare cases — perhaps through no fault of their own, yes, they are probably going to bear some of the brunt.

**Stentzel:** Baroni said that displacement will be the issue of the next decade. Would you minimize that claim?

**Brenneman:** I don't disagree with his statement, simply because displacement is already being made the issue of this decade. But I question the truthfulness of some of the statements made about

**67**

displacement, about the severity of the problem. Yes, it is occurring; and yes, prices are escalating sharply in the city. Those people least able to pay are either going to have to go somewhere else or somebody is going to have to come up with a program to enable them to stay.

Somebody is obviously going to have to go. It is conceivable, however, that developers will be willing to enter voluntarily into agreements with governments whereby people fitting certain descriptions, elderly or infirm, will be able to stay under certain conditions.

From experience, I can tell you that many of the people who claim severe trauma when asked to move are people who have assets that could choke a horse. They're the most vocal group, unfortunately. We're hearing very little from low-income people who don't have that articulateness. They just quietly fade away.

**Stentzel:** Do you think they should have a voice?

**Brenneman:** Oh, yes. I think anybody is entitled to a voice.

**Stentzel:** To what extent do you think that real estate people, for reasons of conscience or whatever, should intervene on behalf of these voiceless people?

**Brenneman:** I'm not sure that I understand your question.

**Stentzel:** Well, you mentioned that the government would have to assume massive responsibility if the poor are to secure good housing. What I'm asking is if the real estate industry also feels any responsibility in this regard.

**Brenneman:** I don't think that the real estate industry, short of compliance with appropriate law, should be asked to take upon itself what is truly a governmental function. Is the grocery store asked to sell food at lower cost to low-or moderate-income people? I think not.

I know of no other segment of the economy that is asked to bear a social burden such as is being borne right now by the landlords in the District *(a reference primarily to rent control — Editor)*. I think it is grossly unfair and immoral. If there is to be a helping hand given to these people economically, then the burden of this should be borne by everybody.

**Stentzel:** I'd be remiss if I didn't ask you if you're a religious person and if and how that relates to this particular problem and to your work in general.

**Brenneman:** I'm sorry, but I don't consider that question to be appropriate in this discussion. My religion and my work are not totally separate; I don't think anybody's are. But I really don't feel compelled to go into that. I'd rather not.

**Stentzel:** To what extent is today the best of times or the worst of times for the real estate industry?

**Brenneman:** I'd say that it certainly leans toward the best of times. In spite of the regulatory problems we're faced with, in spite of the city council that gives us fits, the city is changing. The change is accompanied by profits for developers, profits for brokers, profits for speculators, profits for all people who buy and sell homes.

Obviously, if price levels continue to rise as they have, relatively few people will be able to afford any kind of housing. We see some possibility of things slowing down fairly substantially in 1979. Maybe that kind of thing is needed every few years to kind of bring things back to earth. We'll see.

*Reprinted from SOJOURNERS, November 1978.*

# SECTION III

# WHY RENT CONTROL IS NEEDED

# Moderate Regulations Protect Landlords, As Well as Tenants

## CARY LOWE AND RICHARD BLUMBERG

Rent control is an idea whose time has finally come to California. Tenants throughout the state are demanding relief from unconscionable increases in housing costs and, as a result are turning to rent regulation as the only remedy in sight.

The tenants are opposed, of course, by an eqully determined set of landlords. In 1976, a high-powered real-estate lobby, fueled with nearly $100,000 in campaign contributions, nearly enacted legislation that would have barred local governments from stopping rent gouging. Despite the California Supreme Court's subsequent ruling that local governments do have the power to regulate rents, these same special interests now have pending in Sacramento still another bill to ban such regulation.

When real-estate interests react to rent control, they usually point to the World War II era of rent freezes, particularly those in New York, which did prohibit rent increases for many years at a time. The new so-called "moderate" or second-generation" rent controls, however are totally different. They allow annual rent increases based on increased costs for taxes, utilities, operating expenses and improvements, thereby guaranteeing the landlord a reasonable return on his investment. Modern rent-control plans do not end profits or rent increases, but they do restrict both to prevent blatant gouging.

Second-generation rent controls are operating successfully at present in more than 120 New Jersey cities, four in Massachussetts (including Boston), the District of Columbia and various cities and counties in Alaska, Maine, Virginia, Maryland and Connecticut.

In California, the debate over rent control in 1978 started about a year ago as a battle between "experts." The landlords trotted out industry-financed studies performed in various East Coast cities and loudly proclaimed that New York's economic decline was due primarily to that city's tenant-protection programs.

But tenant advocates, increasingly aware that analyses by real-estate groups consistently support the prejudices of their sponsors, point to another set of studies recently assembled by John Gilderbloom, a California rent-control specialist. Gilderbloom's study declares:

*"During the past year, two non-real-estate sponsored studies using rigorous stastistical techniques have been completed. They have found no negative relationship between moderate rent control and construction, maintenance, demolition or devaluation of rental housing stock. Those studies that do make this claim, all sponsored by real-estate interests, tend to be flawed by unreliable data, fabricated facts, juggled statistics, faulty logic and unrepresentative sampling."*

The myths about rent control perpetuated by landlords and apartment developers comprise an endless, simplistic refrain. But the facts are considerably different.

Landlords argue that rent control inhibits new construction and investment. Most second-generation rent controls, however, explicitly exempt new construction from regulation. Furthermore, housing investment is influenced far more by the costs of labor, materials, land and financing than by the existence of rent control.

The anti-rent-control forces also claim that landlords will undermaintain their properties to preserve a decent profit. But rent controls usually permit the costs of maintenance and improvements to be transferred to tenants in the form of increased rents, thereby removing any lack of incentive for proper upkeep. If undermaintenance does occur, it will be caused by profiteering landlords violating housing and safety codes — not by rent-control advocates.

The foes of control, moveover, sugggest that landlords will abandon apartment houses in droves, largely because of their unprofitability. This argument ignores the assurances built into moderate rent controls that guarantee a reasonable profit level. Nationally, in fact, abandonment is occuring at the same or a greater rate in cities without rent control as in those with it.

Landlords and apartment developers also seek to put homeowners against tenants by claiming that rent control depresses the tax assessments of rental housing. This completely illogical assertion ignores the numerous techniques assessors have for determining the true market value of real estate. There is no basis at all for believing that the value of rented housing will be markedly depressed. Rather than resenting the establishment of some degree of equity for tenants, homeowners fearful of tax shifts should continue to press for the placement of greater tax responsibilty on commercial and industrial properties. Even if taxes are forced up slightly, this is still preferable to — and less costly than — the increase in public assistance payments which inevitiably follows each new jump in rents.

Finally, the opponents of rent control argue that the controls cannot be administered without a costly bureaurcracy. They forget that regulation can be made entirely self-supporting by requiring landlords to pay a registration fee for each rental unit they own and by requiring tenants to pay a nominal filing fee for each complaint they bring to the enforcement board.

Clearly, rent controls achieve an overall positive influence in tenants and landlords, as well as on neighborhoods containing a large volume of rental housing. By assuring renters fair treatment it produces a stabilizing effect by removing incentives to search constantly for a more affordable apartment and by creating more long-term relationships between landlords and tenants. Once landlords surmount their initial paranoia, the results will be not only better overall landlord-tenant relations, but also incentives for both parties to take better care of the properties.

Rent control is not an arbitrary demand. It springs from a genuine crisis in the rental-housing market. California, along with the rest of the nation, is suffering from a well-documented housing shortage and rental inflation. The situation is made even more calamitous by a high level of speculation in rental real estate.

An increased supply of low-cost housing would provide needed relief, but such housing is not being built now, nor is the real-estate industry planning to build such units in the near future.

Many landlords, especially fast-buck speculators and large absentee owners, are taking advantage of this tight market by raising rents to shocking levels, particularly in the Valley and along the coastal area. Yet no significant signs are visible that the industry is willing to police the worst abuses in its own ranks. To date, the real-estate industry has proposed only the creation of voluntary rent-mediation boards that have no enforcement powers.

As long as these conditions persist, rent control continues to remain a necessary weapon against inflated costs for renters.

On a statewide level, the growing movement for rent control is being coordinated by the California Housing Action and Information Network (CHAIN), a coalition of housing-rights groups. Locally, the recently formed United Tenant Organization of Los Angeles is revving up to lead the fight.

Renters, after all, are slowly realizing that, without strong tenant organizations at the state and local level neither rent controls nor any other remedy will provide enforceable relief. Since a majority of Californians will soon be renters, this group will gain the political muscle to become an enormously powerful force in this state in the coming years.

Inadvertently, callous real-estate interests are themselves creating the very interest group that could eventually topple their own previously unbeatable organization. If that happens, rent control will be just the first step in the ascendancy of "tenant power" in California.

**_Reprinted from LOS ANGELES TIMES, November 20, 1977_**

# Rent Control Is a Reform Worth Fighting For

## SHELTERFORCE

Rent control. Why should the housing movement strongly support it? The question is timely, because we increasingly hear housing movement activists playing down rent control's importance. The rap goes something like this: "Rent control is just a reform; it's a stop-gap measure, a temporary solution; it's just too reformist; it won't really accomplish anything in the long run. It's clearly not the answer, but...I think we should fight for it!"

### RENT CONTROL FIRST STEP

Rent control has its limitations. It is not a long term solution and many rent control laws hardly control rents. Also it's difficult to translate rent controls into repairs and improved maintenance without tenants bearing the costs. As long as housing is primarily financed and controlled by private enterprise, there will always be a housing shortage. But calling rent control a reform doesn't help. Every law and any action short of insurrection is a reform.

Should we only give rent control qualified or lukewarm support? We think not. While some reforms are worthless, others can be a necessary and important first step.

### IMMEDIATE BENEFIT TO TENANTS

Rent control is a reform worth fighting for. First of all rent control results in a real and immediate benefit to tenants. Rent control provides a stop-gap measure that protects the poor and moderate income, minorities, and old people on fixed incomes from the brutality of the housing marketplace. This is particularly true in cities and neighborhoods where there are few vacancies and landlords can squeeze rents up astronomically. With over 25% of the population living in shelter poverty, rent control provides real relief.

Second, a reform must be evaluated not only on its content, but within the circumstances in which it is being pushed. When a reform is won by the lower classes through an organized struggle, then those involved in that struggle take a first step toward an understanding that ordinary people, when united, can effect significant change. Also, rent control is an issue that cuts across race, class, sex, age and ethnic lines pitting the people against a class enemy.

A rent control victory reflecting the collective strength of organized tenants in turn spurs more far reaching demands for the fundamental changes we need if people are to live a better life.

## ORGANIZED OPPOSITION TO RENT CONTROL

Third, rent control is the issue around which tenants are mobilizing. High rents charged by landlords is what's in tenants' immediate experience. They do not experience high interest rates charged by the landlord's bank. Tenants won't mobilize against banks who charge high interest rates unless they experience being screwed by banks as homeowners do when they are redlined.

Fourth, rent control does mean a real change in wealth. Tenants pay less rent and landlords and speculators make less profit. If there is any doubt about that just, take a careful look at the extent to which the opposition is organizing to fight it.

The recent formation of the National Rental Housing Council is the best example of how the oppostion perceives rent control. Consisting of landlords, developers and bankers their purpose is to mobilize their vast power and resources to crush any rent control initiative. They know where their self-interest lies. They recognize their shared class interest in the rent control issue. They recognize the explosive impact on controlling profits. They are building a national organization based on collective self-interest and are willing to work with and help each other wherever and whenever it's necessary. Their rallying cry is "defeat rent control."

## PROTECTION FOR ORGANIZING

Fifth, a decent rent control law can give tenants more control over the conditions in which they live. Not only is their rent controlled, but evictions and maintenance have to be regulated as well in order to make rent control workable. Regulation of evictions in turn gives tenant organizers more protection against retaliation by landlords. Any laws that protect organizing are crucial.

## ATTITUDiNAL CHANGE TOWARD PROFITS

Finally, rent control victories effect fundamental changes in people's attitudes about what's right and wrong, what's possible and not possible. In the public mind, it is no longer right for landlords to make as much profit or charge as much rent as they want; the rights of private property are not absolute; a landlord's apartment building is not necessarily his castle; what the market will bear is not a fair measure of what's right.

In those areas where people have fought for rent control, it was attacked as anti-free enterprise and anti-business. Now the debate centers on whether a landlord is entitled to no profit or a fair profit. For example: Five years ago most New Jersey tenants believed landlords could charge as much as they wanted, just like any business. That's the way it had been and that's the way it is. Now many believe a landlord's profit must be balanced against the tenant's needs, even if the landlord goes without a profit.

Furthermore, the fight for rent control educates people as to how landlords profit from housing. Tenants begin to understand that profits are made not only through rents but speculation, tax shelter, appreciation and equity build up. Tenants learn where the government and courts stand. They learn who the housing laws were designed to protect.

## ADVOCATES MUST BECOME ACTIVISTS

Pushing rent control should be seen as part of a strategy to demonstrate the inherent inability of the welfare state in a capitalist economy and social structure to deal with problems that demand a democratic allocation of resources. The strategy is a slow, undramatic building process, but it is a workable strategy in America.

If fundamental and progressive change is to come, then it will come in the course of people struggling to make the welfare state respond to their immediate needs. Fair rent is an immediate need. Housing activists must exercise leadership, not just critical support of those actions that people are mobilizing around. We should not be warning against rent control. In those cities that have none, we should push for it; in those cities that have rent control, we should advocate tighter stronger and more effective controls.

When push comes to shove, when the system amply

**78**

demonstrates its inability to meet the organized demands of housing consumers, then the people will realize they must go beyond the welfare state of a capitalist economy and seek a truly democratic solution.

It's time for tenant leaders and housing activists to get off their disclaimers and get into the forefront of the rent control battles.

*Reprinted from SHELTERFORCE, Spring 1978*

# Rent Control and
# A Fair Return

## DAVID HARVEY

TENANTS ARE IN REVOLT--from Los Angeles to Long Island and from Boston to Baltimore. The explanation is simple enough. Where they once laid out, on average, a quarter of their incomes on rent, tenants now find that 35 per cent, and in some places 50 per cent, of their paycheck is going to the landlord. And that comes hard in times when real incomes are being reduced by rampant inflation.

The rent control which many tenant groups advocate is, of course, a controversial issue, clouded by a smokescreen of rhetoric from both sides. Under such circumstances it is quite proper, as Professor Hanke recently suggested in *The Sun* (September 14, Opinion-Commentary), to seek a sober, "scholarly" evaluation of what the consequences of controls are likely to be.

Unfortunately, the mysterious studies he cites produced a litany of objections to rent control which sounded suspiciously like those trotted out by landlords as they fight well financed and often vicious campaigns--replete with dramatic scare tactics--against proliferating tenants' movements across the country.

Rent control, we are told, will lead to disinvestment and abandonment; it will discourage new investment, diminish the tax base, create housing scarcities and thereby spark a rise in property taxes as well as a whole host of awful bureaucratic and social consequences. All that was lacking was a picture of abandoned dwellings in New York's South Bronx, with the question: "Is this what you want for your community?"

The scholarly studies which I read do not tell so simple a story. The evidence they provide on the actual impacts of rent control is mixed (in part because each study has the curious habit of reflecting the views of those who financed it).

Tales of abandonment deal primarily with New York. But those who wish to attribute abandonment to rent control have a hard time explaining why abandonment rates are much higher in non-rent controlled cities like St. Louis, Cleveland and Chicago.

Tales of disinvestment and a sagging tax base can likewise be documented from New York and Massachusetts. But there are plenty of cities lacking rent control which are plagued by those problems and some rent-controlled communities which are not. And if rent control has such dire consequences, why are the controlled apartments of the affluent on New York's Central Park West or Riverside Drive still standing?

Cities without controls often have as much difficulty attracting new investments as those that do, and it has never actually been proved that investment automatically dries up once controls are imposed.

Two conclusions can be extracted from this confusing array of evidence.

First, the impact of controls varies according to social and economic conditions in particular cities -- vigorous and growing communities can continue merrily on their way, while controls are no palliative for the long-run problems of tenants in declining areas.

Second, the impact depends very much on the kind of controls imposed.

What are known as "restrictive" controls freeze rents for prolonged periods. They tend to squeeze out landlords and create housing shortages unless the government steps in to take up the slack (a solution which some see as not all bad).

"Moderate" rent controls, on the other hand, are designed to avoid such problems. They can often work quite well without requiring any dramatic increase in public spending or incurring the dire consequences which landlords and their economist friends always predict.

The central feature of such "moderate" legislation is that it guarantees landlords a "fair" rate of return and permits rent hikes which can be justified by rising costs or improved maintenance. Rent-gouging and rampant speculation are thereby checked--and that can help stabilize many a threatened neighborhood.

By tying rent increases to maintenance and compliance with housing codes, housing quality can be improved and tenants can be better serviced. For legislation of this sort to work, however, tenants

**81**

must be protected against arbitrary eviction—such protection is a standard feature of the "moderate" rent control package.

Exactly what is "fair" or "moderate" is not easy to determine. In Fort Lee (one of over 100 communities in New Jersey with rent control on the books) rent increases were initially tied to changes in the consumer price index, but subsequently were brought down to 2.5 per cent a year or to the level of the index, whichever was lower. In Washington, rent increases were legislated at from 2 per cent to 10 per cent in 1978 but are tied to the price index this year and next.

Under the Baltimore proposal, determination of what is fair would be left to a tenant-landlord commission to be set up no later than January 1, 1981. In the interim, landlords would be permitted annual rates of increase between 4 per cent and 7 per cent (depending on who pays the utilities). As an interim measure, this is within the middle range of what is being fixed as "moderate" elsewhere.

Tenants, of course, should not be deluded into thinking that moderate rent controls will solve all their problems. Rents will almost certainly continue to rise at a pace which will be exceedingly burdensome for the poor in particular.

Landlords, for their part, abhor moderate rent control in part because the traditional sanctity of private property rights is threatened, but also because the question of what constitutes a "fair" rate of return is opened up for perpetual public scrutiny and debate.

Tenants, for example, might readily agree that rents should rise in line with inflation—provided, that is, wages and salaries, social security and welfare payments also keep pace. But with real incomes declining, tenants might reasonably insist that it is only "fair" that a part of the inflationary burden be passed on to landlords.

The question before the electorate is, therefore, whether such a sharing of the inflationary burden is reasonable in times like these and whether the proposed package of controls is appropriate to such a task given the social and economic conditions which prevail in Baltimore today.

**Reprinted from The Baltimore Sun, September 20, 1979**

# Rent Control is Absolutely Essential

## JAMES O'CONNOR

The orthodox economics argument against rent control is based on a flawed concept of how and why capitalism works. Orthodox economics claims that the free operation of the "laws of supply and demand" removes shortages by driving up prices and profits, encouraging new investments in productive capacity stimulating production, and expanding available commodity supplies, hence alleviating shortages. However, this "micro-economic" analysis tears the whole question out of the context of the operation of capitalism as a whole. USA capitalism today is characterized by profits utilized within the industrialized zones to pay off past indebtedness and other more or less normal expenditures, but also increasingly for speculative purposes. New productive investments are increasingly for speculative rural areas, the sun-belt, and the Third World, "where labor power is cheap and disciplined by authoritarian states." In the economic "recovery" from 1975 to the present, for example, consumer credit and consumption spending has led the way; investment spending is roughly one-half of what it has been during previous post WWII recoveries. Big capital today is practically blackmailing the Federal government to create more tax incentives to invest, attack the welfare state more sharply, etc.

In this context, if rents increase in Santa Cruz, speculative flows of money capital into Santa Cruz increase. This would drive rents and housing prices up still further. The opposite effect predicted by bourgeois economics would occur. Further, to the degree that higher rents and housing prices would actually stimulate new construction, housing would be more and more oriented to individuals and families able to pay higher rents and prices. Given the stagnation and decline of real wages together with the depression in the local job market, the masses of residents in Santa Cruz would effectively be eliminated from the housing market (which of course is already increasingly the case.) Santa Cruz would become a middle and upper-middle class city, which is doubtless one of the aims of the real estate speculators and their political allies.

The only kind of new housing which the majority of Santa Cruz citizens can afford is publicly-built and/or subsidized housing. Meanwhile, rent control *organized by an elected body* to insure popular control is absolutely essential as a holding action against mass impoverishment of Santa Cruz renters. The demand for rent control is at root a demand for decent real wages of the satisfaction of basic needs. The next logical step is the demand for public housing designed by, for, and of ordinary working people and small business-people in the city and county. In cities with strong working class movements or political presences, demands for this kind of public housing have been at times won (e.g., Hunter's Point in San Francisco).

The fact is that the housing question has never been and can never be solved within the confines of the private market. If it could, why is it true that in the richest country in the world, in a period when national income increases, the quality of housing deteriorates, housing prices grow dramatically, rents are pushed up by speculation, and in every city in the country rent strikes, rent control actions, and related actions have occurred in response? This is a basic contradiction which I challenge any bourgeois economist or real estate speculator to "explain away" on the basis of the "laws of supply and demand."

The argument for rent control and public housing organized by, for and of the people ought to appeal not only to renters and potential renters, but also to the average Santa Cruz small business person (just as the argument has appealed to the small business class in other countries). The fact is that wages must be sufficient to cover the cost of reproducing the labor power of workers and their families. The history of capitalist inflation, especially during the past decade or so in the advanced capitalist countries, proves that wage demands, demands for social services, self-reduction of prices, etc. accelerate when the general price level expands at more than a minimal rate. Housing is the most important single commodity in the reproduction of family life. High rents and housing prices in the last analysis mean higher wages, tougher union organizing drives, and more militant wage struggles. These can only be the ruination of local competitive small business already operating on a thin margin of profits, that is small businesses with little or no control over the prices they receive for what they sell. In my judgement, this may be a life and death issue for many small businesses which do not stand to gain directly from high rents, high land prices, high housing prices. Small businesses hiring a few or a few dozens of workers will have to pay higher wages without rent control. This is the price the land and housing speculators extract from their "fellow businessmen." Small businesses all over the advanced capitalist world have learned the hard way that good, low-cost housing, i.e., public housing organized in the interests of ordinary working people, is essential for the survival of their businesses and their survival as a social class.

**Reprinted from: City on a Hill Press, University of California, Santa Cruz, March 1, 1979**

# The Strategic Potential of Rent Control

## PETER MARCUSE

What role is rent control likely to play in current and future political and economic conflicts? How important an issue is it likely to be in future struggles for progressive social change? What characteristics will heighten its importance, and what characteristics will limit it?

The comments that follow must of course be seen in a broader context: housing itself is only a part of a much larger picture, and a rather subsidiary part, it has been previously argued. That broader context is not described here. Further, I have argued elsewhere (Marcuse, 1978) that "housing" is more a convenient category for analysis than a substantive and independent variable on the historical scene; yet some comments on the role of housing itself as a political issue are a necessary part of any comment on the political role of rent control.

### A. The Potential for Major Impact

*Rent control as an issue around which major mobilizations are likely to take place, then, or mass movements to form, has the following positive characteristics:*

1. It deals with housing, one of the most important problems for individuals and families in their everyday lives. Housing consumes 20-30% of average family income; it is the single largest expenditure in the household budget. The residence is the place where most persons spend more time than anywhere else. Its characteristics affect the quality of individual life directly and significantly. Its importance transcends even its critical role of providing shelter, and links it directly to problems of alienation endemic in the social system (Marcuse, 1976).

2. The market, and policies dominated by market forces, are peculiarly unlikely to produce socially desirable housing arrangements. Because of the high capital cost of new housing, as well as its high operating costs, income inequalities will be blatantly exhibited in housing patterns. The demands of production and the demands of consumption conflict directly in the market for land, unlike the market for telephones, for instance. Production dominates, and consumers must buy their way out of the resulting problems with such income as they may have.

Other weaknesses of market allocations are accentuated in housing. Social costs are substantial and have quite different impacts from private costs, major externalities exist that are not captured in market reckonings, the interests of future generations in decisions with long-lasting consequences play less of a role than the profits of present generations, intangibles such as community, friendliness, diversity, beauty, which need social action for their enhancement, are not likely to fare well in a market-dominated housing system. And the negative results, in housing, are not obscure or remote or even debatable. Efforts for better housing may thus readily be used to reveal deeper political and economic problems.

3. Rent control, among housing issues, is one of the most likely to generate mass involvement. At the one extreme, direct action, as via rent strikes, utilities withholding, or squatting, involves high personal risks, risks which for an individual can only be minimized by an already high level of social organization. Where either such social organization already exists from other sources, or where the risks are seen as slim because what may be lost is in any event undesirable, direct action is more likely; thus direct action in the Depression, or in the ghettoes in the 1960's. Otherwise, direct action is unlikely on a continuing basis under normal circumstances.

At the other extreme, campaigns for increased public subsidies are too remote in their targets, too long-term in their potential results, too indirect and diffuse in their impact, and, at least in the United States today, too little based on what is considered politically feasible, to generate major mass involvement.

Rent control has the potential for avoiding both of these weaknesses. Because it is directed at government action, it does not jeopardize the individual's home; because it will directly and immediately affect his or her monthly rent, its potential benefit does strike home. It is local and direct, and the issues are comprehensible in the short run to everyone. It suffers from a lack of acceptability in conventional politics; once legitimately entered onto the political arena, however, it is likely to be a strong issue.

European experience tends to corroborate the foregoing. Council housing in England and social housing in Germany are well accepted in these politically more advanced countries, but rent strikes have not been major weapons there either. Rent controls and subsidies — often linked together — have, however, been the subjects of substantial political pressure.

Coalition building is feasible for rent control. Low-income and middle-income tenants have a common interest in bringing rents down at least to the fair return level. And it is a true common interest, not merely a coalition built on trade-offs and reciprocity. The push to control rents below the fair return level, and to deal with hardship issues, moves from common interest to return level, and to deal with hardship issues, moves from common interest to reciprocity. Middle-income tenants do not suffer from hardship in the same sense as those of low income, and the ideological implications of hardship formulas will not appeal to those already doing well within the system. The dangers of cooptation discussd below thus are of concern. Within such limits, however, effective coalitions can be, and have been, built around rent control.

Such coalitions can be useful even beyond their common ground, by producing successes on which low-income efforts can build to go beyond the issues on which the coalition agrees. Immediate successes are important in the dynamics of mass movements, and coalition possibilities will help provide them for rent control.

5. The oppression of women within the family can serve to heighten the militance of movements around housing issues, although it may also dampen it. Women's traditional role within the family makes them more keenly aware of the irrationalities of the housing system; they are more immediately and more significantly affected by it than are men in the traditional male roles. Women have thus historically played a leading role in tenants movements, and are today.

The home is also, however, the scene of the exploitation of women within the family. The discontent of a woman with her housing, whether she is working outside the house or within it, can be seen by a husband as discontent with him, and what he provides. The response can be his efforts to increase the burden on her, and/or to blame her for the conditions of the house. This will of course be more true of conditions of the individual dwelling unit than of the neighborhood, which are less within the individual family's control; but is at the level of the individual unit that many housing-centered conflicts occur. Again, rent strikes and actions against individual landlords about individual units aggravate the problem; neighborhood actions, and actions directed at public results, such as rent control, are less subject to be vitiated by intra-family sexism, and more likely to call for the the accumulated and repressed leadership, energy, understanding and organizational skill of women.

## B. Limiting Factors

*The factors limiting rent control as a social issue and basis for mass action are as follows:*

1. Controversies about housing take place at the consumption, not the production, end of the economic system. This is not to say that housing does not play a critical role in the production processes, or that state policies affecting housing are not significantly motivated by considerations arising out of the production processes. Nor is it to say that consumption is not a critical variable in the smooth functioning of the productive processes and the economy as a whole. Both of these issues have been the subject of much discussion, and some controversy, in the current literature, and it is not intended to investigate them further here.

The point here is simply that controversies surrounding housing are attenuated in their impact on the fundamental relations of production. While victories on housing issues, such as the imposition of rent controls, may weaken the legitimacy of the dominant relationships, particularly if their full ideological implications are drawn out in the course of the struggle, such victories do not seriously hamper the accumulation process, the economic processes of the system. Concessions can therefore readily be granted, and compromises achieved. Rent control may, from the point of view of the dominant economic groups, appropriately be submitted to the conventional political processes for resolution; whatever that resolution is, only some marginal economic interests will be affected, and that within quite acceptable limits.

European experience certainly bears out this conclusion. All kinds of rent control schemes, from extraordinarily rigid, as during wartime, to very loose, as in Germany today, to repeal, as in Sweden, are consistent with governments running the spectrum from conservative to liberal socialist. The same is true, more broadly, of housing policies in general. Housing is marginal to the productive processes, and a wide range of approaches to housing are compatible with the continued prosperity of a market economy. The ultimate sensitivity of the system to housing issues is thus not great.

2. Housing appears as a private matter at present. The ideological web built up about housing over the last two centuries links it with the sanctity of the individual and the nuclear family, the private personality, the refuge of each person from the outside world. The free-standing single-family house is the symbol of that ideology. The apartment shares it; even the police, the direct agents of the state, need a warrant (theoretically) to violate it. To see this supremely personal adjunct of one's life as a social product, to put its future up to the vagaries of political or legal or direct action controversies, runs against ingrained (in the active sense) convictions.

By the same token, improvements in housing are seen as functions of individual action. Unlike job upgrading or increased pay, which are seen by most workers as functions of collective action, improved housing is seen as moving up — *moving*, not staying and collectively upgrading. The impetus for short-range collective action is thus much reduced. Only for the elderly is this not so; their interest in collective action on housing issues is thus likely to be unusually high. This can be seen both on neighborhood issues and on issues as rent controls both of whose importance is inversely proportional to individual mobility.

3. Ease of coalition-building has disadvantages as well as advantages: the likelihood of submergence of the goals of lower-income tenants to other members of the coalition. History shows a number of examples of such submergence: the events of the 1920's in New York, when after passage of limited rent control legislation tenant groups became virtual administrative adjuncts to the New York State Democratic administration; the shifting emphases of the conflicts of the early 1970's; the erosion of united action after the rental market for higher income tenants had loosened up in Sweden and Germany; the shifting nature of the formulae for limiting rents in the United Kingdom.

4. The subordination of housing to broader issues is as true of specific situations of conflict as it is at a more general and theoretical level. Housing is the focus of few political organizations and few major

political changes are centered around housing-related concerns. Even the ghetto rebellions of the 1960's, which were as directly related to neighborhood-level conditions and took place on as close to a community level as any major social upheavals in recent history, did not focus heavily on housing. Housing problems were high among the complaints of participants, in interviews after the event, but improved housing was hardly seen as the major solution being demanded by those events. Movements originating in housing or rent control problems must be ready to adapt themselves to different demands and confront different challenges as situations develop. This may often mean rent control demands will suffer, as they did when the Socialist Party had to turn to defend its parliamentary legality in 1919 and 1920, or when racial issues took center stage in the 1960's, or perhaps today, with issues of employment at the national level and housing abandonment at the local level have become pre-eminent.

5. Rent control is inherently a quantitative issue; quantitative issues are by nature negotiable; negotiations lend themselves to bureaucratic handling, technical detail, leadership centralization, passive membership, and compromise. Like wage demands in a factory, ceiling rents on housing are as easily seen as matters of mutual adjustment as of principle. There are of course principled issues involved in rent control, as there are in wage demands, but it takes an effort to keep the issues on the plane of principle, to continue to emphasize the issues in the face of the temptation to haggle over amounts. Quantitatively negotiable issues are rarely the bases for fundamental conflicts.

6. Rent control is a device to regulate one aspect of the private market in housing. It assumes the existence of that private market. It simply tries to smoothen out that market, to make it function more effectively, to make it more "orderly."

At the level of liberal/conservative political controversy, rent controls do belong on the liberal end of the spectrum. They suggest that there is some public interest in the regulation of the private market. Their position on the spectrum is akin to that of public utility regulation: fundamental institutions and arrangements are not challenged, but marginal decisions are overseen. That does create some ideological issues of legitimacy, and some opponents of rent control see it clearly: when Frank Kristof speaks of "the institutionalization of the notion that increases in rents...are a privilege and not a right," he is succinctly capturing the political thrust of rent control — more accurately than those opponents who shout loudly of rent control as socialism and a subversion of the free enterprise system.[1] Rent control is a populist issue, in the classical sense, not a radical one.

There is an essential problem in trying to make it a radical issue in any deeper sense. The private market, no matter how regulated, overseen, and controlled, will never meet the housing needs of the poor. The forces that dominate the private market will never allocate land to housing, nor housing among its users, in the same way that democratically, politically determined, methods would. Objectively, rent controls do not, and cannot, no matter how far pushed, lead to a radically different social result than the present market system.

The more radical implications of rent control arise from what it cannot do, not from what it does. if these implications are drawn during particular campaigns, the possibilities for advancing delegitimation exist. In some campaigns, the implications have historically been drawn, and some of the groups involved in current controversies draw them. Urban Planning Aid in Boston, for instance, in analyzing Massachusetts' rent control laws, says, in deliberate and well chosen words:

> Underlying (landlords' opposition to rent control) is the basic assumption that the private market system can be relied upon to meet the housing needs of Commonwealth residents. But the growing scarcity of decent, affordable housing throughout the state casts considerable doubt on this proposition. If the private sector is unable or unwilling to do the job, subject to socially necessary forms of regulation, the solution is not to repeal or modify government controls. Instead, new forms of housing finance, ownership, and control must be created to more adequately serve people's housing needs.[2]

The Metropolitan Council on Housing in New York City is more explicit in what those new forms might be; their program, appropriately entitled "Housing in the Public Domain: The Only Solution," calls for a Housing Board elected by Tenants committees to manage as much housing as is necessary to alleviate the housing shortage and permit every tenant a decent home for 15% of his or her income.[3] The perceived limits of rent control, not its strengths, produce such recommendations.

Within the narrower confines of rent control, aspects that will tend to broaden the issues can be identified:

* Using tenant hardship as the determining criteria for setting rents, rather than returns to landlords;
* acknowledging and highlighting the limitations of rent control;
* developing programs that will increase the redistributive impact of controls;
* using the anomalies produced by rent control to highlight the irrationalities and counter-social results of the private market in housing;
* linking rent controls with the need for immediate subsidies and ulitmately "housing in the public domain."

Because rent control directly affects a poor tenant at the immediate point of hardship, it will be a strongly felt issue at the time of crisis; because rent control assumes the continued existence of the deeper causes of that hardship, it will also be a limited issue. It is likely in the middle range to be preempted by middle-income groups, and to provide few real benefits for the poorest and worst housed. Its fate will in most cases be determined by forces outside of the housing sector, and it will be a primary demand in few major struggles. The history of rent control and its determinants bears out these essentially strategic conclusions.

Rent controls may be presented as the method used by a benevolent state to ameliorate distortions in the housing market in the interests of the poor and the ill-housed. Or they may be presented as a victory of a unitary tenants movement over a set of malevolent interests. In fact, neither explanation is historically correct. Where rent controls have been effectively implemented, it has been because of the needs of accumulation, of production; otherwise, they have helped middle class tenants, and sometimes landlords as well, but had negligible impact on the housing of the poor.

Mass movements of the poor have historically recognized these facts. They have never, in the United States, made rent control a key objective, and where it has been, as in England, its force lay in its intimate connection with the government provision of housing and, ultimately, socialization or municipalization of the housing stock. In the sphere of accumulation then, rent control is not of major import. Some forms of rent control, those basing limits on tenant incomes, have a greater objective potential for redistribution than others, which focus on landlord income. But it is at the level of delegitimation, by using the failure of rent controls to solve the problem at which they are aimed, that its greatest contribution to change will lie.

[1] Kristoff, p. 13
[2] Urban Planning Aid, I-2
[3] Hawley, pp. 55-8

*Reprinted by permission from: The Political Economy of Rent Control: Theory and Strategy, Papers in Planning No. 7, New York, Columbia University, Division of Urban Planning, 1979.*

# Is a Tenant a Second Class Citizen?

## ALLAN DAVID HESKIN

Being a tenant is not part of the American Dream. Tenants are, in an essential way, the unpropertied in a society in which private property is central. Some see their continued existence as a constant contradiction in American life. Periodically, tenants, reacting to their position in society, have acted collectively in their own behalf. Sometimes this action has been violent and other times it has taken the form of orderly political processes.

All Americans are supposed to own their own home. From the very beginning of this country the assumption has been that a burgeoning affluence would erase the categories of landlord and tenant (Starr, 1977, p. 16). The first settlers came here seeking the freedom and independence that landownership necessarily confers in an agricultural economy (Warner, Jr., 1972, p. 16). They built a society that had the ownership of property at its center. People who did not own land could not vote nor could they hold office. It was not until 1860 that tenants received the right to vote in federal elections, and it should be noted that, even today, many tenants continue to be ineligible to vote in bond, property tax and special district elections (Martin, 1976).

Tenants were characterized as second class citizens early in our history. The movements to give suffrage to tenants spread throughout the states before the federal rule was changed. In the 1820's and 30's the constitutions of Massachusetts, New York and Virginia were amended in tenants favor. The list of those opposed to the change in these states is impressive. Among them were John Adams, Daniel Webster, James Madison, James Monroe and John Marshall. Clinton Rossiter reports on their opposition:

There were, for the most part, libertarians who took pride in the "great subdivision of the soil" among the American people and were devoted to the cause of a yeoman republic. But they could not abandon a fundamental teaching of their fathers: that *men without property lack of independence, judgment, and virtue to be participating citizens of a free republic.* They clung tenaciously, like the good conservatives they were, to the inherited doctrine of the *"stake-in-society",* which affirms that office-holding voting should be the concern of those only who have *"a common interest with, and attachment to the community".* Their chief concern, of course, was the rapidly growing urban mass, which they insisted on identifying with "the mobs of Paris and London". (1962, p. 118) (emphasis added).

Despite the fears of many of our founding fathers, tenants became a significant social group in our society. In the 1840's, the first deliberately planned rental units - "tenements" - were built in New York City (Starr, 1977, p. 16). By the 1890's, nearly two-thirds of the residents of our major metropolitan areas were tenants (U.S. Bureau of the Census, 1971, p. 646). This overwhelming number of tenants did not, however, reduce the importance of landownership in American life. With industrialization and urbanization the drive for agricultural land was transformed into the desire to own urban land and especially into a passion for homeownership (Downing, 1969 and Sklar, 1976). In the expansionist period of our history tenants could escape oppressive conditions by claiming the free land to the west (Coker, 1942). At the turn of the century this escape was increasingly accomplished by the upwardly mobile who sought homeownership and a move to the suburbs (Sennett, 1970).

The 20th century has seen the playing out of the pattern set in the late 19th century. By 1950, 55 percent of the population in the standard metropolitan areas owned their homes (U.S. Bureau of the Census, 1977, p. 781). In 1976 this percentage has risen to 64.7 percent (U.S. Bureau of the Census, 1976, p. 1). The substantial increase in homeownership was aided by a continuous policy of the federal government favoring homeownership. The federal intervention began with President Hoover who in 1931 artfully located the place of homeowners and tenants in the American psyche:

> To possess one's own home is the hope and ambition of almost every individual in our country, whether he lives in hotel, apartment or tenement...Those immortal ballards, Home Sweet Home, My Old Kentucky Home, and The Little Gray Home in the West, were not written about tenements or apartment...they never sing songs about a pile of rent receipts (Abrams, 1956, p. 454).

Even with this extraordinary rise in homeownership, the unsung tenant remains in the majority among important segments of our society. In the central cities tenants made up 50.5 percent of the population of 1976 (U.S. Bureau of the Census, 1976, p.1). In the states of New York and Hawaii tenants are in the majority (U.S. Bureau of the Census, 1977). In California, the third most populous tenant state, the percentage of tenants in the population grew from 37.1 percent in 1960 to 45 percent in 1970 (State of California, 1973, p. 18). In the Los Angeles-Long Beach SMSA tenants make up 51.7 percent of the population (U.S. Bureau of the Census, 1974). Los Angeles, itself, is 61.7 percent tenants and smaller cities such as Santa Monica, which is 80.2 percent tenants, have even larger tenant majorities (Southern California Association of Governments, 1978, pp. 58-59).

Tenants are predominant among lower income people. A 1976 study of California's population indicated that tenants were in majority in all income groups up to $10,000 annual income (U.S. Department of Commerce, 1978, p. 163). Among the total of families with up to $15,000 income per year, 51.5 percent are tenants. It is important, however, not to overemphasize the low income tenant for this study also indicated that 26.4 percent of tenants had annual incomes in excess of $20,000.

### History of Tenant Collective Action

The history of tenant collective action is not well documented. Charles Beard gives us only the slighest view of the period in which tenants obtained the vote. He reports that the movements began in the new states: "In none of them was there an upper class of wealth and power comparable to that represented by the great landlords of rich merchants of the original thirteen colonies" - and was aided by the substantial immigration of industrial workers who were forming trade unions and labor parties in the growing industrial cities (Beard, 1944, pp. 212-213).

References to particular collective tenant actions begin in the late 1800's. Burghardt reports that rent strikes were an annual affair in New York City in the 1890's (1967, p. 15). Others have reported on periods of intense tenant activity after World War I and during the depression of the 1930's (Note 1968, p. 1370). Each of these periods was marked by economic crisis and a housing shortage. Each of these periods was also marked by housing reform.

The turn of the century saw the adoption of the "tenement house laws", the forerunner of the housing codes now enacted across the country (Girbetz and Grad, 1966, pp. 1259-67). The end of the First World War brought on the United States' first experience with large scale rent control (Cohen, 1946). The Depression brought on the Federal government's first experiments with public housing (Post, 1938). Following each of these flurries of activity tenant activism faded. The debate about rent control and the issue of its adoption or termination continues to this day. Public housing, which raised many ideological issues contrary to the private property ethic, has fallen into disrepute (Gottlib and Wolt, 1977, pp. 259-262 and the National Commission on Urban Problems, 1968).

The 1960's saw the beginning of another period of increased tenant collective activity. An argument can be made that this period continues through today. The locus of tenant action has moved about the country since the 1960's, and there have been years of more or less activity. Three factors seem to have played a major role in this recent period: 1) the civil rights movement, 2) the war on poverty, particularly the legal services it supported, and 3) the student movement.

This period of tenant activity is generally seen as beginning with the Harlem rent strikes of 1963-65 (Lipsky, 1970). The Harlem strikes, part of the civil rights movement of the time, ended with a reform in landlord-tenant law which is indicative of the period. (Nairson, 1972). The Harlem action also led to the formation of the National Tenants Organization (NTO) (Marcuse, 1971). NTO has been a force of spreading tenant organizing and a lobby in Washington D.C. which has affected federal housing policy (Burghardt, 1972, p. 17).

The war on poverty brought organizers and lawyers to the tenant movement, and the lawyers, in particular, brought major reforms to landlord-tenant law (Hartman, 1975, pp. 81-2). For example, the National Housing Law Project, formed in 1968, joined NTO's effort in Washington and supported the efforts of the many neighborhood legal services programs throughout the country. Major reforms of this period were the warranty of habitability and the protection against retaliatory eviction. These laws allow tenants to withold rent if a landlord fails to maintain the leased property, and protect a tenant against eviction for complaining about the condition of the property and demanding repair. All the major states and many smaller ones now have these reforms (Heskin, 1978).

The student efforts brought rent strikes and rent control drives to college towns such as Cambridge, Berkeley, Ann Arbor and Madison (Burghardt, 1972). There efforts had mixed results, but they did create a group of people trained and involved with housing issues who still play a major role in helping to further define the role of tenants in American Society.

State-wide tenant organizations also emerged in the early 1970's in Massachusetts and New Jersey. New Jersey's organization has served as a model which other states have followed (Hartman, 1975, p. 82). Founded in 1972 following the end of the Nixon rent freeze, it has been successful in winning an extraordinary number of battles in the courts and state legislature, and has helped bring rent control to 102 cities in the state (Gilderbloom, 1978). It has also led to the formation of Shelterforce, a collective, which puts out a national tenant newspaper by the same time. The newspaper reports on tenant activity around the country and expresses tenants' opinions on a broad array of housing and national policy questions.

## Tenant Collective Action in California

Even though California has the third highest proportion of tenant units population among the states, it has not historically been a major scene of tenant organizing. Although there were episodes during difficult years, especially in the college towns, little has been sustained. The California tenant was thought of by aspiring tenant organizers to be too individualistic and too mobile to be organized. In addition, housing conditions have been seen as relatively good, particularly in light of the mild California winter, and urban settlement in the state too spread out and tenant densities too low for collective action.

California, however, has seen a substantial increase in tenant activity over the past few years, and an expolsion in tenant activity over the past few months. A number of factors have led to the dramatic rise in activity. The 1970's have seen a substantial drop in vacancy rates, an unusually rapid rate in rent increases, and an extraordinary rise in the price of houses. The year 1978 brought Proposition 13, known as the property-owners' revolt, which in turn has generated a tenant revolt of unheard of proportions.

## 1. Pressures on California Tenants

The 1979 vacancy rates in the Los Angeles area were around 5 percent, thought by many to be a critical level indicative of a housing shortage. Since 1970, this rate has been steadily dropping. The current Los Angeles vacancy rate is said to be 2.6 percent, and the Santa Monica vacancy rate is at an extraordinary low 1.4 percent (Real Estate Research Council of Southern California, 1978).

It is an unwritten rule in the real estate business that rents increase at a rate less than that of the Consumer Price Index. However, during the 1970's rents have been steadily increasing at a rate approaching that of the Index. And, in 1977, the rate of increase in rents was nearly 13 percent — well above the Index figure (Real Estate Research Council of Southern California, 1978). This figure is even more significant when it is considered that around 30 percent of tenants received no rent increases at all during this period (Community Development Department, City of Los Angeles, 1978).

While rents were climbing rapidly, house prices jumped at an extraordinary rate. In the seven county Los Angeles-Long Beach-San Diego area, prices rose at an annual rate of 23 percent in the period from December 1977 to April 1978 and at the rate of 30 percent per year in the six months previous to that (Real Estate Research Council, 1978). The average price of a house in Santa Monica rose from $95,000 in March 1977 to $125,000 in December of the same year (Santa Monica, Department of Environmental Services, 1978). It is not unusual in the area to find a nearly 300 percent increase in value since 1970.

These figures are particularly important to tenants. The Los Angeles Times reported that an analyst estimated that each time the price of the least expensive home is increased in price by $1,000, about 100,000 Californians are priced out of the market (Los Angeles Times, July 30, 1978). With the present median price for all houses in California at $63,000, the analyst estimated that three-fourths or more of the state's families are unable to break into the homeownership market for the first time. Many families who might, with sacrifice, make the monthly payments do not have the savings necessary to make the downpayment. With homeownership so central to the American image of success and security, one has to wonder what impact this is having on the many young tenant families entering the home buying phase of their lives.

One possible source of relief to prospective homeowners might be the increasingly rapid trend towards converting apartments to condominiums. However, the price of condominiums is also inflating at a rapid rate. The cost of a one bedroom condominium in San Francisco rose from $52,000 to $79,000 in the first six months of 1978. An $80,000 one bedroom condominium in Santa Monica rose to $110,000 in the same period (Sternberg, 1978, p. 11). With the need for a down payment and monthly payments from 30 to 35 percent higher than already inflated rents, only about 20 percent of tenants purchase their converted units (p. 11).

## 2. Proposition 13

With rents rising and homeownership being increasingly cut off, the California tenants received a particularly bad blow. The passage of Proposition 13 was promised as a source of relief. The leaders of the campaign promised that the savings resulting from the tax initiative would be passed on to the tenants. The savings to residential landlords has been estimated to be in excess of one billion dollars (Keating, 1978). Although many tenants doubted that the savings would be passed on, they did believe that rent inceases would be slowed. With this belief, many voted for the initiative.

Following the passage of the initiative, it was not only rare for tax savings to be passed on to tenants, but landlords, in significant numbers, carried on business as usual, raising rents in their normal inflated pattern (Community Development Department, City of Los Angeles, 1978). Tenants in many cities went to their city governments for assistance. The post-Jarvis meeting of the Santa Monica City Council is a good example (Office of the City Clerk, City of Santa Monica, 1978).

Santa Monica has had growing tenant activism over the last few years. Appearances before the Council by tenant activists are not

**101**

unusual. At the post-Jarvis confrontation, however, the somewhat hardened council members were visibly shaken. One council member stated his fear that tenants in the council chambers and those screaming from their overflow positions in the halls, were going to "burn the place down". One tenant did see a Watts style revolt as a possibility:

> There's a problem here, and something has to be done about it. Nobody believed that Watts was going to blow up. Everything was pretty much under control. And this isn't Watts and it's not the sixties, but I think there's a big problem and I think something has to be done about it (Office of the City Clerk, City of Santa Monica, 1978, p. 30).

Tenants repeatedly asserted their attachment to the community. They denied that tenants were second-class citizens and asserted full citizens' status and rights. They referred to their apartments as their homes and indicated that they felt those homes were threatened. One tenant reported that she had had to move three times in one year because of rent increases, and brought a cheer from the crowd when she announced that she was not going to move again. She and others indicated they had just formed tenant organizations to defend themselves.

There were many calls for political action against what they felt was a council dominated by propertied interests. One person captured the sentiment of many, stating, "Government is not interfering in the market. The market is interfering in government. . . " Perhaps loudest reaction of the evening came in response to one tenant's caution to the council: "If you think you've seen a homeowners' revolt, just wait for the coming tenant revolt."

Across Southern California, it appeared that the unorganizable California tenant was beginning to organize. Each news broadcast carried an interview with someone from a newly formed tenant organization. A housing industry analyst reacted, "It has been hard to organize renters because they view themselves as future homeowners. But now with the high cost of housing, a lot of people are viewing themselves as *lifelong renters*. Proposition 13 is the spark that has set off a raging fire." (Los Angeles Times, August 4, 1978). (emphasis added).

The governor of the state, Jerry Brown, was drawn into the protest and began a renters hot line in the State Consumer Affairs Department. The hot line was supposed to gather tenant complaints of rent increases. Staff members of the State Department were then instructed to contact the landlords and attempt to convince them to withdraw the increase. The hot line received nearly 15,000 calls in just three weeks, but very few reductions of rent were obtained (Keating, 1978). Similar hot lines were opened up by landlords and tenant groups across the state with similar results.

Pressure built in the state legislature for relief legislation, as it has in earlier periods of tenant protest. A relief bill passed the more liberal Assembly. With his hot line failing, the governor endorsed the bill. Even with this backing, the real estate lobby was strong enough to defeat the proposal in the more conservative State Senate (Los Angeles Times, August 29, 1978). The defeat of the state bill put the focus back on the cities.

Several months earlier, a rent control proposal had been made by a member of the Los Angeles City Council from the most active tenant district. The proposal failed to receive the vote sufficient to escape a Council Committee. With tenants going through what appeared to be a political awakening, the Council went through its own metamorphosis, and unanimously passed a six-month rent freeze ordinance (Los Angeles Times, August 23, 1978). This was followed by the adoption of full scale rent control ordinance.

The City of Los Angeles was not alone (Los Angeles Times, August 4, 1978). Other city councils are at various stages in considering the issue, and rent freeze and Proposition 13 pass-through initiatives are on the ballot in several cities. In the City of Santa Monica, a rent control measure failed 56% of 44% on the same ballot where the Jarvis initiative succeeded, but passed on the April 1979 election that followed. In addition, the strengthened tenant organizations elected two tenant candidates to a previously all property owner city council and a slate of five tenant sponsored candidates to a rent control board.

## Tenant Movement as Social Movement?

At this point, no one knows the depth of the tenant awakening. This could be another episode that will pass or it could be significant advancement of a building tenant movement. Even before the activists in California, there were those who saw what was happening across the country as an increasingly important social movement (Johnson and Lawson, 1975). The accuracy of this observation will depend on both the size of the latent collectivity of tenants and the ability of that collectivity to mobilize (Olson, 1965, 1971, pp. 50-61). No one knows the potential of tenants to organize. If the potential is there and it is realized, no one knows how significant a change in our society it will bring (Pickvance, 1976).

One of the possible paths for a tenant movement to take is toward unionization in the model of labor unions (Moskovitz and Honisberg, 1970). The relatively new national and even newer state tenant organizations indicate a move in this direction. Chester Hartman has written that such tenant unions could work a profound change not only in the landlord-tenant relationship, but in the entire system of local and national housing policy (Hartman, 1975, p. 84). These reforms could be far reaching.

If being a tenant or having tenant support became a significant advantage when running for office, the security of tenure protection against arbitrary eviction, now present only in New Jersey, could sweep the country. Beyond this, it is not difficult to conceive of a law that would require the sharing of equity build-up between landlords and tenants. The questions posed by state and national tax structures which now favor homeownership would have to be examined, and tenants might press for the right to deduct property taxes just as people now deduct sales tax. At all levels of government, actions could be reviewed for their impact on the tenant population.

Unfortunately the classic studies of American voting behavior have not attempted to separate out the significance of tenant status (Campbell et al, 1954 and Campbell et al, 1960). This information might have indicated the size of an organizable tenant collectivity. The votes of tenants may often decide elections today. If they do, we do not know to what extent the tenant status of the voter determined how the votes are cast. Some pollsters are now collecting data on tenants' voting preferences, but they are not asking the detailed questions necessary for understanding the reasons behind these preferences. In a recent poll by the Times Poll, Governor Brown led challenger Evelle Younger 46 percent to 36 percent (Los Angeles Times, September 1, 1978). While the homeowners vote was nearly evenly split, 70 percent of the tenants interviewed favored Brown over Younger. Did the tenants see Brown as more favorable to tenants? Of the group of tenants supporting Brown, only 59 percent favored rent control. Why did 41 percent of the tenants oppose rent control?

A substantial tenant social movement could have implications beyond a level of reform. Tova Indritz states that tenant action breeds radical political consciousness. In her view, "tenant action and radical political consciousness are mutually reinforcing at least so long as the concept of private property remains so entrenched" (Indritz, 1971, p. 39). Is Indritz correct? Has Proposition 13 cast a new light on this question?

Traditionally, tenants are seen in opposition to landlords. Tenant organizers have consistently attempted to radicalize tenants by linking landlords with judges, and bank officials to provide "important lessons on the nature of capitalism" (Katz, 1972, p. 157 and Henry, 1971, pp. 27-28). They have, however, also consistently acknowledged their limited success in this endeavor (Naison, 1972, p. 31 and Jennings, 1972, pp. 58-59). While the landlords' interests are those of private property, the issues that arise between landlord and tenant can easily be seen as issues of consumer protection or be characterized as a moral question of individual landlords' "greed".

In contrast, Proposition 13 has spotlighted the distinction between those who own real property and those who do not, with landlords and homeowners on one side and tenants on the other. However, the role of the homeowner vis-a-vis the tenant is not yet fully defined. If homeowners continue to act with the landlords, tenants may come to the position that they have to act together, as a group for itself, to confront head on questions regarding the rights and roles of private property in our society.

Leaders of California's new tenants' movement see this confrontation between propertied and non-propertied interests emerging in the state. To capture the essence of the situation they have begun to speak to what they call "tenant consciousness". If such a consciousness is emerging among a substantial number of tenants, this would be a new development in the tenant movement. Without the development of tenant consciousness the tenant movement is not likely to develop into either a reform or radical social movement (Naison, 1972, pp. 31-32). Without the sense of shared identity, interests and goals inherent in a common consciousness, sustained, effective, collective action is not likely (Oberschall, 1973, pp. 118-119).

If I were to predict what the future holds, I would have to see growing tenant consciousness and a growing tenant movement. The primary item of consumption is housing. The inflation in housing costs will only make housing's place in our lives more significant. As such, one would expect that its role in the formation of political consciousness would also be of growing importance.

*Essay completed 1980*

# SECTION IV

# HOW TO WRITE A RENT CONTROL LAW

# A Brief Guide to the Drafting of Rent Control Legislation

## W. DENNIS KEATING

The drafting of a state or local rent control law involves complex legal and political decisions. The form and content of rent control legislation, including that initiated by tenant organizations, must conform to constraints of the political and legal situation confronting tenants, as well as current housing conditions.

Since 1969 there has been a proliferation of state and local rent control legislation in the United States. There was a brief period of Federal rent stabilization (1971-1973). These rent control laws vary and tenant advocates and their legislative allies must carefully consider alternative forms of rent control. There is no accepted "model" rent control law because local housing conditions vary so widely throughout the country and the strength of the tenant movement which advocates rent control varies also. Differing state and local housing laws also affect the drafting of rent control legislation. This brief guide provides a general introduction to those interested in drafting rent control legislation.

### STATEMENT OF PURPOSE

Historically, a housing emergency was legally required to justify the enactment of rent control. However, recently courts have recognized that a legislative body need only find that serious housing problems exist.

Serious housing problems which would justify rent control which are typically included in legislative preambles include:
a) excessive rent increases; b) less than normal (5%) rental vacancy rate; c) a significant

percentage of tenants paying in excess of 25%
of income for rental housing; d) deterioration of
rental housing; e) speculation in rental housing;
and f) abnormally high patterns of tenant
eviction and displacement.

One or more of these serious housing problems which threaten
the general health, safety, and welfare of the people should suffice to
justify rent control. However, landlords often challenge the validity of
such legislative findings so there must be reliable and accessible
evidence to support them. This may be obtained from the Housing
Assistance Plans (HAPs) required by HUD for Community Development Block Grant funding to localities and from local housing,
planning, and community development agencies.

## COVERAGE

Usually, rent control legislation does not universally cover all
rental housing. That housing which is exempted is considered to be
occupied by tenants who do not need legal protection against
excessive rent increases, is exempted as an incentive to landlords to
develop additional rental housing, or is exempted for expedient
political reasons. Typical exemptions are:

a) **New Construction:** this can be a blanket exemption (to
encourage new construction) or a conditional exemption (e.g. only the
first rent charged for initial occupancy is exempted);

b) **Owner-Occupied** (2, 3, or 4-unit buildings): owner-occupied
units are usually exempted based on the assumption that, since the
landlord and the tenant live together, the housing should be well-
maintained, rental disputes can be resolved by the landlord and tenant
occupants, and non-professional resident landlords will be less able to
comply with complex rent regulations, thereby causing administrative
problems. (N.B. While an exemption for "mom and pop" resident
landlords is politically popular, small buildings which are owned by
absentee landlords are usually regulated.);

c) **Substantially-rehabilitated housing**: this is sometimes
exempted to encourage the rehabilitation of seriously substandard
housing;

d) **Publicly-owned, operated, or subsidized housing**:
public housing and privately-owned but publicly subsidized housing
(e.g. HUD's Sections 8 and 236 rental housing programs) are
considered to be regulated already by the public agencies which

administer the subsidies. HUD and many State Housing Finance Agencies have legally or administratively exempted housing assisted through their programs from state and local rent control;

e) **Transient and Institutional housing**: hotels, motels, dormitories, hospitals, convalescent homes are usually exempted, as are cooperatives. (N.B. residential hotels have often been regulated);

f) **Luxury housing**: high-rent housing is sometimes exempted because it is not believed that its assumed upper-income occupants need protection against exorbitant rents; what constitutes luxury rental housing can either be defined in the statute or determined administratively (usually according to levels of monthly contract rent);

g) **Existing long-term leases**: these are usually not exempted but instead are considered void upon the enactment of rent control;

h) **Vacancy Decontrol**: If forced to accept rent control, landlords advocate vacancy decontrol. This exempts from any further rent control a vacated apartment. This represents piecemeal decontrol. Landlords are encouraged to harass tenants into vacating "voluntarily", tenants are reluctant to move, rents are skewed in the same building depending upon the length of tenant occupancy, the Rent Control Board has difficulty determining which units are still controlled, and rent increases in decontrolled apartments are all too often exorbitant. Vacancy decontrol should not be included in a rent control law. Instead, uniform decontrol standards should be included (see Decontrol).[1]

## BASE RENT, ROLLBACK, AND TEMPORARY RENT FREEZE
### BASE RENT AND ROLLBACK

All rent control laws include a "base" rent. This serves as the initial level of controlled rents. While this can be the rents as of the date of enactment of rent control, this allows landlords to increase rents in anticipation of rent control. To nullify such distortions in an already tight rental housing market characterized by high and excessive rents, most rent control laws roll back rents prior to the date of adoption. The rollback period varies from a few months up to a year. The choice of the rollback base rent date is usually arbitrary but is intended to reflect a more normal rental housing market and fairer rents generally. Individual determination of a fair base rent is much too cumbersome administratively and should not be allowed.

### TEMPORARY RENT FREEZE

**110**

Rents are often frozen temporarily from the date of enactment of rent control until the rollback, if there is one, or until the appointment of a rent control board and/or the first general rent increase is authorized. Temporary rent freezes lasting several months are justifiable.

## ADMINISTRATION OF RENT CONTROL
## RENT CONTROL AGENCIES AND BOARDS

Rent control policy is usually determined by a citizen board appointed by the Mayor or City Council. Some laws specify qualifications for appointees (e.g. designating proportional representation of landlords and tenants). Since elected local officials are all too often hostile to rent control, allied with real estate interests, and not accountable to tenants, appointed rent control boards may act inimically to tenant interest. If it is legally possible, tenant advocates should consider the alternative of an elected rent control board (modeled after elected School Boards). This will probably require an amendment to the City Charter. Berkeley, California in 1973 briefly had an elected Rent Control Board (until that law was invalidated). In June 1979 Santa Monica elected a 5-member Rent Control Board with broad powers to regulate rents, demolitions, and condominium conversions. Arguably, if tenants can elect a majority of a Rent Control Board, then it will be more accountable to tenant interests (e.g. in determining general rent increase guidelines).

Whether appointed or elected, Rent Control Board members usually receive nominal compensation. Most of New Jersey's local boards consist solely of unpaid volunteers. Rent Control Board members should be required to disclose any real estate holdings.

Rent Control Boards can be staffed by existing local housing and planning agency and City Attorney staff. Preferably, they will have their own independent staff. Hearing examiners and attorneys familiar with housing law and real estate economics will be critical to the efficient functioning of a Rent Control Board.

There have been self-enforcing rent control laws. Landlords are not required to register, compliance is voluntary, and tenants must enforce such laws through appeals boards or in the courts. Several California cities (San Francisco, San Jose, Berkeley, and Davis) have recently passed such laws. While these laws are relatively simple and less expensive to administer, they are usually too weak to protect tenants adequately and are not a model to emulate.

## RENT CONTROL BOARD FINANCING

Local rent control can be financed from municipal general funds or from annual registration fees charged to landlords (these nominal per unit fees can usually be passed on to tenants). Landlords and tenants can also be charged fees for filing appeals. If rent control boards are financed through fees, cities should be prepared to lend them "start-up" funds until they can collect their initial registration fees. (N.B. New York State has partially subsidized New York City rent control since 1962 when New York City assumed responsibility for administering rent control.).

## LANDLORD REGISTRATION

Landlord registration is a key element of rent control. Rent Control Boards should be given broad discretion to require all relevant information from landlords, including operating and maintenance costs. N.B. Requiring landlords to supply information concerning their Federal and state income tax benefits from ownership of rent-controlled apartments (e.g. depreciation) may be challenged as an invasion of privacy.

## RENT ADJUSTMENT METHODS

Rent Control Boards can adjust rents through several alternate methods. Each must be analyzed in terms of fairness to tenants, administrative efficiency, and legality.

### a) Individual Building Petitions

Given the peculiarities of real estate financing and the rent-setting policies of landlords, this is a valid approach. However, given the characteristic diffusion of the housing stock, including fragmented ownership, this is a cumbersome and inefficient method and, for that reason, has been declared unconstitutional.

### b) Cost of Living Index

A relatively simple but misleading rent increase standard is the Consumer Price Index (CPI) or the CPI Rent Index issued bi-monthly by the Bureau of Labor Statistics (BLS) of the U.S. Department of Labor. While landlords argue that they should be allowed to raise rents automatically by at least the CPI, where a building has a mortgaged indebtedness, a significant part of the landlords' costs is fixed and does not vary as do their other expenses because mortgages usually are long-term and at fixed interest rates. Therefore, a CPI standard in an inflationary economy provides a built-in windfall for most landlords.

For this reason, many rent control laws allow landlords only a percentage of the CPI.

### c) Percentage Increases

Many rent control laws include a maximum allowable percentage rent increase annually or empower a Rent Control Board to determine this.

### d) Cost Pass-along

Some rent control laws tie rent increase to landlords' increased costs. Generally, landlords are allowed to pass onto tenants all normal and reasonable increased operating and maintenance costs and amortized capital improvements. However, often mortgage debt financing costs and "depreciation" are disallowed because the former represents "equity" to the landlord and the latter is not necessarily a real expense. New York City's Rent Stabilization system is unique because rent increases are based on an operating cost index (in reality a price index of selected landlord costs compiled annually by the BLS).

Some rent control laws condition landlords' right to general rent increase adjustments to registration and some also condition it to "substantial" compliance with local housing and health codes and maintenance of existing or essential services.

## FAIR RETURN AND HARDSHIP ADJUSTMENTS

Perhaps the most difficult issue to be addressed in the drafting of rent control legislation is how to define and determine the fair return on investment guaranteed to landlord by the courts. Virtually all rent control laws provide hardship adjustment mechanisms for landlords who claim that generally allowable rent increases are not sufficient to provide them with a fair rate of return on investment.

Fair return formulas can be provided in the law. The alternative approach is to give a Rent Control Board discretion to determine a fair return formula, providing it with general guidelines or factors to consider. There are several fair return formulas, each of which presents difficulties in application.

Ideally, a fair return on investment formula would be the most equitable approach. However, the definition and determination of landlord's actual investment (original down payment, appreciation, labor) is usually complex. Some purchasers make only nominal downpayments. Other purchasers have no cash invested as a result of refinancing, years after the original purchase, or inheriting the property. Inclusion of actual tax benefits makes a return on equity formula even more difficult to calculate, even if landlords cooperate in making this information available. Furthermore, the tying of maximum rents to the owner's peculiar financial situation would not be desirable.

The return on market or assessed value approach is not an acceptable alternative, despite its appealing simplicity. This approach, leads to to circular results since present market value is based on a multiple of the gross rents, whose excessive and exorbitant levels are the reason for the imposition of rent control. Use of market value would reward speculation and lead to continuing excessive rent spirals.

An alternate approach is to allow landlords to pass on most increased operating and maintenance costs in order to maintain a reasonable level of net operating income. Financing costs and increases in interest payments would be excluded from allowable operating costs since their inclusion would cause rents to reflect the financing peculiarities of a building, including rising interest rates, and would further encourage speculative selling in rent controlled markets. Tenants should not automatically be forced to bear the burden of refinancing by landlords. Such increases could be limited to refinancing upon a bona fide sale. Rent-controlled landlords should not automatically be guaranteed a positive cash flow, since the free market does not guarantee a positive cash flow.

Whatever formula is used, there is little agreement on a fair and reasonable rate of return on whatever is defined a investment. A range of 8-9% rate of return seems typical where such formulas are in use.[2]

## EVICTION CONTROLS

In order to prevent landlord retaliation against tenants exercising their rights under rent control, most include a "just" cause. Just causes can be few or many. This may be done by the state legislature without rent control but to date only New Jersey has done this (see "New Rights for New Jersey Tenants - 'Good Cause' Eviction and 'Reasonable Rents', 6 RUTGERS-CAMDEN LAW JOURNAL 565 (1975) ).

However, the adoption of municipal rent controls as part of a rent control law may be pre-empted by state law (see, e.g. Michael Marowitz, *Birkenfeld v. Berkeley:* Blueprint for Rent Control in California," 7 GOLDEN GATE UNIVERSITY LAW REVIEW 677 (1977) and Hank Lerner, "The Right to Reasonable Rent Regulation: a Newer Economic Due Process," 65 CALIFORNIA LAW REVIEW 304 (1977) ).

## DECONTROL

Rent control laws typically have a limited duration. Either they are renewable (after 1, 2 or 3 years) or there is a decontrol provision included. Renewal or decontrol is usually tied to a normal annual average rental vacancy rate (e.g. 5%).

## RELATED CONTROLS

There are several related types of controls which this brief guide does not discuss that may be relevant to rent control proponents. This may be included in a rent control law, although they typically comprise separate legislation.

**COOPERATIVE AND CONDOMINIUM CONVERSION CONTROL:** Many landlords may try to evade rent control by converting their apartments into cooperatives or condominiums and reaping short-term windfall profits, thereby aggravating a shortage of affordable apartments. In response, companion laws to control conversions have been enacted, administered by state and/or local planning and housing agencies. These conversion controls typically condition approval of conversion on tenant approval, guarantee some sitting tenants longterm leases, provide relocation benefits, and may limit landlords' prices and profits.

**DEMOLITION CONTROL:** Landlords may also try to demolish rent-controlled buildings in order to convert the land to more profitable use, including newly-constructed luxury housing which is exempt from rent control. This may necessitate strict demolition controls, including the requirement of the replacement of any demolished low and moderate-income housing.

**COMMERCIAL RENT CONTROL:** Only New York City (for a period after World War II) has had commercial rent control.

**RENTERS' TAX RELIEF:** In those jurisdictions where property tax reform has reduced property taxes for landlords without requiring them to pass on these savings to tenants, limited legislation mandating a full or partial pass-along of these savings to tenants may be appropriate as an alternative to rent control. Several California cities have passed such renter tax relief measures in the wake of landlords' windfall profits from Proposition 13 after similar legislation was defeated in the California Legislature.

**MEDIATION BOARDS:** As an alternative to rent control, landlords often propose landlord-tenant mediation boards. Lacking any legal authority to set fair rents or prevent unjust evictions (including those in retaliation against tenants who file complaints) the mediation boards are too weak to present a viable alternative to rent control. Cities like Chicago, San Diego, and Madison have established these boards rather than adopt rent control.

[1] Single-family housing: houses which are rented are often exempted to ensure that they will not be withdrawn from the rental market and to avoid complicating administration by covering single units; however, if single-family rental units constitute a significant proportion of the rental housing market, this exemption may be inadvisable.

[2] Whatever formula is adopted, tenant, as well as landlord, hardship should be considered through the following provisions:

1) hardship rent adjustments should only be allowed if the landlord has fully complied with the law, including local housing codes;

2) tenant hardship should be considered;

3) a ceiling (e.g. 10-15%) should be placed on cumulative annual rent adjustments;

4) only necessary and unavoidable landlord operating and maintenance cost increases should be considered

***Essay completed June 1980***

# Items for Inclusion In a Model Rent Control Law

## EVELYN ONWUACHI AND TIM SIEGEL

The following are items to consider for inclusion in a model rent law. Asterisked (*) items are presently existing in the district of Columbia's Rental Housing Act of 1977. Non-asterisked items have been drawn from the shortcomings of the D.C. law.

1) **Opportunity to Purchase*** Tenants in single-family and multi-family housing should have the legal right to be the very first to be offered the opportunity to purchase the building when the landlord is intending to sell the building. Tenants in single-family housing should be given a minimum of 60 days to consider whether or not they wish or can purchase the building. Tenants in multi-family housing should be given at least 90 days to consider. In either situation, tenants do not need to be incorporated to receive this offer. During this time the landlord may not mention the possibility of sale to the public or show the property to potential outside buyers. Should tenants be unwilling or unable to purchase the building and the building is put on the market for a period of six months but not sold, tenants then have an exclusive opportunity again to purchase the building.

D.C. does not have any provision saying that the landlord's selling price cannot be highly speculative. Activists may wish to include some mechanism for assuring that the landlord's offer will not be absurdly inflated.

2) **No Demolition of Sound Units** Rental housing units that are in rather sound condition may not be demolished.

**117**

This item is to prevent landlords from demolishing perfectly useful, livable units for replacement with a parking lot or office building or even higher grade, luxury rental units. With a severe shortage of rental units, with a growing loss of moderate-rent units in town and across the city, we must try to preserve the stock of apartments that we have.

3) **No Shutdown of Sound Units** Likewise as in 2, sound units should not be allowed to be emptied & boarded up while speculators realize accelerated depreciation. Fines could be imposed for every month that such units were boarded up. After six months or a year, the city could inherit the units.

4) **Relocation Expenses*** Where landlords legally evict tenants (due to substantial rehabilitation for repairs, landlord to move into the unit or demolition) landlords must pay up to $125 per room in relocation costs to tenants. Example: a tenant in an apartment having 1 kitchen, 1 living room, 1 bedroom and 1 den would receive 4 X $125 or $500.

5) **Small Landlord Exemption** In D.C. "small landlords", those owning 5 units or less, are exempt from all rent increase provisions. A model law should not exempt small landlord units. The units in D.C. are notorious for being the first to convert to non-rental use. Some units have received annual increases of over 200%. If we don't want small landlords, the supposed mom and pops, to be submitted to an involved rent increase process we could simply provide for a reasonable automatic rent increase, say, an annual increase of 6 or 8%.

6) **Penalties and Fines** Mandatory fines should be imposed on landlords who knowingly violate the law. False information submitted in the securing of an eviction, bribing a housing inspector, discriminating against tenants, etc. D.C. does provide for fines, but they are not mandatory.

7) **Interest Paid on Illegally-High Rents** Tenants who paid illegally-high rents should receive the illegal portion payments, but with interest. A tenant who paid $250 per month for 6 months when♦the legal rent was $200 per month should receive a refund of $300 plus a compounded interest of at least 6% on the $300.

8) **Public Posting of Rent Levels and Ownership** In the lobby of every apartment building or building containing a rental unit, there should be posted two documents. The first would clearly show the legal rent levels for each apartment. Also included in this notice would be a statement telling tenants that they are entitled to certain rights and to call or write the local rent control agency for more information. A separate notice would inform the tenants of the management company, if any and its phone number and address along with a statement of the true owners, a corporation would have to show its address and its principal officers. The first item would prevent landlords from illegally jacking up the rents whenever a new tenant moved in. The ability to do this would discourage upward filtration of a building. Also tenants could begin to see the amounts of rent monies the owners receive. The second item would provide easier access to the management company (versus just the property manager) and especially to the landlord or true owner. Tenants could better identify and organize against horrible landlords. Hours of time and frustration could be saved in researching just who does own the property. A great deal could be learned about the housing power structure.

9) **Duties and Responsibilities of the Rent Control Office** Any rent control or rental accommodations or tenant-landlord office created by the city would be required to do the following; print all materials in all languages represented in that city, establish a tenant hotline open five days a week to specifically assist tenants in need, release monthly public service announcements on renter rights to the media, produce necessary materials informing the

renting public of their rights, hold monthly or quarterly public forums to explain the law, publish a regular newspaper to inform the public of latest interpretations, actions by the rent office, and keep careful track of the number and nature of complaints and cases it receives. These are rather self-explanatory. Where applicable, materials should be available in Spanish, Chinese, etc. The tenant needs a hotline for quick information — otherwise s/he will be discouraged from asserting their rights. PSA's are cheap and easy ways of informing the public of their rights. Public forums around the city are needed to get the word out. Employees should not confine themselves to the rent control office. Statistics on the work of the office can be of great value in documenting the crisis, displacement, continuing trends. These figures can provide needed ammunition for acquiring future legislation.

But unless these points are spelled out in the law they may never be done. D.C. had a rent control law for three years (1974-1977) before any public information was printed about it!

10) **Retaliatory Eviction\*** Tenants may not be harassed or evicted because they choose to assert their rights. This includes the right to summon housing inspector and to call a meeting of the tenants. Where this occurs landlords may be fined.

*Essay completed May 1980*

# Writing a Strong But Legal Rent Control Law

## John Atlas

The toughest rent control system in the country can be found in Fort Lee, New Jersey, birthplace of that state's tenant movement and headquarters of the powerful New Jersey Tenants Organization. Since its enactment in 1972, landlords have attempted to skirt the democratic process by appealing to the courts to invalidate or weaken Fort Lee's rent control. Its most recent, and somewhat successful attempt was in the 1978 New Jersey Supreme Court case called *Helmsley v. Fort Lee,* No. 5 A 163, 164, 165, 166, and 167 (Sup. Ct. N.J. Oct. 17, 1978). Litigation is a tactic we can expect from landlords all across the county.

Accordingly, the following article will examine not only the desirability of rent control but its legality. I will summarize the *Helmsley* case and then examine some of the major legal issues raised by it and other rent control cases. I hope this will aid local activists and their lawyers in avoiding any legal pitfalls when drafting local and state legislation.

### N.J. DECISION

The *Helmsley.* case involved a challenge to the rent control ordinance in Fort Lee. The ordinance limited automatic yearly rent increases to 2½%. If the landlord believed he was not making a fair profit, he could apply for hardship relief. Hardship increases, however, expired at the end of one year. These hardship adjustments did not become adjustments to the old rent. In addition, there was no automatic pass through of operating cost increases and landlords were prohibited from passing on property tax increases to their tenants.

The landlords did not argue that the law was unconstitutional on its face. Rather, they tried to prove that the Fort Lee ordinance as applied to all landlords in Fort Lee was confiscatory. This meant that despite the diversity in Fort Lee's apartments which varied in size, age, and financial histories, the landlords had to prove widespread deprivation of profits upon these diverse buildings.

At the trial, the landlords presented numerous expert witnesses and offered volumes of documents and statistics into evidence. Fort Lee, the named defendant, managed one witness on its behalf. The tenants who were really on trial, but not a party to the suit, had limited participation. In an unanimous 71 page opinion the court held that strict rent control schemes are permissible as long as municipalities provide an efficient and fair method of granting hardship relief to owners of efficiently managed apartments who allege they are not making a profit.

The 2½% Fort Lee limitation on rent hikes was ruled constitutional through December 31, 1976, but unconstitutional as applied after that date. This was based on the Court's prediction that the administration of the ordinance could not provide for prompt and efficient "hardship" relief for landlords. The Court perceived that after December 31, 1976 it was inevitable that the combined effect of the 2½% limit and a faulty hardship procedure would end up denying landlords even the bare minimum "just and reasonable return" (profit) required by the New Jersey Constitution. Landlords looking for hardship relief had to seek it from Fort Lee's Rent Control Board. The Court found that the Board lacked the professional expertise, resources and time "to support a sophisticated administrative relief system." For example, it took several months to grant individual hardship relief.

In sum, the Court ruled that any town can enact strict rent controls, but if it does it had better be prepared to provide prompt, fair, and efficient hardship relief, preferably by a professionally staffed rent board.


## WHAT FACTORS WILL JUSTIFY THE ENACTMENT OF RENT CONTROL?

The first line of attack by landlords attempting to invalidate rent control through the courts is that there is no emergency and/or no rational basis for enacting rent control. Therefore, it is arbitrary and in violation of the Due Process clause of the United States Constitution.

The U.S. constitutional requirement that rent controls were valid only in an emergency ended in the 1930s. In the 20s and 30s the U.S. Supreme Court repeatedly held that legislation regulating the price charged for goods and services was unconstitutional as a violation of due process unless there was an emergency necessitating the legislation. Commonly known as the "Economic Due Process" theory it was used by a conservative Supreme Court to invalidate social legislation. The demise of this theory came with a series of cases in the 30s, beginning with *Nebbia v. New York,* 291 U.S. 50, (1934), which held that a price control law like most regulatory legislation was valid provided a rational basis for it existed. (See Barr and Keating, *The Last Stand of Economic Substantive Due Process--The Housing Emergency Requirement for Rent Control.* 7 Urban Lawyer 447 (1975).

In short, the burden on landlords challenging the need for rent control has sharply increased since the United States Supreme Court's first decision on rent control, *Black v. Hirsch,* 256 U.S. 135 (1921) which required an emergency to exist.

The New Jersey Supreme Court has ruled that municipalities may adopt rent control if they have any rational basis for their action. A housing shortage or widespread substantial rent increases are usual reasons. Other reasons might include monopoly control of rental housing, the prevalence of substandard housing, or a large number of tenants paying a high percentage (over 30%) of their income toward rent. Landlords must prove that there are no facts which would support any possible rationale for adopting rent control, *Brunetti v. New Milford* 68 N.J. 576 at 594 (1975).

But as I previously said, this has not always been the law and it still may not be the law in your state.

Be forewarned! State courts with conservative judges might be free to remain in the early 20th century. However, the New Jersey Court as well as the Maryland Court of Appeals has held that a housing emergency is not the test under either Federal or State Consititution. The standard for rent control is the same for any other exercise of police power. Does the governing body have a rational basis for imposing control?

The landlords in *Helmsley* argued that there was no rational basis for enacting rent control However, based on their observations and facts presented by the landlords the court found a vacancy rate of 1.5 to 2.6%. This is below a 3% rate which is sufficient to justify legislation. In addition, the court stated that since landlords were able to keep profits even with or ahead of inflation, there is sufficient reason to believe that rent increases of a substantial or blatant nature did in fact take place.

## CAN RENT CONTROL LAW BE ATTACKED AS UNCONSTITUTIONAL "ON ITS FACE"?

Yes. A rent control ordinance can be challenged as facially unconstitutional as applied. The court in *Hutton Court Gardens v. West Orange* 68 N.J. 543 at 571 (1975) gives examples of laws which would be facially unconstitutional: a law which continued for fourteen years without any provision for rent increases, a price which was set so low that *all* landlords in a city would have to operate at a loss. Only such a drastic law which obviously precludes any possibility of fair return can be held facially invalid. *Hutton Park supra,* 68 at 571.

Since the Supreme Court of New Jersey ruled that all New Jersey ordinances must permit landlords to apply to rent control boards for a hardship increase on grounds that they are entitled to a "fair return," it seems highly unlikely that a rent control ordinance could even be facially invalid.

The lesson is that it might be wise to include that kind of language in your law.

## MUST RENT CONTROL PROVIDE ADMINISTRATIVE REMEDIES?

To properly protect tenants, rent controls should be as tough as possible, limiting annual rent increases to some rate below the rate of inflation and force landlords to prove they need rent increases. Therefore, administrative remedies must be available for landlords who believe they are not making a "fair profit."

## MUST A LANDLORD EXHAUST ADMINISTRATIVE REMEDIES BEFORE CHALLENGING A RENT CONTROL ORDINANCE IN COURT?

No, if this landlord is challenging the law as unconstitutional on its face. (see above.) However, if the landlords are challenging the law as unconstitutional "as applied" the answer is -- it depends.

There are two types of unconstitutional as applied arguments. A plaintiff can argue that an ordinance as applied denies *all* landlords in town a fair return or he can claim that the ordinance as applied to him is confiscatory. In the first case, there is no need to exhaust administrative remedies; in the latter, they must be exhausted.

The landlords in *Helmsley* used the former approach.

## CAN A RENT CONTROL LAW PLACE STRICT LIMITS ON ANNUAL RENT INCREASES?

Only by fixing an absolute ceiling on annual rent increases that is less than the increases in a landlord's operating costs, will your rent law protect tenants. If the ceilings are as high as, or higher than real cost increases, cost pass through provisions may be a positive advantage for landlords, as well as others who profit from rents such as oil, gas and electric companies. At the same time it removes the landlord's incentive to economize and ends up protecting inefficient management.

New Jersey municipalities have used flat percentage increases to regulate automatic increases. In other words a landlord can receive an automatic annual rent increase equal to 2½ % or 4% or a percentage increase measured by the consumer price index (CPI), or ½ the CPI or any other percentage, depending on the city's ordinance.

In the *Brunetti* case the court stated that a municipality could constitutionally freeze all rents, dispense with all automatic increases and require a landlord to prove that he was not making a fair return prior to allowing any rent increase. *Brunetti,* 68 N.J. at 590 n, 16.

In Helmsley the courts affirmed and refined this position. While reiterating that a municipality could constitutionally freeze rents or impose strict limitations on automatic increases, (decision p. 69) it imposed a caveat. Such a stringent limitation on automatic increases is valid only if the muncipality provides "prompt, fair and efficacious administrative relief." to landlords seeking hardship relief (slip option p. 69). If a municipality is unable or unwilling to develop such an administrative system, then it must provide a more moderate formula which ties automatic rent increases more closely to increases in operating costs without lengthy administrative proceedings.

*Reprinted from SHELTERFORCE, Spring 1979*

# Los Angeles Faces Up to Rent-Curb Issue

## CARY LOWE

Tenant-activist leaders have presented the City Council with a logical and comprehensive set of proposals aimed at both the immediate problem of inflated rental-housing costs and the longer-term issue of increasing the supply of affordable housing. The current rent freeze/rollback was enacted by the City Council because the vast majority of Los Angeles landlords failed to pass on to their tenants an equitable share of Proposition 13 tax savings. Now renters seek a program of flexible regulation that would protect tenants from unjustifiable rent increases, while assuring landlords sufficient income from their buildings. Such "second generation" rent regulation, unlike the freeze-type controls associated with New York City (and which are now in effect here), is operating successfully in cities in New Jersey, Massachusetts, Alaska, Connecticut, Maine, Maryland and Virginia.

Under the tenant proposal, rents could not be raised more frequently than once a year. Ideally, the rate of increase should be limited to the President's 5.7% inflation-control guideline, and absolutely should not exceed 7%.

Landlords who incur extraordinary costs, or who make capital improvements that clearly inure to the benefit of their tenants, should be permitted to petition for higher increases. These adjustments would be handled on a case-by-case basis, by an appointed board representing all interest groups.

Some housing could be exempted from the regulations. since the goal is primarily to protect low- and moderate-income households from burdensome costs, luxury-class units could be exempted. It is critical, however, that the definition of "luxury" be realistic, to avoid the prospect of tenants being further impoverished as a result of being legislatively assigned to "luxury." An exemption should be extended

126

to all rental housing built after implementation of the regulations, so as not to deter new constuction.

The proposed controls should stay in force as long as the city's low vacancy rate- currently about 2.5%- allows landlords to dominate the market. The regulation program could be lifted when the vacancy rate rises to 5%. This should also act as an incentive to the real-estate industry to build the increment of new housing necessary to lift the controls.

It is imperative that the City Council reject the removal of vacated rental units from control. Such a gaping loophole would rapidly undercut the effectiveness of the regulation program, especially in lower-income areas where transiency is common.

Most important, tenants need protection from retaliation for exercising their rights under this program, or otherwise. Evictions should be permissible only in cases in which the landlord could demonstrate good cause, such as nonpayment of rent, serious property damage, illegal use of the premises or conversion of the unit to nonresidential use. The lack of such a provision has critically flawed the current ordinance, leaving tenants afraid to even complain of illegal rent increases.

The enforcement of the program could be facilitated by establishing penalties for landlords who illegally raise rents. And the victimized tenants should have the opportunity to sue an offending landlord for damages.

Specific actions could be taken to create the kinds of housing most critically needed:

— The public-housing inventory currently managed by the City Housing Authority needs to be greatly expanded. Thousands of units authorized nearly two years ago by referendum remain unbuilt, despite the clear need for both the housing units and the jobs that the projects could generate.

— The Community Redevelopment Agency, which in the past has sold public land at bargain rates to developers of upper-income condominiums, should contract for construction of low-cost housing.

— To preserve the existing supply of low- and middle-income rental housing, conversion of apartments to condominiums or cooperatives should be strictly regulated. Conversions that would remove units from the lower-cost housing supply should be banned altogether during periods of severe shortage.

— The city should substantially increase its allocation of federal

**127**

community-development funds for the rehabilitation of older housing which comprises most of the low-cost stock.

— The city should streamline building-permit processing and environmental reviews for developments meeting high-priority needs.

— Rampant real-estate speculation, especially in rental housing, must be prohibited. A high graduated fee imposed on repeated real-estate sales would remove most of the financial incentive in speculation.

These measures would protect all the parties involved in the current debate over Los Angeles' housing policy. The critical question now is whether City Council members will accept this challenge when they vote in the coming days.

*Reprinted from LOS ANGELES TIMES, January 19, 1979*

# Private Real Estate Interests and the Details of Rent Control Laws

## PETER MARCUSE

The bewildering variety of formulas used to establish rent limits under rent control laws can be neatly categorized conceptually to show the exact nature of the impact on the economic position of landlords. The relevant categories are:

**"Fair return" formulas** - under which rents are fixed so as to provide a "fair return" to the landlord on investment, on equity, or consistent with past returns, or on some similar base. This formula effects no redistribution whatsoever, and may even benefit landlords.

**"Market" formulas** - under which rents are fixed so as to be consistent with what they would be were a free market operating, based on comparable rents, on standards established by size, amenity, and location, by past rental levels, or on some similar base. This formula effects no general redistribution, and may, at most, limit returns in exceptional situations to those prevailing in the market generally.

**"Tenant hardship"** formulas - under which rents are fixed in relation to tenant income, on the basis of percentage of earnings, welfare standards, changes in the cost of living, or on some similar base. This formula, if effectively administered, may in fact provide for limited redistribution from landlord to tenant.

Rent freezes, depending on their level, can come in any category. All sorts of combinations are of course possible, and laws as complex as New York's contain elements of all three (the last being the weakest and applying only to elderly residents where rent increases are limited based on income).

Generally, reference to one or another of these standards can be readily found in the text of the legislation establishing controls. Monica Lett, for instance, classifies 17 different criteria used to indicate the existence of a housing emergency in contemporary United States rent control laws and ordinances into two broad groupings: those relying on a "rent factor...placing decent housing beyond the means of a large portion of the population," (what is here called "tenant hardship"), and those relying on a "vacancy factor...leading to abuses in the housing market, i.e., rent gouging," which can comprehend both fair return and market rent formulas.[1] The quite different impact of the two theories is not alluded to.

In England, the distinctions are more clearly recognized, and tenant hardship, the only significantly redistribute formula, has been explicitly rejected as the determinative criterion. In the words of the Milner Holland report in 1965, exorbitant rents should be defined as

> 'rents...grossly out of keeping with the age and condition of the property.' (It excludes) cases where the rent was high only in relation to the tenant's means, which we treated as hardship and not as abuse.

The Rent Act of 1968 gives a crystal clear definition (conceptually, if not practically) of its linking of rent controls to the market rent:

> In determining...what...would be a fair rent,...regard shall be had,...to all circumstances (other than personal circumstances) and in particular to the age, character, locality and state repair of the dwelling house....

The parentheses excluding "personal circumstances" make it clear that hardship on the tenant is not a factor, and no redistributive effect is intended. But neither is the landlord's profit to be protected beyond what the open market would provide, for the Act goes on to say:

> ...it shall be assumed that the number of persons seeking to become tenants of similar dwelling-houses in the locality on the terms (other than those relating to rent) of the regulated tenancy is not substantially greater than the number of such dwelling-houses in the locality which are available for letting on such terms.

The inescapable empirical impossibility of trying to determine how many persons would seek a given dwelling-house, rent not being a factor (parentheses in English legislation seem to contain unusually interesting matter), when in fact rent is the most important factor that *more than any other* determines what type of dwelling a person seeks, has understandably caused substantial difficulty, although again the conceptual root of the problem does not appear to be generally discussed.

The German formula is today likewise a market rent formula, explicitly. A "miete-spiegel," rent-mirror, is established for each community, in which prevailing rents are reflected, separately by size, amenity, and age. Ceilings are then based on that standard, and only evidence of changes in amenities, or market trends requiring modification of the mirror, can substantiate a request for an increase.[2]

What such market formulas thus do is to smoothen out the rental housing market, to standardize prices and perhaps quality. The logical extension of the concept would be to permit housing-market-wide bargaining to determine the level of rents. That system is in fact permitted locally in West Germany, and is established nationally in Sweden, where national organizations of landlords and tenants meet annually to establish and revise rent charges.

The fair return formula, the least redistributive of all, is predictably the most widely used in the United States, where the over-all strength of the forces for redistribution are weakest. Where market formulas are used in the U.S., they are likely to permit increases, rather than hold them down. New York City's rent stablilization law, for instance, permits individual adjustments beyond those generally given where the rent would otherwise be:

> substantially different from the rents generally prevailing in the same area for substantially similar housing accommodations.

Three features are characteristic of fair return formula, and together ensure that rent controls will act redistributively only in the case of the severest shortage and most flagrant abuses. The three identifying characteristics are:

> A formula to provide for a fair return;
> Automatic pass-through of operating cost increases;

Adjustments permitted for individual hardships to landlords.

Provision of a fair return to landlords has been held constitutionally required in rent controls under the due process clause by a number of courts,[3] although there are also cases holding to the contrary.[4] In any event, almost all U.S. rent control legislation includes them. In a few, where the definition of a fair return is based on some historic return earned at a given point in time, the assumption is explicit that that historic return was fair:

The Director shall presume that rents for housing accommodations in the City in effect on October 16, 1974, were established at levels which yielded to owners a fair rate of return for such units.

The manner of definition of "fair return" varies substantially from law to law. In some it is based on the owner's equity; in others on the value of the property, which may in turn be based on assessed value (as it is for many purposes in Great Britain) or on appraisals made for the purpose; it may carry forward a dollar return from a prior period, adjusting for inflation; or it may be calculated as a constant percent of gross rent. Herbert Selesnick lists no less than seven different variations of these formulas used in four communities under the Massachusetts local option law over a four year period.

Fair return provisions seem to provide a limit on rent levels in the long run by freezing the amount of profits that can be derived from a given piece of real estate to some figure determined at a given point in time and then frozen there, possibly with an adjustment for inflation. The speculative element at least seems thus to be removed from the market for residential real estate by fair return rent control laws.

But this conclusion is erroneous. Capital gains on the sale of such property are not controlled by any rent control law in any jurisdiction in the U.S., nor, to my knowledge, in any European country. Reasonable calculations as to the likely ending or weakening of rent control - calculations soundly based in past history - make continued speculation in the appreciation of property values continue unabated. One major source of landlord profit is thus entirely unaffected by temporary rent controls, or controls expected to be temporary.

132

Beyond this, even during the temporary period of subjection to rent controls, the failure to limit speculation in fair return rent control laws permits immediate rent increases to take place that reflect the impact of such speculation. This is because most of the fair return formulas are in fact circular. They base the permitted return of some assessment of "value," "fair market price," or "equity"; these figures are determined by appraisals, comparable market prices, or the price paid for the actual unit. But in turn the market price of that property as well as of comparable properties based on the return expected from it; the amount of equity will be likewise influenced by anticipated return. Value is based on expected return, and permitted return is based on value. Thus, permitted return is based on expected return, and the market determines rents just as if there were no rent controls at all.

The pass-through of operating costs from landlord to tenant is a standard feature of fair return rent control laws. Under some, a Fair Net Operating Income (FNOI is a recurrent term) is determined on a case by case basis; in others, an annual increase is allowed based on some price index for standard components of operating expenses; in still others, a flat percentage increase is allowed, based on estimates of cost increases. If an absolute ceiling is fixed on increases which is less than the real increase in costs, there may be a redistributive aspect of pass-through provisions. If the ceilings are as high as, or higher than, real increases (and most are, partly under pressure of court rulings, and if not, they permit hardship adjustments of the type described below to avoid their effects), pass-through provisions may be a positive advantage for landlords.

The automatic pass-through of operating cost increases removes the incentive to economize, and can protect, if it does not reward, inefficient management. More important, it removes from the bargaining arena what might otherwise be a very touchy issue: the rising cost of utilities and other operating supplies and materials. Oil companies, in this sense, are the biggest beneficiaries of rent control: landlords no longer have any incentive to argue over price increases, nor to explore the feasibility of alternative sources of fuel. At the same time, tenants are hamstrung in their opposition because of the intervening landlord and rent control regulations, which seem to render official and inevitable fuel cost increases. Pass-through formulas in rent control ordinances thus are likely a blessing in disguise for landlords and suppliers.[5]

Adjustments for hardships to landlords are a final component of almost all U.S. rent control laws. In New Jersey, they have even been held to be essential if rent control is to meet constitutional tests of due process. They permit any landlord who can show that the combination of statutory fair return formulas with operating cost pass-through provisions are still inadequate to provide an adequate return on the facts of that landlord's particular case to obtain an adjustment in rent to provide it.

All in all, the net result of fair return rent control ordinances in the sphere of accumulation is negligible. They tend to even out the market, to bring temporary or isolated high rents more into line with prevailing ones. They rationalize the market for residential rental properties. They even have some advantages for landlords that may arguably contribute to increased net profits. The rents fixed under them achieve a status of a legal sanction, that makes individual efforts to bargain for lower rents more difficult. The vagaries of the atomistic free market are reduced; while upper limits are set on current profits, lower limits are also de facto established. Although data are not readily available, the likelihood is that most apartments in middle income communities subject to rent control are in fact collecting rents at the rent control levels. J. G. Cragg's essentially anti-rent control report for the Rentalsman in British Columbia makes both these points:

> ...rent control...may be beneficial at the present time in providing a more orderly market. The Allowable Rent Increase can be used to indicate in general terms what would be a reasonable figure. The justification procedure at least indicates to tenants that a further increase is not completely arbitrary.

One final bit of fragmentary evidence supports this conclusion about the essentially neutral, rationalizing function of rent control in the middle income market, and the lack of impact in the low income market: cities under rent control seem to show the same patterns of increases in rent levels as cities not under rent cotrol. The one detailed study readily available compares Vancouver, with a fluctuating history of rent control over 5 years, with Toronto, without such controls: rents in fact went higher in the former than the latter. One may speculate that the housing market in Vancouver grew tight in the late 50's; that some agitation among lower income and politically progressive forces took place, gaining some support from middle income tenants that the issue was seen as an appealing one for political leaders, in conventional vote-getting terms; that a weak rent control measure was enacted, achieving some rationalization of the housing market, avoiding some temporary excess profits of landlords in the middle income housing market, but having virtually no effect on low income rents; and that the underlying circumstances that began forcing rents up to begin with continued, only trivially moderated by rent controls, to produce increasing rents, on a par with what was happening elsewhere in Canada.

There is some fragmentary evidence to the contrary in Massachusetts but it is based on too small a sample to be reliable;[6] (it is reported that rents increased by 30% in one year after New York rent control laws expired in 1929);[7] and there is evidence, again unsatisfactory, that rents are being kept below their market levels in New York by controls. But that is not the point here; it is rather that rents are at best kept to "normal" market levels (normal in the economy as a whole) by controls, although below the levels abnormal conditions might make possible without controls. Controls thus function to even out rents and permit a readier integration of the economy spatially.

But the needs of private accumulation are not only consistent with the fair return model of rent controls; they are consistent, depending on the specific and in fact with the ultimate elimination of the private residential landlord entirely from the housing market. Hitler, Churchill, Nixon are the national leaders who have been responsible for the most recent stringent rent controls in their respective nations; they are hardly among the most militant challengers to the prevailing economic order. Britain has seen the virtual elimination of the private landlord from the low-income housing market, and all-together private rentals now account for less than 13% of the total stock of dwellings, compared to 44.6% in 1950; yet Britain is still clearly a free market economy. In other western European countries, the private landlord has been in David Donnison's words, "both regulated and subsidized...he has been employed, unwillingly perhaps as an instrument of housing policy." In the broader picture, the role of the private landlord, and the particular profits associated with various permutations of that role, are not indispensable to the accumulation function of a private market economy; landlords may be entirely unfettered, virtually eliminated, or regulated and controlled, and yet the system prospers. Rent controls are as likely to serve more smoothly to integrate the functioning of the private landlord with the needs of accumulation of the economy as a whole, as they are to redistribute normal rental market profits from landlord to tenant; at least in the United States, that conclusion hardly seems in doubt.

[1] Lett, pp. 35-7
[2] Brenner and Franklin
[3] Hutton Park vs. West Orange, (1975) 68 NJ 543
[4] Bowles vs. Willingham, (1974) 321 US 503
[5] Urban Planning Aid, 1975
[6] Selesnick, 1976
[7] McLoughlin, John J. and Ronald Lawson, 1975, History of Tenant Organizing in New York City in the Twentieth Century. Paper presented at the Eighteenth Annual Meeting of the Missouri Valley History Conference, Omaha Nebraska, March 7, 1975

*Reprinted by permission: THE POLITICAL ECONOMY OF RENT CONTROL: THEORY AND STRATEGY, Papers in Planning No. 7, New York, Columbia University, Division of Urban Planning, 1979*

# Rent Controls Impact on the Quality and Quantity of the Housing Stock

## JOHN INGRAM GILDERBLOOM

### Rent Control in America

It is simply impossible to generalize about rent control, without making important distinctions about the type of rent control being discussed. Indeed one type of rent control can be disastrous, while another type of rent control is not. Any debate on the merits or demerits of rent control is useless unless distinctions are made as to the kind of rent control being discussed. In other words, you cannot generalize about rent control as such; the types of rent control are as varied as the kinds of cars on the road--some work, some don't. The detractors of rent control would like us to believe that all rent control systems are a disaster by simply pointing the finger at New York's restrictive rent control laws of the 1950's and early 1960's. Such an argument is as absurd as claiming all cars are bad based on what happened with the Edsel.

### Restrictive Rent Control

Rent control programs in the United States can be classified into two broad subgroups: restrictive and moderate. World War I and World War II and New York City rent control programs, up until 1969, fall into the restrictive category; while the stabilization programs in New Jersey, Maryland, Massachusetts, and Washington, D.C. are generally considered moderate.

Restrictive rent controls seemed to have led eventually to serious problems such as little or no new construction, declining maintenance and valuation of rental property (Friedman and Stigler, 1946; Hayek, 1972; de Jouvenel, 1948; Paish, 1950; Rydenfelt, 1949;

Samuelson, 1967; Willis, 1950; Seldon, 1972; Pennance, 1972; Keating, 1976). World War I and II rent controls put a virtual freeze on rents (Blumberg, et al., 1974). New York City's own rent control program, from 1949-1969, followed the federal government's termination of controls. Prior to reforms in 1970, according to Emily Achtenberg (1976:10), New York's rent control program "may have accelerated the process of private disinvestment by making it difficult for many owners to earn a reasonable return on investment". This inability for the landlord to earn a fair rate of return was affirmed by the New York Court of Appeals in *Teeval Company v. Stern* when it ruled that rent control, "even though it may now and then compel an owner to operate his real property at a loss, the statute for that reason is not to be condemned as an arbitrary use of police power" (Note, 1967). Lowry and Teitz (1970) argue that New York's program had prevented landlords from increasing rents sufficiently to meet escalating costs. Lowry (1970:12) argues, "by preventing rents from rising in step with the costs of supplying rental housing, it (New York's rent control program) has left owners with few alternatives to undermaintenance and reduction of building services."

**Moderate Rent Control**

To avoid such problems, moderate rent controls were developed. As mandated by the ordinances, moderate rent controls must provide for annual rent adjustments to compensate for escalating costs and "guarantee a fair and reasonable return on investment." In general, the courts have defined that a just and reasonable return be commensurate with returns on investment in other enterprises having similar risks. For example, in Hoboken, New Jersey, "a fair return on the equity investment in real property shall be considered to be six percent (6%) above the maximum passbook demand deposit savings account interest rate available in the municipality." Thus rather than holding rent levels relatively constant, moderate rent controls attempt to regulate the increase on a year-to-year basis. Such controls provide owners with annual rent increases to compensate for increases in operating costs and taxes. The law also provides incentives for capital improvements (Blumberg, 1974: 242; Lett, 1976: 91). If the allowable rent fails to provide for a reasonable return on investment or to cover costs for major capital improvements, the landlord may apply for a "hardship increase" in rents charged. On the other hand, should maintenance or services decline or code violations exist in the building, the rent control board can either reduce the amount of rent collected, or prohibit future rent increases until the problems are corrected. In addition, all new construction and other substantially rehabilitated housing are excluded from regulation, with the exclusion ranging from the initial setting of rents to an indefinite exemption (Blumberg, 1974: 244; Lett, 1976: 91).

In sum, moderate rent control has the following features: (1) a guarantee of a fair and reasonable return on investment (2) all increases in a landlord's operating costs must be passed along to tenants in the form of increased rents (3) all new multi-family construction is exempt from controls. A moderate rent control ordinance is not "moderate" simply by definition alone but also by the equitable administration of the law by the elected rent control board (Lett, 1976:89). In New Jersey and Massachusetts all the evidence seems to indicate that short-term, moderate rent controls have not caused a decline in construction, maintenance, or valuation of controlled apartments relative to non-controlled units. However, in attempting to avoid the problems traditionally associated with restrictive controls, moderate controls do not necessarily result in across the board general rent relief for tenants, but instead work mostly to control extreme or erratic rent increases. In other words moderate rent controls will only provide protection against rent gouging and, in general, will not affect those tenants whose landlords are earning a fair and reasonable return on investment.

But despite the non-restrictive nature of these moderate controls, the real estate industry has made the unsupported claim that moderate controls lead to a decline in construction, maintenance and valuation of apartments and increase in demolitions and abandonments. Upon closer scrutiny, however, the empirical evidence on which these views are based proves weak because of faulty methodological and statistical procedures, which serve to bias their results (Gilderbloom, 1978,1980; Achtenberg, 1975). Principal among these defects are the failure to systematically examine a comparable set of rent and non-rent controlled cities, and in those few studies that attempt such comparisons--the failure to control adequately for potentially confounding effects. Moreover, these biases appear to flow directly from its sponsorship--real estate interests which have supplied the data and funding for most of these reports. Studies that have avoided the above problems have found no evidence of a negative relationship between moderate controls and the quality and quantity of the housing stock.

## Multi-family Housing Starts

Data from five different sources show that short term moderate rent controls have no net effect on new conventional multiple-family construction. Gruen and Gruen's recent study of New Jersey rent control found no statistically significant shift in apartment construction from rent controlled cities to non-rent controlled cities. Urban Planning Aid reports that after enactment of controls in four Massachusetts cities, multi-family construction in rent controlled cities increased. The California Department of Housing and Community Development's analysis of 26 rent controlled and 37 non-rent controlled cities over a three year period in New Jersey found that the existence of moderate rent control had no net impact on construction. In fact, 11 of the rent controlled cities actually showed increases in multifamily housing starts after controls were enacted. A recent update of this study published by the Conference on State and Local Public Policies examining the impact of controls over a five year period found that multifamily construction has not slowed in rent controlled cities relative to non-rent control cities. A recent study by the U.C.L.A. Institute for Social Science Research (1980;114) for the City of Los Angeles found that new multifamily housing in that rent controlled city were "consistent with a statewide trend." The Institute (1980;11) also found that "condominium conversions have increased over the past year, in Los Angeles and nationwide, regardless of rent controls or construction activity." This study successfully replicated the results of an earlier study done by the Community Development Department (1979) on the effect of moderate rent control on the quantity of the rental housing stock. According to interviews, builders continue to build in rent controlled cities for two reasons. First, it is difficult for the builder to leave a community which she/he is already familiar with. Understanding of future developments, knowledge of business trends, planned externalities (parks, schools, churches, etc.) and other builders' plans are essential to a builder's success. Such knowledge comes from a long and direct involvement in the community. Second, the nature of moderate rent control also contributes to a builder's decision to stay and build in the community. Naturally, the exemption of all new construction is an inducement to continue building. But since new construction might eventually fall under rent controls, the guarantee of a "reasonable return on profit" is also crucial to a builder's decision to stay and build in rent controlled areas. As one builder put it, (moderate) "rent controls don't bother me, I'm not a gouger, just a guy trying to make an honest buck."

## Maintenance and Capital Improvements

Statistics also show that maintenance has not declined in cities where moderate rent controls have been enacted. Sternlieb's study of Fort Lee, New Jersey and Boston, Massachusetts show that maintenance expenditures have remained constant since the enactment of controls. Another study by Joseph Eckert found in Brookline, Massachusetts that the percentage of the rent dollar going into maintenance has not declined since the enactment of rent control six years ago. Similar findings were found by the Apartment and Office Building Association report of rent control in Montgomery County, Maryland. In 1972, according to the data, 4.8% of the rent dollar went into maintenance and repairs; by 1974 the distribution of the rent dollar going into this category increased to 6.4%. In addition, the percentage of the rent dollar going into painting and decorating remained the same. Lastly, a study by Urban Planning Aid examining permits issued for "Additions, Alterations and Repairs" in Massachusetts rent controlled cities found that permits for upgrading of rental units are on the upswing. Another study by the U.C.L.A. Institute of Social Science Research (1980:119) reported that after the enactment of rent control in Los Angeles, "there has been an increase in the number of permits issued for alterations, additions and repairs in apartment buildings..."

On the basis of these data it seems that moderate rent control has not caused a reduction in the amount of money going into maintenance, and in certain cases maintenance has increased. The reason for this--according to those rent control board members and analysts interviewed in New Jersey, Massachusetts, and Florida--is that the law allows for landlords to pass the full costs of repairs and improvements on to the tenant. According to Eckert 1977:324),

> One positive and successful Board policy for encouraging maintenance involves a provision for special limited hearing for landlords who wish to make major repairs, capital improvements or renovations (previously outlined in Chapter I). These hearings result in the landlord receiving a guarantee from the Rent Board as to the amount of

additional rent he can charge once the capital improvements are made.

Moreover, almost all the ordinances in New Jersey and Massachusetts mandate that landlords must retain the same level of services and maintenance as that existing before the enactment of moderate controls. If, for some reason, maintenance declines, the tenants can file a complaint with the rent control board. According to Eckert (1977),

> Tenants proving negligence in maintenance can expect a rent reduction until the problem is corrected, and in some cases the Board might initiate a full building hearing if tenants' complaints seem particularly widespread in a particular building. It is probable that in this atmosphere landlords simply are not able to cut maintenance or capital improvements significantly without the Board taking action to stop this reduction in services.

According to Shirley Green, former Rent Control Director of Newark, New Jersey, if a landlord wants to increase his or her rent in excess of maximum allowable increase, the property must be without code violations. According to Sylvia Aranow, the Rent Control Chairperson for Fort Lee, before rent control was enacted, it was difficult to get a landlord to fix code violations.

> Before rent controls, landlords could easily overlook bad conditions if there was a violation in existence just by ignoring it. Finally, the building inspector would get fed up with it and haul him into court, and the judge would fine him $15. Big deal, it didn't correct the violations. It was easier to pay that than to go out and pay $1,000 to correct what really was the problem to begin with--lack of maintenance.

Eckert (1977:324) concludes by arguing that it is these positive and negative inducements that cause maintenance to remain stable.

## Valuation of Rental Housing

Many claim that rent control causes the local tax base to decline. Both the construction of new rental housing and the condition of the existing stock determine the size and health of a city's rental property base.

The notion of an eroding tax base is plausible only to the extent

**142**

that the alleged adverse effects of rent control upon new construction and maintenance are accepted. Sternlieb and others have argued that declining construction and maintenance in cities makes the erosion of the tax base "imminent" (Sternlieb, 1975:VII-23). However, the foregoing pages demonstrate that moderate rent control has not adversely affected new construction and maintenance. Therefore, in the absence of any other generally accepted correlation between controls and ill effects, the claim that rent control causes an erosion of the tax base should be reexamined. Data indicate that controlled rental property has continued to appreciate in value and this rise in value has been about parallel to cities where the market is free and competitive. The Institute for Social Science Research (1980:105) found that market values for apartments of ten units or less in Los Angeles continued to increase at a rate similar to the non-rent controlled period, while the market valuation of large buildings of ten units or more have declined. This decline, however, is attributed to "changing investor sentiment and/or increasing interest rates", a fact that has negatively affected both rent controlled and non-rent controlled cities during 1979 and 1980. A report by the Massachusetts Department of Corporations and Taxation found that rent control had no systematic effect on property valuation. Similarly, a study by the City of Brookline Revenue and Rent Control Study Committee reported that gross rent multiplier has remained about the same since the enactment of rent control. Eckert's study of Brookline, Massachusetts found that rent control has not caused the burden of taxes to be shifted from landlords to homeowners. The California Department of Housing and Community Development Study of 26 rent controlled and 37 nonrent controlled cities in New Jersey using multiple regression techniques found that the rise in value of rent controlled apartments was about the same as in noncontrolled apartments. A recent update of this study published by the Conference of Alternative State and Local Public Policies reports that the percentage of taxes paid by the rental housing sector has remained unchanged since the enactment of controls five years ago.

Under moderate rent control, valuation of rental property will continue to increase at about the same pace as other nonrent controlled apartments where the market is free and competitive. Moderate rent controls are typically introduced where the market mechanism has been impeded from functioning correctly and, consequently, landlords have taken advantage of a tight housing situation by charging exorbitant rents. With the introduction of moderate rent controls, the increase in the valuation of the rental stock has been slowed only to the approximate level at what the market would bear under normal conditions.

## Conclusion

This paper found that short-term, moderate rent controls had little or no impact on the amount of construction, maintenance, or taxable valuation of rental properties. Such a finding is due primarily to the non-restrictive nature of moderate controls which exempt all newly constructed housing, guarantee a fair and reasonable return on investment parallel to other investments with similar risks, and allow for all increases in a landlord's operating costs to be passed along to the tenant in the form of increased rents. This type of non-restrictive rent control has resulted only in controls over extreme rent increases. Still to be studied are the political, sociological and psychological impacts of moderate controls. In general, it seems that the aim of most of the reports reviewed in this paper is to focus only on the possible negative aspects of moderate rent controls so that the real estate industry can mobilize other interest groups (construction trades, homeowners associations, etc.) to oppose moderate controls. These studies typically exclude from examination possible positive aspects of moderate controls. While we have been able to argue that moderate controls have not had any negative effect on the quality or quantity of housing stock, its positive aspects have yet to be studied. Further examination is needed to study these aspects of moderate controls.

*Essay written September 1980*

144

# How Rent Control Works in Massachusetts

## EMILY PARADISE ACHTENBERG

**HISTORY:**

Massachusetts' rent control law (Chapter 842, Acts of 1970) was adopted by the state legislature in 1970 in response to pressures created by a severe rental housing shortage. As the Act's preamble notes:

(A) Serious public emergency exists with respect to the housing of a substantial number of citizens in certain areas of the Commonwealth…which…has been created by housing demolition, deterioration of a substantial portion of the existing housing stock, insufficient new housing construction, increased costs of construction and finance, inflation and the effects of the Vietnam War.[1]

Chapter 842 is an 'enabling' law which can be implemented only on a local option basis. Any city in the Commonwealth, and any town with a population of 50,000 or more residents, may adopt the state law by a majority vote of the local legislative body. Forty-three cities and towns presently qualify for rent control under Chapter 842, and 5 have chosen to adopt it.

The city of Cambridge and the town of Brookline were first to implement rent control in 1970, followed by Somerville in 1971. These communities, situated adjacent to Boston, have experienced extremely low vacancy rates and rapidly rising rents since the mid-1960's. In the city of Boston itself, rents were initially regulated under a separate local system which provided for rent review only upon the initiation of complaints by individual tenants. This limited approach, which lasted from 1970 through the end of 1972, proved to be quite ineffective in controlling overall rent levels. Thus chapter 842 was adopted in Boston in December 1972.

The city of Lynn also adopted Chapter 842 in 1972, when a new popular slate gained control of the municipal government. However, when the reform party lost its majority in 1974, rent control was revoked despite a city-wide referendum in which voters overwhelmingly favored its retention.

Presently, an estimated 166,000 rental units are subject to the provisions of Chapter 842 in the four communities, including 125,000 in Boston, 20,000 in Cambridge, 11,000 in Brookline, and 10,000 in Somerville. In addition, the city of Boston, under a separate local regulatory scheme, controls rents in another 12,000 units which are subsidized and insured by the Federal Housing Administration (FHA). Approximately one-half of all rental units in the Boston metropolitan area are thus covered by some form of local rent control.

Widespread public debate over the future and effectiveness of rent conrol occurred during 1974 and 1975, when the renewal of Chapter 842 was considered by the state legislature. While the scheduled expiration date of the law was extended, the legislature commissioned a comprehensive review of rent control by a local consulting firm. This study concluded that rent control has generally worked well in the cities and towns where it has been adopted, and recommended extension of Chapter 842 as well as expansion of its scope of coverage

> The statistical evidence... indicates that there is no sound justification for the repeal of Chapter 842. None of the available data demonstrates that rent control harms more people than it helps, or that it significantly impairs the supply of rental housing. In the light of the continuing shortage of affordable rental housing also demonstrated by the statistical evidence in this study, we recommend the extension of Chapter 842.[2]

At the same time, a study commissioned by the Rental Housing Association, representing property owners, was quite critical of rent control and recommended various measures to modify the impact of the present statute. A variety of amendments are presently being considered by the State Legislature, which is expected to act by the end of the year.

## PROVISIONS OF THE RENT CONTROL ACT:

The overall regulatory scheme established by Chapter 842 is applicable to all municipalities choosing to adopt the legislation. The major provisions of the Act are as follows:

## A. Rent Regulation

### 1. Coverage:

Rent control covers all rental housing in the locality except:

- rental units in two or three-family houses, if the owner is a resident landlord;
- new housing constructed on or after January 1, 1969;
- rental units in hotels, motels, inns, and rooming houses which are rented primarily to transient guests for less than 14 days;
- government-owned or operated housing, e.g. public housing. Privately owned rental developments subsidized by the state or federal government are also exempt under this legislation;
- rental units in any hospital, public institution, or dormitory operated exclusively for charitable or educational purposes;
- rental units in co-operatives.

The city or town may also choose to exempt up to one-quarter of the rental units in the municipality which exceed rental cut-off limits as defined by the local government. The local rent control office may also exempt any "class" of rental units, upon a finding that there is no longer a shortage of apartments in that category.

### 2. Administration:

Chapter 842 may be enforced either by a board or by an administrator at the option of the locality. The administrator or board must be appointed by the mayor, city manager, or town board of selectmen. The composition of the board is not specified by the legislation. Rent board members may not be paid for their services, but may be reimbursed for expenses.

### 3. Method of Rent Adjustment:

**a) Rollback.** 30 days after a community adopts rent control, all rents must be "rolled back" to what they were six months prior to the date of local adoption. The intent of this provision is to eliminate unwarranted rent increases imposed in anticipation of local rent legislation.

**b) Rent Adjustments.** Once rent control is enacted, the rent cannot be raised above the "rollback" level without the approval of the rent control office. Rent adjustments may be made in one or two ways. First, any landlord or tenant may petition for an *individual* rent adjustment applicable to the rental unit or units in a particular building. If either side requests it, a hearing must be held where both sides may present arguments. Second, the rent control office can make a *general* adjustment of rents in all controlled units or in specific building categories, after holding a public hearing.

    **c) Grounds for Rent Adjustment.** The standards for rent adjustment are defined only broadly by the rent control statute. Landlords are entitled to receive a "fair net operating income" from their apartments as defined by the rent control office. In determining whether an apartment is currently yielding a "fair net operating income", the rent control office must take into acount the following factors:

- increase or decrease in property taxes;
- *unavoidable* increases, or any decreases, in operating and maintenance expenses;
- capital improvements, as distinguished from ordinary repairs, replacement, and maintenance;
- increases or decreases in living space, services, furniture, or equipment;
- failure to perform ordinary repair, replacement, and maintenance.

    The rent control office also has the power to refuse to grant a rent increase if violations of state and local housing codes exist in the apartment or building, or if a hearing has been held for the building within the past year.

    **d) Rent Adjustment Hearings.** The law prescribes certain standards to be followed in individual rent adjustment hearings. For example, both tenant and landlord must receive adequate notice of the hearing time and place, and of the evidence and arguments to be used by the other side. Each party is entitled to have representation, to call witnesses, and to conduct cross-examination. An official record of the case must be made and transcribed at the request of either side.

## B. Security of Tenure

    The rent control law also regulates security of tenure, by requiring a landlord of a controlled rental unit to obtain a "certificate of eviction" from the rent control agency before he can go to court to evict a tenant. Certificates of eviction may be issued only for one of 9 specific "just causes." These include non-payment of rent, other substantial violations of the tenancy agreement, nuisance or damage caused by the tenant, demolition, and use and occupancy of the apartment desired by the landlord for himself or close relatives. In addition, a certificate of eviction may be issued for "any other just cause," provided that it does not conflict with the purposes of the rent control statute.

When a landlord applies to the rent control office for a certificate of eviction, the tenant is entitled to receive a copy of his application and adequate notice of his right to challenge it. Hearings are not explicitly required but are generally held upon request. Once a certificate of eviction is obtained, the landlord must still go through regular court proceedings in order to legally evict the tenant.

## C. Appeals

Rent control decisions may be appealed by either side to the local district court.

## D. Enforcement

### 1. Registration

All owners are required to register their rent controlled buildings with the local rent control office. The scope of registration information required is a matter of local determination.

### 2. Penalties

Willful violations of the law are punishable in two ways. First, if the landlord "demands, accepts, receives, or retains" any payment in excess of the maximum lawful rent, he can be sued by the tenant or rent control office for triple damages. The landlord is also liable for court costs and reasonable attorney's fees. The rent control office may also choose to award triple damages itself. Second, convictions under the rent control law are punishable by a fine of up to $500 or a 90-day jail sentence for the first offense; for a second offense, the maximum fine is $3,000 or a one-year jail sentence.

## LOCAL RENT CONTROL POLICIES AND PRACTICES:

In the absence of state administrative guidelines, and as a result of the flexibility in Chapter 842, the Massachusetts communities which have adopted rent control have varied considerably in their methods of implementing the statute. Each locality has followed its own approach to registration, the rollback, hearings, rent adjustments, evictions, and enforcement, as well as in the organizational structures established to administer these functions, some of the more significant policy and administrative differences which have arisen are described in this section.

## A. Individual and General Rent Adjustment Methods

While each locality has utilized both the individual and general approach to rent adjustments, the relative emphasis placed upon each method varies considerably (see Table 1-1). With the pressures of rapidly rising property taxes and fuel costs, three of the four communities have come to rely increasingly on general adjustments as a vehicle for reducing the individual review caseload.

In contrast, Boston has relied on the individual case-by-case method of rent adjustment almost exclusively. This approach must be viewed in the context of several factors unique to the Boston situation. First, the property tax rate has remained stable for the past 3 years; in 1972, when the tax rate increased, a general adjustment was authorized for tax purposes. Second, many controlled properties in Boston are small buildings where tenants pay directly for heat and their utility costs; owners have not felt the impact of cost escalation in this area. Finally, Boston has developed an effective administrative capability which has permitted the office to process individual cases with considerable speed and efficiency.

## B. Allowable Costs

With respect to individual rent adjustments, the overall approach in each community has been to permit owners to "pass-through" increased costs in certain "allowable" operating expense categories, as specified by the legislation. Depreciation and debt service are not considered allowable expenses. Generally, the increase in allowable costs is determined by comparing the most recent year's operating experience with a previous year's, on the basis of audited financial statements or documented expenses. However, within this general framework there were notable community differences.

For example, Cambridge places a great deal of emphasis on ascertaining the "reasonableness" of claimed expense increases. Each expense item is analyzed with respect to its consistency and recurring nature as part of the owner's normal expenditure pattern. This approach minimizes the problem of an owner withholding bills for the previous year's expenditures in order to overstate operating cost increases. By contrast, the tendency in Brookline has been to accept actual operating cost increases which can be substantiated by the owner. Procedures for cost verification also vary. While Brookline requires a full audit and documentation for all claimed expenditures, Boston requires substantiation only for selected items "flagged" by tenants or hearing examiners.

Capital improvements are another item treated differently by

**150**

# Table 1-1

## General Adjustments Authorized by Municipalities Under CH-842

| Effective Data | Stated Purpose | Units Affected | Avg. % Increase Over Previous Rents |
|---|---|---|---|
| **Cambridge** | | | |
| Dec., 1972 | 9/67 rents + 30% | 10,788 | 13.18% (over 3/70) |
| Jan., 1974 | 1973 taxes | 17,000 | 1.15% |
| May, 1975 | 1974 taxes, fuel & profits | NA | 10-15%* |
| **Brookline** | | | |
| Aug., 1971 | 1/68 rents + 25% | 7,348 | 9.45% (over 3/70) |
| Sep., 1972 | 1972 taxes | 10,047 | 2.94% |
| Sep., 1973 | 1973 taxes | 10,432 | 1.20% |
| Sep., 1973 | 1973 operating costs | 9,312 | 1.80% |
| **Somerville** | | | |
| Mar., 1971 | 1970 taxes | NA | 7 % (over 6/70) |
| May, 1972 | 1971 taxes | NA | 2% |
| Jan., 1973 | 1972 taxes | NA | 0.6%* |
| Jan., 1974 | 1973 taxes | NA | 1.4%* |
| Apr., 1974 | 1972-3 fuel | NA | 5-7% |
| Mar., 1975 | 1970-4 taxes & operating costs | NA | 10-20% |
| **Boston** | | | |
| Mar., 1973 | 1972 taxes | NA | 4.5% |

* General adjustment based on actual dollar increase in stated costs experienced by each owner, provided automatically for all qualifying owners. Average percentage increases are estimates only.

Source: Emily Achtenberg, "A Critique of the Rental Housing Association Rent Control Study", Urban Planning Aid, Inc., unpublished mimeo, May 1975, Table 3.

each locality. In Boston and Cambridge, the cost of capital improvements, plus allowable interest charges, is amortized over the useful life of the item. In Brookline the approach is similar except that the interest expenses are actually incurred. In addition, Brookline holds preliminary "advisory hearings" in order to determine the eligibility of proposed work for a capital improvements increase and the probability of increased amount. In Somerville, capital improvements are treated on a "return to capital" basis; that is, the cost of the improvement is added to the value of the property and the owner is permitted to earn an additional return on it.

Another major area of divergence is the treatment of legal and administrative costs. While Boston permits all legal expenses to be passed on to tenants, Brookline disallows legal fees incurred in connection with challenges to rent control decision, on the grounds that such a cost is not "unavoidable" as required by the statute. Allowable components of management expenses are also defined differently by each locality.

## C. Fair Net Operating Income

The concept of "fair net operating income" is uniquely defined by each community. In combination with the variations in treatment of allowable costs, these policy differences have resulted in quite different approaches to individual rent adjustments in each of the four communities.

In Boston, fair net operating income was defined, until quite recently, as the dollar net operating income (gross revenues minus operating expenses) yielded by the building in the month of December 1971 (annualized).[3] This amount was further subject to a minimum and maximum ratio, applied to net operating income as a percentage of 1971 gross revenues. This relatively stringent definition was designed to limit rent increases to the amount actually justified by rising costs on a dollar-for-dollar basis, and to stabilize or reduce grossly inflated property values. It further reflected the Boston Rent Control Administration's view that most Boston landlords are either small, long-term owners seeking a fixed dollar return on investment (similar to a bond) or large investors interested primarily in the tax shelter aspects of real estate. In neither case does the structure of investment motivation justify more than a modest return from ongoing rental operations.[4]

Cambridge defines "fair net operating income" as the dollar by revenues earned in 1967, the local rent control "base-year", adjusted

152

by the Consumer Price Index to maintain the constant value of 1967 purchasing power. The theory of this approach is that since many tenants receive salary increases pegged to the general rate of inflation, landlords' incomes should be permitted to rise accordingly. This formula permits rent increases considerably larger in magnitude than those allowable under the Boston approach, while at the same time allowing property values generally to rise with the rate of inflation.

Both Somerville and Brookline utilize a return on current market value formula to define fair net operating income. In Somerville, a standardized index figure is used to adjust the most recent purchase price forward. In Brookline, current appraisals, tax assessments, gross rent multipliers, and other criteria are reviewed in detail. As well, the owner's allowed rate of return is adjusted to reflect the condition of the property, as an incentive to improved maintenance. This complex approach, particularly with respect to the determination of market value, has resulted in numerous legal challenges and delays in the processing of individual adjustment cases.[5] Both of these formulas permit generally larger rent increases and introduce an element of circularity into the rent regulation process. Thus rents rise generally to reflect the increase in market values, which in turn justify higher rents.

## D. Decision Making Authority

In all communities except Boston, Chapter 842 is administered by a Rent Control Board. The Cambridge Rent Control Board has 5 members, the Brookline Rent Board has 9, and the Somerville Rent Board has 11. Cambridge formerly had an Administrator, and in Boston, an Administrator is currently responsible for implementing the rent control program under Chapter 842. (There is also a special Boston rent board with jurisdiction over FHA units; see Section IV below.)

Each of these administrative mechanisms appears to have its advantages and limitations. With a rent board, landlord-tenant conflicts are internalized within the decision-making process, and responsibility tends to be more diffuse as well as publicly exercised (e.g. through board meetings). This has had the advantage of providing more balanced policy decisions, while at the same time rendering the decision-making process itself more cumbersome. The Administrator approach has tended to be efficient; but it has also contained the drawbacks of bias (real or perceived) in one-man decision-making and of focusing local political opposition to rent control on a single individual.

**Table 1-2 Cost of Rent Control Administration**

| Municipality | Estimated No. Of Controlled Units | Total Administrative Costs | Cost/Unit | Estimated Rent of On Local Tax | Cost Control Tax Rate* | 1973 Tax Rate* |
|---|---|---|---|---|---|---|
| Boston | 125,000 | $873,800 | $6.99 | | 49¢ | $196.70 |
| Brookline | 11,300 | 126,448 | 11.19 | | 31¢ | 73.00 |
| Cambridge | 20,424 | 252,341 | 12.36 | | 76¢ | 152.30 |
| Somerville | 10,000 | 46,986 | 4.70 | | 34¢ | 171.60 |

* Per $1,000 of assessed valuation.

**Sources:** Joint Legislative Committee on Local Affairs, **A Study of Rent and Eviction Controls in the Commonwealth of Massachusetts,** p. V-16.

Urban Planning Aid, Inc., "Why Rent Control is Needed," April 10, 1974.

The type of decision-making body and, if a Board, the number of members appointed, has also played a significant role in shaping individual rent adjustment procedures. For example, in Boston, rent adjustment hearings are conducted by paid officers, who make recommendations to the Administrator. In Cambridge, where the board is small, hearing officers serve a similar function, except that the Board hears their recommendations publicly and either the landlord or tenant may appeal before the full Board to plead his case (in effect, a form of second hearing). In Brookline, individual Board members are responsible for holding hearings, in conjunction with staff hearing officers who perform all the initial administrative and investigative work required. In Somerville, a low-budget program, there are no hearing officers and only minimal staff; the 11 individual Board members serve as hearing officers and do all of the work performed by administrative staff in the other communities.

## E. The Cost of Rent Control Administration

In Massachusetts, the cost of rent control administration is financed by each locality out of general tax revenues. Table I-2 shows the approximate cost incurred in 1973. Brookline and Cambridge had the most expensive systems in terms of the average cost per controlled rental unit. Many factors have an important bearing on the differences in unit costs: the type of "fair net operating income" fomula used (some formulas are easier to administer than others); the size of the staff; the number of hearings conducted, etc.

The institution of rent control in Massachusetts has not imposed a heavy burden on taxpayers. In fact, the cost of administering rent control amounts to an insignificant fraction of the local tax rate. For example, in 1973, about 49¢ of Boston's total tax rate of $196.70 (per $1,000 of assessed valuation) was attributable to rent control; in Cambridge it was 76¢, in Brookline it was 31¢ and in Somerville it was 34¢.

## IV. ADMINISTRATION OF RENT CONTROL IN BOSTON:
## A. Administrative Structure

Rent regulation in Boston is carried out under chapter 843 of the state law and chapter 19 of the City Ordinances which applies strictly to control of rents in FHA units. The city has an Administrator of Chapter 843, and a Rent Board which administers Chapter 19. The Administrator also serves as the Executive Director of the FHA Rent Board. The members of the FHA Rent Board and the Administrator are appointed by the Mayor.

The Administrator is supported by two staff offices — operations and legal counsel — and by five line offices or sections — rent, evictions, compliance, registration and inspections. The Administrator, assisted by a Deputy and two Assistant Administrators who provide general advice and consultation, is the final decision-maker. A total of 11 Hearing Officers and an equivalent number of assistants report to the Assistant Administrator for rents. The Assistant Administrator for Evictions also serves as a backup attorney on court cases. The Deputy Adminstrator concentrates on program management and administration (personnel office systems and procedures, etc.)

Figure 1-3 shows the organization structure and staffing pattern of the Boston Rent Control Administration.

## B. Systems and Procedures

The five line sections reflect the major functions performed by the Rent Control Administration. Each section will be discussed in terms of the systems and procedures developed to handle the function.

## 1. Rent Adjustment Section

Landlords who wish to petition for rent increases are required to file both a "Property Financial Statement" and "Landlord Petition for Rent Adjustment with the rent control office. These forms are reviewed for substance and, if accepted, the case is assigned to a hearing officer. The hearing officer conducts a preliminary financial analysis and may ask the landlord to substantiate selected expense figures.

At the same time, the tenant is notified of the landlord's petition and of his right to request a hearing. If a hearing is requested, the hearing officer informs both parties of the date, time, and place, allowing 14 days notice. The tenant is asked to note any problems with respect to housing conditions. The hearing officer may request an inspection prior to the hearing if he feels that one is warranted.

Rent adjustment hearings are informal; they are not conducted in accordance with strict rules of evidence. The Hearing officer is responsible for conducting the hearing, although some hearings are attended by the Administrator and many are attended by the Assistant Administrator for rents. Most hearings are held during the day at the rent control office. Some are held at night at the building site, especially where many tenants are involved.

The hearing officer makes a recommendation on the case, which is then reviewed by the Assistant Administrator for rents. The Administrator makes the final decision and notice is sent to both

Figure 1-3

Organization and Staffing of the Boston Rent Control Administration

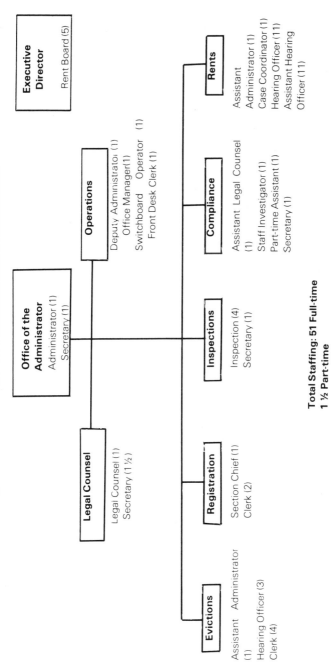

**Office of the Administrator**
Administrator (1)
Secretary (1)

**Executive Director**
Rent Board (5)

**Legal Counsel**
Legal Counsel (1)
Secretary (1½)

**Operations**
Deputy Administrator (1)
Office Manager (1)
Switchboard Operator (1)
Front Desk Clerk (1)

**Evictions**
Assistant Administrator (1)
Hearing Officer (3)
Clerk (4)

**Registration**
Section Chief (1)
Clerk (2)

**Inspections**
Inspection (4)
Secretary (1)

**Compliance**
Assistant Legal Counsel (1)
Staff Investigator (1)
Part-time Assistant (1)
Secretary (1)

**Rents**
Assistant Administrator (1)
Case Coordinator (1)
Hearing Officer (11)
Assistant Hearing Officer (11)

**Total Staffing: 51 Full-time**
**1 ½ Part-time**

Source: Joint Legislative Committee on Local Affairs, *A Study of Rent And Eviction controls in the Commowealth of Massachusetts*, prepared by Harbridge House, Inc., Boston, December, 1974, p. IV-122.

157

parties. If the landlord is entitled to a rent increase but has failed to comply with the housing code, the Administrator generally grants the increase conditional upon correction of all code violations. When the work has been completed and reinspected, a Certificate of Compliance is issued and the new maximum rent becomes effective.

Tenants may also petition for rent reduction on variety of grounds. These include: decline in services or deterioration of the housing unit, decreases in operating expenses, rent charged in excess of the legal maximum, or excessive "fair net operating income." The first reason is most frequently cited.

When a tenant petition is filed, it is assigned to a hearing officer who makes the initial determination with respect to acceptance or rejection of the petition. If the petition claims that housing code violations exist in the apartment, an inspection is automatically scheduled. The landlord is also asked to provide any relevant financial information.

Rent reduction hearings are scheduled automatically. Recommendations on the case are made by the hearing officer, and the final decision is issued by the Rent Control Administrator. If no information is received from the landlord within 15 days, the Administrator may automatically order a 10% rent reduction.

## 2. Eviction Section

The Eviction Section handles landlord petitions for certificates of eviction. When a petition is received, the tenant is notified of the landlord's request and of the alleged grounds for eviction. Hearings are generally held only at the request of the tenant, although the Administrator reserves the option of holding a hearing on his own initiative. Most eviction cases involve non-payment of rent and are relatively straight-forward; however in the less clear-cut cases, information provided at hearings is essential.

Hearing officers assigned to the evictions section are responsible for conducting hearings and for making recommendations on the case to the Assistant Administrator for evictions. He in turn summarizes the findings and presents them to the Administrator for approval. This dual review of eviction proceedings provides an important safeguard against capricious approval of eviction certificates.

## 3. Inspection Section

If a hearing officer determines that an inspection of the property is required, he asks the Inspection Section to check with the City's code enforcement department for outstanding violations. If there are violations of record, no further inspection is necessary. If none are found, either the code enforcement department or the Inspection Section will visit the property. While some duplication of effort is involved in this function, the heavy workload of the city's code enforcement agency has made it necessary for the rent control office to train and utilize its own inspection staff.

## 4. Registration Section

The object of registration is to obtain full and complete information on all properties subject to control under Chapter 842. There are two separate forms, one for individual units and another which provides comprehensive data on each controlled building. Registration forms were mailed to landlords at the start of the rent control program.

The rent control office relies primarily on tenant complaints to identify unregistered buildings. Continued failure of a landlord to register results ultimately in court action by the Compliance Section. However, an estimated 97% of all controlled units are currently registered.

All registration information is stored in computer files and is treated as public information.

## 5. Compliance Section

This section of the rent control office is responsible for enforcement of Chapter 842. The main types of violations encountered are: illegal rent overcharges, illegal evictions, false or incomplete information on forms, non-registration and violation of one of the Administrator's orders. The Compliance Section learns of violations either through a tenant's complaint or as a result of investigation carried out on its own initiative. For example, the compliance section may discover that a landlord, in petitioning for a rent increase, is already charging more than the maximum rent; the Section would then investigate the illegal rent charge.

Most of the illegal rent over-charges discovered are not of the willful variety. They are typically generated by absentee landlords who were either unaware that their properties were subject to rent control or did not understand how Chapter 842 worked. The Compliance Officer asks the landlord to return the overpayment to the tenant and if the landlord refuses he is prosecuted. Seldom is prosecution necessary, as the money is usually returned.

If a landlord is found to be willfully charging illegal rents, the Compliance Officer files a complaint with the Boston Housing Court. The judge hears the case and imposes a fine. The case is usually dismissed when the landlord pays the fine and returns the rent overpayment to the tenant; the landlord will have no criminal record.

## C. Workload

In 1974, the rent control office received a total of 2429 individual rent adjustment petitions, inlcuding 1640 landlord petitions for rent increases and 789 tenant petitions for rent reductions. 1306 hearings were held, including 635 for rent increases and 671 for rent decreases. The Eviction Section received about 800 applications per month for certificates of eviction. The Compliance Section handled about 300 prosecutions in 1973.

The average time required for processing rent adjustment cases in Boston has been 4-6 weeks, as compared to 6-8 weeks in Cambridge and up to 12 weeks in Brookline. At the same time, Boston has many more appeals of its decisions to the courts, on a percentage basis, than either the Cambridge or Somerville Boards. This may be explained by: (a) landlord or tenant dissatisifaction with the Administrator's approach to decision-making which may be viewed as biased; and (b) the accessibility of the Boston Housing Court to landlords and tenants.

[1] Chapter 842, Acts of 1970, Section

[2] Joint Legislative Committee on Local Affairs, *A Study of Rent and Eviction Controls in the Commonwealth of Massachusetts,* prepared by Harbridge house, Inc., Boston, December, 1974.

[3] The Rent Control Administration was recently forced to modify this approach by a court order from the Boston Housing Court. The court arbitrarily required a formula providing a 7.5% return on current market value, defined as 3 x assessed valuation. This decision has not been tested in the higher courts.

[4] Joint Legislative Committee on Local Affairs, *op. cit.,* p. IV-139.

[5] *Ibid.,* p. V-16.

[6] *Ibid.,* p. IV-124.

[7] Boston Rent Control Administration Memorandum, January 10, 1975, "Number of Petitions Received for 1974"; and "1974 Hearings" (undated).

[8] Joint Legislative Committee on Local Affairs, *op. cit.,* p. IV-128.

[9] *Ibid.,* p. V-127.

[10] *Ibid.,* p. III-115.

*Reprinted from "Housing and Rent Control in British Columbia," Interdepartment Study Team on Housing and Rents, Vancouver, B.C., Canada, 1977*

# SECTION V

# HOW TO WIN A RENT CONTROL CAMPAIGN

# The Politics of Rent Control

## PETER DREIER

The issue of rent control is primarily political, and is perceived as such by both tenants' groups and the housing industry. Its success or failure depends on the extent to which organized tenants' movements can neutralize the obvious economic and political strength of their more powerful opponents. Rent control has worked best where well-organized tenant groups exert a steady pressure on elected officials, landlords, and rent control boards.

In Washington, D.C. — where seventy percent of the population are renters — the Rental Accommodations Office (RAO — the rent control agency) was understaffed and intimidated by the housing industry throughout its first four years; only during the past two years has it been able to efficiently and effectively administer the city's six year old rent control law. This is due in part to pressures put on the RAO by Washington tenants' groups, and in part to internal reorganization of the agency itself — in which the director and top staff were recruited from citizens' and tenants' associations, the RAO now sees itself in an advocate role, actively involved in outreach and public education. But none of this would have occurred — nor would the agency's level of funding have increased — had not the City Wide Housing Coalition exerted political pressure. The Coalition pressured the district government in 1978 to beef up the law, mandate more funding, and hire a competent staff. The RAO was reorganized in March 1978 and its performance since then has demonstrated that rent control need not be a morass of red tape and confusion. Rent control is relatively easy to administer in Washington because nearly all of the city's rental units fall under the law (150,000 of the 180,000). Only landlords who own four units or less are exempted. The RAO now operates on an annual budget of $750,000, or about $3 per unit under control (compared to 85¢ during 1973-1974). This figure is about average for rent control administrations around the country. The big difference in Washington is the skill and commitment of the staff.

As part of the RAO reorganization, Bowles Ford — former director of the Metropolitan Washington Planning and Housing Association, a citizen advocacy group — was brought in to head the office. Statistician Jim Burns was hired to computerize data on code enforcement, housing sales, and rents; previously, the only source of statistical information on the Washington housing market was the Apartment and Office Building Association, an industry group. John Hampton, the new client services director for RAO, had been director of the National Tenants Organization. There are ten hearing officers — all lawyers — to process petitions by landlords and tenants, The backlog of cases — once almost a year long — was reduced in the first few months after reorganization despite a sharp increase in new cases.

The increased caseload was a result of RAO's recent efforts at outreach and public education. Again, it took pressure from the City Wide Housing Coalition before the rent control office was mandated (and funded) to spread the work. A tenant hotline (advertised on radio) now offers emergency housing information and advice on landlord-tenant law. An easy-to-read 21-page pamphlet on the city's housing law is free on request. Billboards and posters on trash cans urge residents to contact RAO. A bimonthly newsletter keeps both landlords and tenant groups up-to-date on legal and administrative matters.

Tim Siegel of the City Wide Housing Coalition gives Bowles Ford and his staff high marks, but he also emphasizes the critical role of organized tenant groups. "If tenants are scared, don't know their rights, aren't together, or are willing to leave their apartments without putting up a fight, then the landlords will win regardless of what the law says." The RAO's John Hampton agrees: "Tenant groups are extremely important especially in educating tenants and enforcing compliance by landlords."

Tenant groups often report building code violations, landlords' inflated statements of the costs of repairs and maintenance, and landlords that have failed to register with the rent control board. This day-to-day enforcement is as important as any victory in the court or at the ballot box.

In East Orange, New Jersey, too, a strong rent control law

reflects the influence of a strong tenant group, · the East Orange Tenants Association (EOTA). East Orange landlords are not permitted to pass on tax increases, which may simply reflect land speculation, not an increase in the cost of city services. Yet careful inspection by EOTA of landlords' statements to the rent control board demonstrates a remarkable fact: the board has never granted a "hardship" increase beyond the maximum annual increase. In fact, it has ordered rent reductions where landlords have reduced maintenance. Two of EOTA's members sit on the five-member board. With a full-time staff of seven (funded in part with CETA and community block grant money), EOTA has organized tenants in as many as 100 buildings and set up an "abandonment alert" to monitor landlords who fail to comply with local regulations. Where landlords have been found delinquent, tenants have been allowed to name a receiver, who is then authorized by the court to collect rents and manage the building. Rent control gives EOTA leverage in organizing tenants and serves an educational purpose as well: "We show how rent is only one source of a landlord's profits," explains EOTA's Woody Widrow. "Speculation and tax shelters are just as important."

Rent control enforcement is only one of EOTA's activities. It is affiliated with the New Jersey Tenants Organization (NJTO), the largest and most powerful tenants group in the country. Started in 1969, and made up predominantly of middle-income renters, the NJTO is responsible for the fact that some 110 New Jersey municipalities have rent control laws. The group has also lobbied the state legislature to pass some of the toughest landlord-tenant laws in the country. State law now prohibits eviction of tenants who complain about housing conditions, bars landlords from refusing to review a lease without "just cause," permits courts (with tenant approval) to collect rents until repairs are made, and requires that landlords pay interest on security deposits.

The absence of a strong tenants movement has visible consequences just across the border in New York. There, rent control has been passed like political hot potato from federal to state to city agencies. Over the years it has become a hodgepodge of regulations and formulas, making administration the kind of bureaucratic nightmare landlords warn against.

During the past few years the reaction to rent control on the part of the housing and business communities has been strong and, in many instances, effective in reversing earlier gains made by tenants and their organizations. For example, in Boston, which introduced rent control in 1969, property owners considerably undermined the city's rent control law by prevailing on the city council to pass "vacancy decontrol" — a measure that permanently removes an apartment from controls whenever a tenant moves out. When the vacancy decontrol law took effect in January 1976 there were 95,000 units under rent control. In the next two-and-a-half years, nearly 30,000 units were removed from control as they became vacant. In the fall of 1977, a report by Andrew Olins, housing adviser to Boston Mayor Kevin White, recommended ending rent control altogether (except for apartments occupied by senior citizens on fixed incomes). But White was facing a tough re-election campaign. When the Boston Committee for Rent Control and Massachussetts Fair Share (a citizen action group that includes more homeowners than renters) mobilized to dispute Olins' conclusions — that rent control hurt the city's tax base and housing stock — the mayor backed away from repeal. During the summer and fall of 1979, community groups in Boston once again mobilized for a long battle in anticipation of the expiration of the city's rent control ordinance on December 31. Real estate interests lobbied to do away with the program altogether. Tenants groups kept the issue alive during the fall 1979 mayoral elections, forcing the mayoral candidates to shift ground. They sponsored a bill in the city council that would reinstate all the "de-controlled" apartments to controlled status, regulate evictions due to condominium conversion, and mandate rent control's continuation until the vacancy rate reaches 8 percent. In the end, the mayor and city council decided to continue the "vacancy decontrol" status quo.

The Boston groups did not want to repeat the experiences of Lynn, Massachusetts (1974), Miami Beach, Florida (1976), and Somerville, Massachusetts (1978), where the local business community convinced the city council to end rent controls.

The experience of Somerville reveals how the administration of rent control is itself a political issue. Rent control was introduced in 1971 in the midst of a flurry of tenant activism. But poor administration of the program eroded support for and the credibility of rent control. A pro-landlord mayor appointed opponents of rent control to a majority of the seats on the rent control board, and underfunded and understaffed the agency. Tenants and landlords alike complained of staff indifference and excessive delays in processing petitions. When landlords and business groups pressured the Board of

**165**

Aldermen to end rent control in this working class city of 80,000 outside Boston, the tenants groups were not well-organized enough to make the politicians fear that opposition to rent control would hurt their chances for re-election.

In Boston, the former deputy director and a hearing officer for the Rent Control Administration were both recently indicted for tampering the rent control records. According to the *Boston Globe (July 17, 1979)*, the alleged tampering may have resulted in more than $1 million in illegal rent charges, but none of the eight landlords implicated in the allegations were indicted. Some individuals could recover up to $1,500 if all the excess rent is returned to them.

In California in 1976, landlord groups pushed a bill through the state legislature that would have prohibited municipalities from imposing rent control, but Governor Brown vetoed the measure. In New Jersey, landlord groups have brought suits in the state courts challenging local formulas for granting rent increases.

Real estate groups have succeeded in keeping rent control out of Philadelphia, Minneapolis, Madison, New Orleans, Chicago, Seattle, and other cities. But most groups are well organized. When the two sides faced off in three citywide referenda on rent control in Berkeley (April 1977) and Santa Monica and Santa Barbara (June 1978), rent control was defeated all three times.

Rent control advocates in Berkeley made a number of strategic mistakes (their proposal, for example, extended controls to small "mom and pop" landlords as well as property owners). But they were also badly outspent. The Berkeley Housing Coalition operated on about $5,000. The Berkeley Committee Against Rent Control raised $150,000 — or about $8 a vote as it turned out — 80 percent of which came from out of town. The money financed direct mail, billboard, radio and newspaper ads, and 15,000 phone calls to voters.

Chastened by the Berkeley defeat, rent control activists in Santa Monica and Santa Barbara started early and mounted precinct-by-precinct campaigns. Both towns seemed ripe for controls. They are medium-sized coastal communities that have experienced enormous land speculation in recent years, and both have been strongholds of progressive political activity. Tenants make up 80 percent of the population in Santa Monica and about 60 percent in Santa Barbara. In both cities, the rent control proposals were of the moderate form discussed earlier: they exempted newly constructed buildings — both to avoid the hostility of the building trades union and to counter the charge that rent control discourages new construction. But unlike most rent control ordinances, the Santa Monica and Santa Barbara measures called for elected boards, in hopes of short-circuiting an unfriendly mayor or city council.

The pro-rent control forces managed to raise about $10,000 in Santa Monica and $21,000 in Santa Barbara. Two groups, the Santa Monica Residents and Taxpayers Committee and the Santa Barbara Housing Council, were set up by local real estate interests specifically for the rent control fight. The money they raised — $257,000 in Santa Monica and $160,000 in Santa Barbara — was more than had ever been spent for a referendum or election campaign in either city. Part of that money came from the newly formed California Housing Council (CHC), a statewide organization of the state's 200 largest landlords, which raised half a million dollars by levying members $2.50 per apartment. The anti-rent control organizations hired professional consultants, who drew on previous successes and ran a slick advertising campaign. In Santa Monica, pamphlets with a photograph of a burned-out tenement in New York warned that "rent control will turn Santa Monica into a slum." Eight separate mailings went out to every voter in the city, followed up by phone calls from "opinion researchers" asking questions like, "Did you know that New York-style rent control is being proposed to Santa Monica?" In Santa Barbara, special mailings were tailored to Democrats, Republicans, Spanish-speaking citizens, homeowners, and senior citizens. Voters received copies of a *Readers Digest* article by liberal senator Thomas Eagleton (D-Mo.), called "Why Rent Controls Don't Work." The mailings were reinforced by ads in the local media. And in an unusual move, almost the entire Department of Economics at the University of California's Santa Barbara campus spoke out publicly against the rent control initiative. The *Los Angeles Times,* as well as local dailies in Santa Monica and Santa Barbara, opposed rent control in editorials and one-sided news coverage.

The money spent by anti-rent control forces had a dramatic effect. Polls showed that only a few months before the initiative, a majority of voters in both cities favored rent control. On election day, though, it was defeated by a 55-45 margin in Santa Monica and by a 64-36 margin in Santa Barbara. Money was not the only reason for the loss; however, the timing of the elections was also bad. The rent control issue went to the voters the same day as the Proposition 13 Tax cut, which triggered a strong voter turnout among homeowners and conservatives and focused a general feeling against any forms of additional governmental bureaucracy. Many tenants figured that landlords' Proposition 13 tax cuts would be passed on to renters in the form of lower rents, making rent control unnecessary.

Indeed, the tax revolt gave new impetus to the rent control movement in California. There, renters were chagrined to find that the significant tax cuts in many cases amounting to hundreds of thousands of dollars for large apartment complexes — did not produce rent rebates: in fact, many of California's 3.5 million tenants received notices for rent increases shortly after Proposition 13 passed. Ironically, the tax cut measure — which had contributed to the defeat of rent control in Santa Monica and Santa Barbara by bringing out the "anti-government" vote — also set the stage for a significant tenant backlash in the weeks following the election. And as a result, tenant leaders in California are calling Howard Jarvis, author of Proposition 13, the "Father of Rent Control."

Throughout California, tenants who had been hit by increases organized meetings to demand that landlords share the property tax bonanza. Newspapers were filled with stories of outraged renters, embarassed landlords, and politicians jumping on the bandwagon. For example Los Angeles Mayor Thomas Bradley, who had earlier lent his name to the anti-rent control campaign in Santa Monica and Santa Barbara, called for a citywide rent freeze ordinance.

Amid the public clamor, Governor Brown and Howard Jarvis appeared at a joint press conference to "jawbone" landlords into sharing their 1.2-billion windfall — or risk mandatory rent rollbacks and freezes. As the pressure mounted, many landlords did agree to voluntarily take action in order to avoid controls; they announced that they would reduce rents to May 31 levels and freeze them for six months.

But tenant pressure did not subside. Oakland Assemblyman Tom Bates introduced a bill in the California legislature that would have required all landlords to pass on Proposition 13 savings in reduced rents. The measure was defeated 21 to 12 in late August, after heavy lobbying by real estate groups. The battle then shifted to the local level, and temporary rent freezes were passed by the city councils of San Francisco, Beverly Hills, Los Angeles, El Monte, and Cotati. Similar local ballot measures were narrowly defeated in November in San Francisco and Santa Cruz, overwhelmingly defeated in Palo Alto, and victorious in Berkeley and Davis. And lastly, Santa

Monica voters went back to the polls in 1979 and overwhelmingly passed the most restrictive rent control now currently on the books in the United States.

Tenant groups across the state reported a flurry of interest in their activities, and have added full-time organizers to their staffs. Rent strikes by angry tenants have provided impetus to the movement. Tenants' groups in such California cities as San Diego, Santa Barbara, Napa, Hayward, Salinas, Burlingame, Arcata, San Jose, Milpitas, Mountain View and Santa Cruz are renewing their efforts and plan future rent control campaigns. Across California, it seems, the aftermath of Proposition 13 is creating a new consciousness.

Elsewhere around the country, rent control initiatives are gaining momentum even without the impetus of a Jarvis-Gann backlash. The issue is being actively debated (as of late-1979) by tenant groups, city councils, and state legislatures, in New Mexico, Nevada, Oregon, Washington, Illinois, Wisconsin, Louisiana, Ohio, Florida, Massachusetts, Colorado, Texas, Michigan, Georgia, Pennsylvania, Iowa, Minnesota, and Hawaii.

The importance of grass-roots organization is best-illustrated by the contrasting experience of San Francisco and Baltimore on November 6, 1979.

On that day, San Franciscans for Affordable Housing suffered a stunning defeat when its comprehensive housing referendum — which included rent control, moderate income housing — lost 59-41 percent at the polls. The group, a coalition of labor, tenants, church, women's, gay and senior citizen organizations, was outspent by approximately $600,000 to $45,000. The landlords warchest came from landlord groups across the nation and was used to finance a slick media campaign coordinated by Solem and Associates, a campaign management firm that had helped defeat rent control in other cities.

That same day, however, voters in Baltimore approved a strict rent control ordinance by a 52-48 margin, despite being outspent at least $400,000 to $10,000 by landlords. Solem and Associates orchestrated the landlords campaign in Baltimore, too, using the same tactics.

The financial advantage of the landlords and their allies may make some tenant and community groups gun-shy. Certainly they will never be able to outspend the real estate interests so long as campaign finance laws remain as they are. But it is important to remember that in most medium-and large-sized cities, tenants comprise a majority (between 50 and 75 percent) of the population. They do tend to vote less frequently (28 percent, compared with 59 percent for homeowners in November 1978 elections) unless mobilized around specific issues. But experience suggests that such a mobilization is possible. In the case of Baltimore's success, it helped to have a prominent black Congressman, Parren Mitchell, and well-established civil rights groups, strongly endorsing and working on rent control's behalf. In San Francisco, several conditions hurt the rent control vote; a rainy day kept voters from the polls; several other progressive initiatives on the ballot may have confused voters; and a short rent freeze prior to the vote may have knocked the winds out of the tenants' sails. In general, the financial deck is stacked in favor of the landlords and real estate interests, but the political potential of tenants and their allies is significant if they are well-organized.

Groups attempting to introduce rent control in a city for the first time should therefore be careful when considering the referendum strategy. The disparities in campaign spending can be expected to reappear whenever rent control is on the ballot. Viewing Madison, Berkeley, Santa Barbara, and Santa Monica as initial skirmishes, The National Association of Realtors, The National Association of Home Builders, and other groups are now preparing a national campaign against controls to be coordinated by a new organization, the National Multi-Housing Council (NMHC). An article in *Multi-Family News,* a trade journal, reports that NMHC plans to create a national lobby to provide local anti-rent control groups with research, legal assistance, campaign advice, and to improve media coverage. The NMHC has been pressuring bond-rating services such as Moody's to include rent control as a reason for lowering a city's credit rating. It also hopes to make repeal of rent control a precondition for federal aid to cities — a formula endorsed by treasury secretary William Simon. Public officials in cities that have or are considering rent control are being supplied with a six-inch thick looseleaf notebook filled with news clips from around the country, academic studies, and statements by politicians, all with the same message: rent control doesn't work. Although each notebook bears the imprint of a local real estate group, it comes compliments of NMHC. Solem and Associates of San Francisco has published a how-to manual that sells for $90.

If the landlords' arguments against rent control have a ring of common sense about them, it is due in part to their frequent repetition by the news media. Even where they report the difficult plight of inflation-squeezed tenants and the organizing efforts of tenant groups, the news media consistently editorialize *against* rent control. Reporters and editorial writers bow to academic "experts" who oppose rent control. "Wherever they have been tried," editorialized the *Los Angeles Times,* "the controls have made housing shortages worse and sick cities sicker." The *Washington Post* called rent control a "bureaucratic nightmare." The *Boston Globe* published an article, "The Dark Side of Rent Control," by Roger Starr, former New York City housing commissioner. *Time (April 30, 1979) and Newsweek* (June 4, 1979) magazines recently featured long articles on the growing movement for rent control. Both articles quoted George Sternlieb, Rutgers University professor and the real estate industry's leading "expert" opposing rent control, who repeated his standard criticisms of rent control, without citing studies that seriously question Sternlieb's findings. Both articles linked New York City's housing problems to its long-term rent control program, despite a rent study by Peter Marcuse of Columbia University that finds no link between the two. *Time* even titled its story, "Catching the New York Disease."

While rent control advocates can use the news media to give their efforts visibility, they cannot rely on them to present an even-handed view of the pros and cons of rent control. Tenant groups have to find ways to reach tenants through grass-roots organizing and their own literature.

Organizing at the state and local level is necessary because housing in America — except for the poor and the elderly — has remained a local issue. The federal government has continued to rely on private initiative and voluntary local participation in public subsidy programs despite the fact that the United States over the last decade has fallen far short of the goals set in 1968 by the Kaiser Committee, a blue-ribbon presidential panel that called for 26 million new units to meet the nation's housing crisis. In Europe, by contrast, national governments took the lead in housing following the wide-spread destruction of housing stock during World War II. Now both government and quasi-public bodies such as cooperatives finance, build, and manage much of the housing. Rent controls in West European countries operate as part of a national housing policy. (Even though for-profit housing is a shrinking proportion of the total housing stock in these countries, rent controls have such widespread support that no governments want to take the political risk of abolishing them.)

In this country, opponents of rent control have favored new

federal initiatives that would continue the pattern of subsidizing private developers and mortgage lenders without coming to terms with the fact that investors as a class have a stake in keeping housing in short supply. The policy most often suggested as an alternative to controls is rent allowances to low and moderate-income families. But a number of pilot programs initiated by the Nixon administration have demonstrated that direct cash grants don't work. They do not increase or improve the housing stock. Far from giving the low-income consumer more freedom of choice, they simply provide an additional government subsidy to landlords and lenders.

Rent control, too, can only be a stop-gap measure. It cannot build more housing. Nor can it affect the utility costs, property taxes, and mortgage interest rates that force up rents. But it does give some protection to those who suffer most from the absence of a national commitment to ensure a supply of moderately priced housing — minorities, old people on fixed incomes, low- and middle-income families. Particularly in cities and neighborhoods where few vacancies would allow landlords to squeeze rents up astronomically, rent control shields tenants from the brutality of the housing marketplace. "Rent control offers an immediate benefit to people," says Boston's Emily Achtenberg. "It gives people a certain amount of control and security over their housing that they didn't have before. It shows how the housing system works. So it provides a basis for organizing and common action."

As an organizing issue, rent control makes sense as well. It shifts the balance of power between landlords and tenants. And the fight for stronger housing codes, more equitable leases, and greater public scrutiny of the movements of capital in the housing market can be of assistance on other fronts: the homesteading movement to revive abandoned buildings through "sweat equity," efforts to control the process of "gentrification." Rent control advocates have natural allies among other groups fighting urban decay — citizens who have organized around property tax and utility rate reform, opponents of redlining, condo conversion, and gentrification, groups who are trying to halt the flight of industry from older urban areas.

Landlord and real estate groups have recognized that action at the national level can affect the outcome of local housing struggles and have begun pooling their resources to defeat local initiatives. The housing movement for the most part remains locally based (only New Jersey and California have active statewide coalitions) though a number of progressive federal measures would make life easier for local activists: lower interest rates, more funds for rehabilitiation, risk capital for housing cooperatives, perhaps even an agency to protect the rights of tenants unions much as the National Labor Relations Board protects labor organizing. Unions, environmentalists, Pentagon critics, and other groups working to reorder national priorities would all endorse job-creating programs to build and rehabilitate energy-efficient, affordable housing. But such programs will require a well-organized and well-informed constituency to challenge private interests in housing. One step in that direction is "less rent and more control."

*Adapted from Dreier, Peter, John Gilderbloom and Richard Appelbaum, 1980. "Rising Rents and Rent Control: Issues in Urban Reform" in Pierre Clavel, John Forester and William W. Goldsmith, "Urban Planning in an Age of Austerity." Pergamon Press, New York.*

# Rent Control Surge May Be Just a Start

## CARY LOWE

Rent control is the hottest political issue in California today. From San Diego to Humboldt County, renters are locked in combat with real estate interests and public officials over the future of the rental housing industry in California.

What has made rent control a continuing subject of attention, from newspaper headlines to dinner conversation, is not merely the fact that it is being proposed, but rather that its proponents are winning. Nearly 2 million California tenants have already won the protections of rent control, and that number could double by the end of this year. In the process, rent control is becoming the opening wedge in a political campaign against massive inflation in the costs of basic economic necessities.

While the tenant movement, and the drive for rent control, have been underway in California for several years, they have gathered real momentum only recently. Vacancy rates have been too low, creating a landlords' market in most areas for more than a decade, and rents have been increasing nearly 40 percent faster than renter income since 1970. Those factors helped spawn rent control proposals in Berkeley, Santa Barbara and Santa Monica in past years.

The real catalyst for the rent control movement, however, was provided by the passage of Proposition 13 in June 1978. Howard Jarvis and other proponents of the initiative repeatedly assured renters that a vote for lower property taxes would mean immediate rent reductions as well. That was not to be the case, despite the fact that a majority of renters voted in favor of the measure. A survey conducted by the City of Los Angeles three months after the passage of Proposition 13, for example, revealed that fewer than 20 percent of tenants could expect to have the financial benefits of the tax reduction passed through to them by their landlords.

The realization that they had been duped by Jarvis and the landlords galvanized thousands of renters throughout the state into action. As it became clear that financial relief for renters would have to be aggressively fought for, existing tenant organizations were besieged with calls and letters from people ready to do battle with the real estate industry. This seemingly spontaneous uprising has already brought rent control to Los Angeles, Santa Monica, Berkeley, Davis and several smaller cities, and has campaigns underway in many more, including San Francisco and San Diego.

The scene for this reaction had been set by a continuing, critical development in the housing market. As home prices have soared in recent years, enormous numbers of middle-income households have been locked into renter status. More affluent, better educated and more politically sophisticated than their counterparts of a decade ago, they have brought to the rental housing market higher expectations of fair treatment and a willingness to respond to denial of their rights. These changes in composition and style have also increased the attention they receive from both elected officials and the media.

In the midst of the resulting political furor, the merits of rent control as an anti-inflation measure continue to be hotly debated. At the simplest level, the real estate lobby seeks to associate rent control with the abandoned tenements of the South Bronx. The landlords go on to argue that controls will put an end to new rental construction, cause a reduction in maintenance and improvement of existing structures, and foster a costly administrative bureaucracy.

Tenant advocates respond that the type of controls being implemented in California are distinctly different from the problematic version associated with New York. The new, so-called "second-generation" rent controls not only exempt all new constructions from regulation, but also allow annual rent increases, based on rising operating costs and pass-through of extraordinary expenses such as capital improvements. Modern rent controls do not end profits or rent increases, but they do restrict both to prevent blatant gouging, while still assuring honest landlords a reasonable return on their investment.

As for administrative costs, the Los Angeles program, for example, is being entirely funded by an annual registration fee of just $3 on each rental unit, plus an appeals fee for landlords requesting special consideration from the Rent Adjustment Commission.

Tenants also note that, in housing markets where conditions

**175**

have necessitated rent controls, there has been little construction of affordable housing in recent years anyway. The tenant strategy, therefore, is to ensure that the existing housing supply remains affordable, while seeking to expedite development of new low and moderate income housing.

The moderate, but effective, impact of these second-generation controls has been well documented in two studies prepared by the California Department of Housing and Community Development. Those analyses were based on the positive record of such laws in more than 125 New Jersey cities, four in Massachusetts (including Boston), the District of Columbia, and various cities and counties in Alaska, Connecticut, Maine, Maryland and Virginia.

Despite these assurances, however, landlords are grossly overreacting. Los Angeles, for example, has seen large-scale conversions of apartment houses to condominiums, and in Santa Monica some landlords actually demolished buildings on the eve of enactment of controls. Such behavior has, in turn, generated public demands for controls on conversions and other practices which deplete the rental housing supply.

The economic implications of these issues have elevated them to a level of political conflict beyond mere landlord-tenant disputes. As Tom Hayden, head of the activist Campaign for Economic Democracy, explains it, "What really scares the real estate industry about rent control is not that it reduces their profits, but that it takes away their unilateral power to control the costs of a critical resource like housing."

CED's decision to make tenant organizing and rent control major priorities brought a dramatically increased level of political sophistication and resources to the tenant movement in California. Based to a large extent on that infusion, the movement is now riding on a solid series of electoral and lobbying victories.

With the tide turning sharply against the landlords at the local level, they are seeking a new strategy to regain their fading political dominance. They have already attempted three times to push through state legislation which would outlaw local rent control in California. One of those efforts succeeded, but was vetoed by Governor Brown, whose position has consistently been that rent control is an issue to be resolved at the local level.

Now, stymied in Sacramento as well, the landlords are preparing a statewide initiative which would place strict limits on local rent controls, and nullify all the existing ordinances. Interestingly, one renter organization is already countering this with a proposed statewide pro-rent control initiative.

All sides in the rent control conflict agree that the present crisis would be considerably alleviated if the supply of affordable rental housing were dramatically increased. Unfortunately, the real estate industry representatives and government officials who now claim that the existence of controls will deter new construction showed little interest in developing such housing until the tenant movement began to score some victories. Their belated concern over a long-standing problem is understandably greeted with skepticism by tenant leaders.

As Hayden says, "We acknowledge that rent control is only an interim solution, but until local government and real estate developers show a real commitment to producing affordable housing no one can blame tenants for seizing the opportunity to bring some economic justice to the housing market."

*Reprinted from SAN DIEGO UNION, July 1, 1979*

# How Rent Control Passed in Santa Monica

## Mike Jacob

Three weeks before the April 10 election, Mayor Donna Swink of Santa Monica evicted the tenants of her apartment building, so she could get a permit to demolish the structure and build condominiums.

Among the tenants evicted was her 72 year-old aunt Ruth Whetsell--"Aunt Ruthie".

According to the L.A. Times' coverage, neighbors reported Aunt Ruthie to be hysterical when she was evicted – not unusual in such a situation. Reporters couldn't verify this, because Mayor Swink wouldn't allow them to talk with Ms. Whetsell. "It's none of your damn business if you're going to make a stink of it."

Aunt Ruthie shared her plight with some 900 other households in Santa Monica.

### THE BATTLE OF SANTA MONICA

The READER, a Los Angeles free weekly referred to the struggle as the "Battle of Santa Monica." The neighborhood where the "demolition derby" of the 900 units took place was referred to as the "war zone."

Speculators had declared war on the city of 95,000 with its 36,000 housing units and 80% of its residents, tenants.

Over the past year, more than 3,000 conversions of apartments to condominiums could be added to the demolition derby thus taking the housing units off the market for Santa Monica tenants. The tenant population was being driven out of town, decimated; speculators were bleeding the city for the most profitable use of land while the bloodletting was easy.

## AND THEY WERE IN A HURRY

If the rent control ordinance passed--the game would not be easy. Demolitions, for example would be tightly controlled. (Later landlord interests will undoubtedly say that the spectre of rent control caused these and other outrageous landlord actions--blaming, as usual, the victims--tenants responding to the housing crisis--as the the cause of their own criminal actions. Rent control does not cause demolitions. Landlords do.)

## LANDLORD ACTS BACKFIRE

But landlord misanthropic actions only served to more deeply unify the outraged tenant population of Santa Monica. And as it was, this was no easy task, because Santa Monica landlords already faced one of the best-organized, well-financed, experienced grass-roots campaign machines ever to knock out a flyer.

Almost as fast as outrageous landlord actions hit the newspapers, organizers took the clippings and turned them into effective leaflets, all tied to the message: SO YOU'VE GOT TO VOTE FOR RENT CONTROL.

An army of precinct workers--perhaps 1,000 people working on the campaign at one time or another--distributed the literature. Where they walked, they were often received like guerrilla regulars in a friendly countryside.

## TENANTS WIN THE VOTE, TOO

While securing the streets in this amazing struggle, tenants won the vote too: 14,053 in favor; 11,786 against--54 to 46%--close to an exact turn-around from 9 months before.

Longtime campaigner Ruth Yannatta, who had spoken for rent control in the 1978 Santa Monica campaign, captured the most votes in the City Council election. William Jennings, who ran with Ms. Yannatta and Proposition A on the renters' ticket, also captured a City Council Seat. Together, Yannatta and Jennings won by landslide margin over their competitors, in what Council Watchers called the most impressive victory in City history.

## ONWARD AND UPWARD

But even as an election night party bubbled onward towards the morning the later speakers were careful to mention the next campaign, coming up within the next three months. A special election must be held to elect the rent control board, if tenants do not control that election, watch out.

To Denny Zane, Park Skelton, Cheryl Rhoden, and others who have not taken a breather from the issue since it began over two years ago, all this must go to prove there is no rest for the organizer, not to mention the wicked.

## HISTORY OF THE
## SANTA MONICA CAMPAIGN GRASSROOTS

The first time around for Santa Monica was in June, 1978. The tenants were split into two groups, each kind-of running a campaign. Tenant activists raised $11,000 while the opposition spent $260,000. Proponents put together a series of 8½ x 11 leaflets explaining that rent controls actually do work, and that maintenance hasn't declined in Brookline, Massachusetts. Thirty to forty people worked in the streets. Lacking enough volunteers to walk the precincts, people staffed tables' at the major shopping outlets. In other words, the normal progressive grassroots election campaign was launched. With normal results.

Landlords designed slick pieces, and mailed several to every voter. Everywhere you turned, you learned that rent control would turn Santa Monica into a bombed out South Bronx, or rent control was a communist plot straight from the USSR, via New York.

In a town where 80% of the population was renters, and many, 80% seniors on low or fixed incomes, being slowly driven out of Southern California by price displacement, the rent control initiative still failed, 47%-53%.

The landlords had done what they did in Santa Barbara, Berkeley, and Cotati in the tradition set by the California Housing Council, the group of large landlords organized to fight rent control. They used their overwhelming dollars to spread fear and confusion about rent controls. Damn the facts, was the motto, some good horror stories will win the votes.

It was the same in Santa Monica the second time around--for the landlords. They had raised $188,000 by the last filing before the election, were mailing scare literature as normal.

One newspaper ad ran: DON'T ALLOW SANTA MONICA TO BECOME...ANOTHER NEW YORK FULL OF SLUMS AND ABAN-DONED BUILDINGS...WHERE RAPISTS, MUGGERS, ROBBERS, AND MURDERERS WILL INCREASE...PROTECT YOUR COMMUNI-TY...VOTE AGAINST RENT CONTROL.

In another standard tactic, the landlords had designed a flyer to look "grassrootsy"-- hand drawn and lettered printed on 8½ x 11 paper in green ink. Showing a scene of demolition of Santa Monica, it said: "It's not too late to stop the demolition derby which has levelled hundreds of apartments in Santa Monica and will continue to destroy the community if Prop. A passes. Vote No on Prop. A."

Prop. A, of course had an anti-demolition provision, which would quickly put an end to the demolitions landlords had been perpetrating upon the city's housing. It took a strange and malicious sense of humor to demolish hundreds of units, then tell neighborhood residents that the measure to stop demolition will cause more demolition.

But the tenant organizations and others who had seen the June, 1978 debacle, had learned from the landlords. Serious about fundraising, $28,000 was listed as of the filing before the election, and organizer Park Skelton thinks the total will top $37,000 by final count. That's a large amount of money for an election in a city of 95,000.

Some of the fundraising was done by direct mailing to tenants in the city, raising consciousness of the rent control issue at the same time. Other methods included fundraising dinners and events, and letters to traditional political contributors.

Santa Monica's campaign also didn't lack for workers this time around. Inviting activists from all over Southern Califonia to join in the battle, and combining these forces with the many Santa Monica volunteers, perhaps 1,000 people were active at one time or another, either in the phone campaign or on the streets.

On election day volunteers swarmed over the city, reminding people to vote. The spring election saw an unusually high 45% turnout, when the rest of the greater Los Angeles was seeing record lows of less than 30%.

But perhaps the keenest difference between the 1978 and the 1979 Santa Monica campaigns was in the literature. Organizers Denny Zane and Park Skelton, and others who designed or had a hand in most of the literature in both campaigns, had learned a lot.

With $30,000 plus, several different pieces were designed-- some geared to tenants, others to homeowners-some playing up the rent control measure on the ballot, others highlighting the City Council candidates on the renter's ticket.

Gone were scholarly explanations of "reasonable rate of return." One flyer carried a picture of an old man, saying "My last act will be to vote yes on Prop. A." Inside the headline was, "Evicted and Dying of Cancer," His Santa Monica landlord had been ruthless, as the reprinted story from the Herald-Examiner clearly told.

On the back of the flyer, "Let's show we still care—Vote Yes on A." Putting this piece together with the landlord equivalent mentioned above, one observer was prompted to quip: "Well rent control may cause rape and murder, but it cures cancer."

The piece Park Skelton called the most effective of the campaign was a simple postcard. A photo on the front of an elderly man and woman was labeled "Just Evicted."

On the back was a short note from the old couple's son, telling of the eviction and asking for donations to the campaign for the law that would, besides controlling rents, end unjust evictions. It achieved a high response, according to Park.

Despite a more gut-level approach to the campaign, educational values were not forgotten as far as the issue itself went, one precinct worker remarked that, after about two years of hot public controversy, walking Santa Monica streets was "like talking to a town full of rent control experts."

And as far as other educational value to the campaign, there was graffiti in a Santa Monica restaurant bathroom that summed it up: *"The lines are drawn/By now you've got to know what side you're on/ Vote Yes an A."*

All in all, the Santa Monica rent control campaign was rather symbolic of California's tenant and housing movement as a whole—it's growing up! The grassroots are losing naivete and growing muscle.

*Reprinted from CHAIN Letter, May 1979*

# A Curious Voter Proves That Where There's Smoke, There's...Smoke

## CHUCK ROSS

The voters of Los Angeles and Santa Monica have just weathered another season of political mailbox pollution. Day after day, we received ever-bigger bundles of "voter information" — pamphlets, postcards, invitations, exhortations, endorsements of this candidate and that, the "truth" about this issue and that.

In Santa Monica, where I live, the issue last Tuesday was whether to impose rent controls on apartments. Predictably, the pro and con campaign literature reached a peak in volume and emotion just before election day. What's a voter to believe? Aren't there laws about this sort of thing.

Astonishingly, no. And it's all but impossible for the Average Voter to ascertain the truth, as I found out last year when my curiosity about one small campaign postcard led me on a 8-month telephone odyssey from Santa Monica to New York and back.

The postcard was one I received from the Santa Monica Taxpayers and Residents Committee the day before a similar rent control measure was to be decided in the June primary. The front of the card had the word "Abandoned!" superimposed on a photograph of a five-story brick tenement, its ground-floor windows boarded up. On the reverse side of the card, a printed message warned: "This could be Santa Monica! It isn't. It's a New York City apartment building, devastated by the neglect and decay caused by rent control. Don't let this happen in our city!"

I decided it was time to test whether the claims of campaign literature were true. I called the committee and told the woman who answered that I'd like to have the address of the "apartment building

**183**

devastated by the neglect and decay caused by rent control,'' so that I could check it out myself. She curtly refused, and told me to call back on Wednesday, the day after the election.

I complained to the consumer affairs specialist in the Santa Monica City Attorney's office. She suggested that I contact someone in the state election-controls office, but by then it was too late in the day.

On Wednesday, I called the taxpayers' committee again. The rent control measure had lost, and the woman who was so abrupt with me on Monday very pleasantly informed me that the address of the building pictured on the postcard was 246 Pacific St., Brooklyn, New York.

I phoned Rent Control Registration in Brooklyn to find out whether the building had indeed been devastated as a result of conditions caused by rent control. If so, my search would be over and I would think better of claims on campaign literature in the future.

I was in for my first awakening. Not only was 246 Pacific St. occupied; the landlord had been granted a rent increase only six months before I had received the postcard. Perhaps the building had been abandoned since...

The New York City Department of Finance, which keeps such records, sent me the name of the building's current owner. His secretary confirmed that 246 Pacific St. was not the vacant tenement pictured on the postcard.

Back to the Santa Monica committee. As is common after an election, their number was no longer in operation. I called the chairman at his residence and found that the woman who had given me the address worked for Braun Campaigns, Inc., a consultant firm that worked on the committee's campaign.

At Braun, an executive said she could not identify the exact location of the building but would check it out. Some days later, she sent me a map of the Bronx, with a red line circling about half the area, covering 100 or so square city blocks. In an accompanying letter, she said that the building depicted on the postcard was one of the 17 locations inside the circled area. The 17 locations were listed simply as street corners — 3rd Ave. & 166th St., etc., making it virtually impossible for me to find out which was the building in question and whether its ''neglect and decay'' was due to rent control.

(Braun has since told *The L.A. Times* that the photograph was provided by Community Housing Improvement Program, Inc., of New

York, an association of apartment owners, which verified the photograph's authenticity to Braun's satisfaction. But no one has yet to provide the address of the building).

Still believing that statements of fact in campaign literature have to be substantiated, I decided it was time to take up the matter with public agencies.

I went to the state Attorney General's Los Angeles office, where a deputy said that Braun was not in violation of any statute. He further explained that there is a reluctance to interfere with campaign literature claims because of First Amendment guarantees of free speech. Before leaving, I took a form to fill out to make an official complaint to the Attorney General's office in Sacramento.

Next stop was the local office of the state Fair Political Practices Commission. But there I learned that its function does not include monitoring campaign literature.

The state election code does have some regulations regarding campaign literature, but does not address the type of problem I had uncovered.

Almost out of public agency doors to knock on, I tried the Los Angeles County District Attorney's office. There, a deputy said he would look into my complaint.

Meanwhile, the state Attorney General's office replied to my official complaint, explaining that they had forwarded it to the Fair Practices Commission. Two months later, I was told that my complaint to the Attorney General also had been sent to the district attorney's office. Months later, I was informed that they were sending my complaint back to the Attorney General.

A deputy attorney general who had been assigned to my complaint reiterated that there had been no violation of any state law. He also doubted that there had been any violation of postal regulations, but said he would inform postal authorities of my complaint.

Another month went by. An investigator with the Department of Justice phoned to tell me that the Postal Service had no record of the deputy attorney general's letter to them. He would...

Wait. The cast is getting too large, the plot too complex. This is not an absurdist work by Ionesco. The action has been well played, the point has been made. The truth is that neither side of a ballot initiative has to substantiate statements made in its campaign literature.

The opponents of rent control won last June, and the loser blamed emotional, misleading campaigning. Last week, rent control was approved by a 3,000 vote margin — and it was the opponents turn to blame emotional factors.

The only way to prevent an emotional response in the voting booth is to campaign on facts. Campaigners on either side of an issue should be required to document their claims of facts, and this information should be available for inspection by anyone who is interested. After all, we have laws that require proof of claims made in the marketplace, why not in the packaging and selling of government?

Buyer beware...Voter beware.

*Reprinted from LOS ANGELES TIMES, April 15, 1979*

# Rent Control Wins in Baltimore

## CLAUDIA LEIGHT, ELLIOT LIEBERMAN, JERRY KURTZ AND DEAN PAPPAS

In an upset victory that could have national significance, Baltimore voters approved 74,000 to 69,000 a charter amendment establishing rent control in this city of 860,000, eighth largest in the nation. It was the first time in recent years that rent control has been enacted by referendum in a major U.S. city.

Less than two weeks later, a Maryland judge ruled unconstitutional the right to institute rent control in Baltimore by initiative. The State Court of Appeals upheld that decision.

Although we do not yet have rent control in Baltimore, the campaign and electoral victory were in themselves significant.

The November 6, 1979 victory handed Solem and Associates, a San Francisco consulting firm that specializes in high-powered, anti-rent control campaigns, their first defeat. Prior to the Baltimore setback the firm could boast a perfect 7-0 record in defeating similar initiatives in other cities.

The odds against a rent control victory were high.

The city newspapers and television stations had come out against rent control. So did the mayor, city council president and 15 of the 18 members of city council. And the opponents of rent control spent nearly $400,000, while the proponents could raise only $10,000.

### HOW WE WON

The upset can be attributed to several factors:

**(1) The severity of the housing situation.** Baltimore is a

187

majority-renter city. The U.S. calls a 5% vacancy rate an "emergency" and Baltimore, with less than 2%, is a "No Vacancy" town. Many tenants have seen their rents rise 70% in the past year and do not have the alternative of leaving for cheaper apartments — they don't exist. On top of this, even the city admits 71,000 units are substandard, and 28,000 families are waiting on line for public housing.

In recent years the housing squeeze has been further aggravated by real estate speculators' and developers' new-found interest in Baltimore. They have been encouraged by the city's downtown redevelopment program — an intense promotional effort — and Baltimore's nearness to the ballooning Washington market. The result has been a dramatic rise in housing costs.

Within this context many saw rent control as an important step in relieving the pressure on housing.

**(2) A broad-based, racially integrated, grassroots, pro-rent control campaign.** In the course of the six-month campaign, pro-rent control forces enlisted the support of over sixty groups including community organizations, labor unions, women's organizations, church groups, the NAACP, tenants' organizations and political groups like NAM. Each was represented at bi-weekly steering committee meetings and each played a distinct role in mobilizing a particular constituency. Hundreds of workers went into communities the weekend before the elections and thousands worked cn Election Day itself. In contrast, the anti-rent control forces were narrowly organized around the real estate industry and their supporters in political establishment.

**(3) Mobilization of the Black electorate.** Baltimore's population is 55% Black. The rent control campaign succeeded in turning out the Black vote as few other issues have. The major factors figured in the turnout. First, key organizations with roots deep in the Black community — the NAACP, the City Tenants Association, the Welfare Rights Organization and the Interdenominational Ministerial Alliance — actively supported the rent control initiative. Secondly, the campaign made turning out the Black vote a cornerstone of its Election Day strategy. Precincts were targeted and 20 sound trucks drove through them all day while 200 youths organized into "blitz" teams— knocked on doors and dropped flyers.

**(4) An aggressive, conscious, creative campaign strategy.** The campaign saw as its prime constituencies tenants, the

Blacks, and moderate-income homeowners. To reach them, rent control advocates devised a range of tactics, including speaking engagements, leafleting, church services and a pre-Election Day car caravan through city neighborhoods.

A very bold media committee worked out how to use our scarce resources. Talk shows, debates and media events were the staples. During the last two weeks of the campaign we managed, using the FCC "Fairness Doctrine," to force television and radio stations to give us free advertising time. This helped counter the thousands of dollars spent on advertising by the opposition.

**(5) Taking advantage of the excesses of the opposition.** The anti-rent control forces outspent rent control advocates by 40 to 1. In a city where high budget campaigns are not the norm, the spending disparity created suspicions among voters that grew as Election Day approached. Following a pattern that had been successful in previous campaigns and that has become the hallmark of the Right's anti-tax movement, consultants Solem and Associates designed a campaign based on saturation targeted mailings and television and radio advertising. By Election Day voters had received as many as five separate slick direct mailings. Offensive in themselves, the excesses became doubly offensive to Baltimore's electorate when the "anti" forces attempted to disguise their propaganda as a community newsletter and sent personalized computer typed letters in envelopes that looked exactly like city tax bills.

The pro-rent control forces were quick to react to these tricks. We called on the media and filed mail fraud charges with the Maryland Attorney General. So successful was the counter-attack that politicians supporting the landlords were obliged to publicly disown the mailing.

## CAMPAIGN ORGANIZATIONS

The organizational structure of the pro- and anti-rent control forces was indicative of differing campaign strategies. Early in the campaign, pro-rent control forces could not avoid splitting into two groupings though many were afraid we could not beat landlords with a divided campaign. Baltimore Welfare Rights Organizations and Youth Against War and Fascism split from the original coalition to form the People's Campaign for Rent Control. They tried to gear their campaign exclusively to Black and poor people, using the slogan, "People before profits."

The Baltimore Rent Control Campaign, by far the larger of the two "pro " groupings, set out to create a multi-racial coalition of organizations and individuals. While stressing the importance of rent control for the city's poor, elderly, and Blacks, the Rent Control Campaign saw the need to build broad-based support for the issue.

Among the Campaign's endorsing organizations, Baltimore NAM and to a lesser extent the Democratic Socialist Organizing Committee provided an openly socialist presence. When some in the campaign, angered by the disruptiveness of the split into two groups, reacted with anti-communism, NAM people made it clear that the issue was really differences in strategy and tactics. These two remaining socialist groups helped bring a long-range organizational perspective to the campaign and offered support through the active involvement of many of our members.

NAM members worked throughout the campaign; every member of the Baltimore chapter did some work. About 10 members have met regularly as a chapter rent control caucus to guide and elevate our involvement in the campaign and to organize other chapter members. Our contributions as a group were substantial and recognized. We organized a number of all-day blitzes, mobilizing primarily our friends and associate members. One of our members served on both the research and media committees of the campaign. Another was a full-time volunteer office co-ordinator for the campaign. NAM also played an important role in pushing for strategy that went beyond what seemed most immediate.

The pro-rent control camp stressed grassroots, community-based organizing. By contrast the "Anti-s' " Keep Baltimore Best Committee relied on telephone surveys, direct mailings and saturation media coverage. Their supporters read like a *Who's Who* of the Baltimore real estate industry. They hired a large paid staff to carry out their campaign. Their tactics, familiar in other cities, were designed to heighten fears — of higher taxes for home-owners, evictions for the elderly, fewer apartments for tenants. They also tried to create confusion and doubt to the point that the voter would choose the status quo rather than risk the uncertainty of a rent control remedy.

## THE SITUATION NOW

As people in Baltimore await the appeal ruling we are working to keep the issue alive by pressuring city council to pass a comparable rent control bill. Supporters of the referendum are determined to preserve the most crucial of its components:

*(1) rent rollbacks to alleviate recent gouging;*

*(2) rent increases limited to a percentage to be fixed each year;*

*(3) no rent increases at all for units with substantial housing code violations;*

*(4) real penalties for landlords who don't comply with rent control laws.*

The Rent Control Campaign is considering its future as a citywide housing organization. Building on strengths developed in the campaign, the coalition believes it can be the basis of a powerful, continuing bi-racial movement in Baltimore.

Thus far we have run a campaign that was both grassroots and sophisticated. We beat a well-financed and unscrupulous enemy. We foiled the predictions that we would get slaughtered at the polls. We think we've been able to show that the local government is rigged against democracy. Even though this particular victory has been snatched away temporarily, our new-found confidence will be hard to shake. We are the majority.

**Reprinted from MOVING ON, March 1980**

# Winning Rent Control in a Working Class City

## MARY JO KIRSCHMAN

The Baltimore Rent Control Campaign began organizing in March, 1979 and won its election in November, 1979. We were (and are) a coalition of about 50 community, labor and church organizations which came together around the single issue of rent control. We had about 300 volunteers during the campaign, and spent about $8000. The anti-rent control group spent about $500,000.

Our campaign was a joy, not just because we won, but also because it was a true multi-racial people's victory, unlike anything Baltimore has ever seen before. And that is why, even though the landlords then stole Question K from us in Court, we are still around, still winning battles. And that is why we have decided to take our single issue campaign and turn it into a citywide housing organization which will continue to expand the work which the press said "turned around politics as usual" in this working class city.

## ROUGH CHRONOLOGY OF ACTIVITY DURING THE BALTIMORE CAMPAIGN:

February      Idea of rent control campaign conceived at meeting of 4 community groups. Initiative strategy chosen because of previous negative experience with our City Council (Mayor dominated) and advice of our political allies.

March      Initiating groups called 1st citywide meeting of tenants and community organizations to lay out proposal for initiative campaign, including strategy and structure. This meeting was attended by about 80 people.

| | |
|---|---|
| April & May | We then debated the contents of the petitions. Committees (steering, media, research, districts) began outreach to recruit volunteers and organizational endorsements. |
| June | A team of lawyers drafted the petition; meanwhile outreach continued. |
| July | Petition drive kicked off. Fundraising person brought in to work for 10% of whatever he raised. |
| August | Petitions finished and turned in to Board of Elections. Between the two organizations (two original member groups splintered off from what was now a coalition of about 50 groups), 35,000 signatures were turned in with only 10,000 valid ones required. Party thrown by and for volunteers. Lawyers for unnamed client tries legal maneuver to keep Question K off the ballot, but fails. |
| September to November | Question K o.k'd by Board of Elections for November ballot. Massive outreach to get out the vote. Media — using F.C.C. Fairness Doctrine for free time; debates; talk shows, letters to editor, etc. Leaflet drops in target precincts where our supporters should be recruiting volunteers for Election Day. Fundraising continued with mailings to many petition signers, receipt of a grant from the Youth Project, a party with Jane Fonda, Tom Hayden and Cong. Parren Mitchell, discos, raffles. Motorcade thru city, ending with church service. |
| November 6 | Election Day. This day had its own elaborate strategy, with a committee just for this purpose. Sound trucks followed by "blitz" leaflet droppers in key precincts all day. Pollwatchers in key precincts at least for opening and closing times. Special Election Day literature. VICTORY BY 5000 VOTES! |

**SINCE THE ELECTION...**

| December | Lower court rules Question K unconstitutional, saying Baltimore citizens do not have right to initiative. |
|---|---|
| January | Campaign works for passage of rent freeze bill (and tenants first right of refusal). The latter passes. |
| February | Our appeal is heard. |
| May | We put out pro-rent control workers in primary election judicial race. The lawyer who took us to Court was now running for judge, and press gives us great credit for his defeat, as well as for the election of judge who had helped us during our campaign. |
| June | Appeals Court upholds lower Court. Three City Council members introduce Question K in Council. We continue to raise money and plan for the formal formation of a citywide housing coalition. |

## OUR BEST MOVES DURING CAMPAIGN

In general, organizing a multiracial, mixed income campaign of "real people" who know Baltimore, its problems, and its style.

**Media** — The following moves were successful:

Switching our style of literature from long, discursive pieces to short, snappy copy.

Playing up the opposition's overkill and slickness.

Using the Federal Communications Commission "Fairness Doctrine" (and a lawyer with a lot of assertiveness) to get free air time.

Following the opposition everywhere — making sure that whenever they had a press conference, we were there to challenge their statements and to get covered too.

Exposing the opposition's conflicts of interest regularly (such as who was contributing to their campaign, how many code violations their big supporters had). We found this to be more effective than arguing the technicalities of our own bill.

Aggressively appealing to homeowners, women, seniors, blacks with specialized literature.

Suing the anti-rent control campaign for mail fraud for some of their tactics, and calling it to the media's attention.

## Organizing

Building a broadbased coalition of community, labor and church organizations.

Using "blitzes" - teams of canvassers at shopping centers and neighborhood fairs to collect signatures, register voters (about 5000) and to go door-to-door in communities dropping literature before Election Day.

Getting lots of new people involved.

Using the same public events and mailings and speaking engagements to community groups to recruit volunteers. Getting back to them with a job right away. (We had a core of about 75 key workers, 300 canvassers and 2000 people without literature at the polls on Election Day.)

Enlisting the support of black ministers and many Catholic clergy who talked from the pulpit and handed out literature.

## Speakers Bureau

Soliciting invitations to speak at all kinds of community, church and labor groups.

Engaging landlords in public debate, wherever possible. This worked to our advantage because: 1) They don't know the facts like we do 2) The facts prove them wrong anyway 3) Our interest in housing as shelter is more appealing than their interest in housing as profit.

## Research

Researching the opposition's conflicts of interest (and they were many) using all available public information such as: lists of housing code violations, assessment records, lists of campaign contributions, candidates' and politicians' financial disclosure statements. Funnelling this information to the media committee.

## Fundraising

Having creative events: raffle of 1 month's free rent or mortgage, selling food at Oriole game concessions, the Fonda, Hayden, Mitchell party.

Grant from Youth Project.

Having all staff be either in-kind or volunteer.

**Election Day**

Having a strong, separate Election Day Committee, with a fresh strategy.

## OUR WEAKEST MOVES & MISTAKES
### Media

Not enough tenant exposure. Too much political coverage and not enough of the human stories. Needed to work harder at getting tenants who were not afraid to speak out.

### Organizing

Not getting enough of our endorsing groups to produce work for us.

Not handling a split campaign with "grace under pressure."

Difficulty with tension between being a democratically run organizing effort and an efficient campaign organization.

Too formal and big a structure too soon.

### Research

Took too long to draft the petition. The Research committee should have given its ideas to the lawyers sooner so we would not have wasted time arguing the merits of a provision which they could have told us was unconstitutional to begin with.

### Fundraising

Did not start early enough.

Never had a consistant Fundraising Committee.

Kept taking the fundraiser off his job to do organizing.

Too many fundraisers which required ticket sales instead of, for example, flea markets or other "attractions."

*Excerpted from "Winning Rent Control in a Working Class City," Baltimore Rent Control Campaign, July, 1980*

# Landlord Money Defeats Rent Control in San Francisco

## CHESTER HARTMAN

San Francisco may well be on its way to losing its reputation as a politically progressive city. November 6th was a clear disaster for the left. Voter initiatives on housing cost controls, high-rise height limits, shifting the local tax base to large businesses, and abolishing the police vice squad all lost. In the mayor's race, ultra-conservative Supervisor Quentin Kopp trailed incumbent moderate Dianne Feinstein by just 3300 votes and probably has a better than even chance of winding up mayor in the December 11 runoff.

The city's voters even approved (although by only 54%, compared with its 3:1 statewide margin) the local spending control initiative pushed by Proposition 13 co-author Paul Gann. All in all, not a terrific day out here.

The fact that it was not a terrific day weather-wise either lent these results a natural as well as political explanation. The threatening skies began to open up around 2:30 and by 6 o'clock it was raining hard, leading many folks to head directly home after work instead of making a quick polling booth stop. The 54% turnout — incredibly low for a San Francisco mayoral election — was in part attributable to this, in part to the lack of exciting candidates, particularly for the citywide offices. Curiously, although the left placed some provocative and important initiatives on the ballot, there were no citywide candidates who served to bring out progressive voters.

Perhaps most painful was the defeat of Proposition R — the Affordable Housing Initiative. Only 41% of the voters said yes, in a 70% renter city. The measure was put together by a broad coalition of fifty labor, neighborhood, church and other groups, working together

since January. It was a comprehensive housing reform proposal —
controls over rents, evictions, condominium conversions and housing
speculation, with provisions also to aid homeowners and add to the
housing supply. Two weeks before the election most polls predicted it
would pass.

What happened in the final two weeks reflects the power of big
money. Real estate interests (aided by brethren in other parts of
California and the nation) spent over a half million dollars on a media
blitz of unprecedented proportions for San Francisco politics. Based
on reports filed two weeks before Election Day (and representing
about two thirds of what will finally be reported), the No on R
campaign had secured 191 $500 contributions (the legal maximum),
and 407 contributions in excess of $200. Over 10% of their money
(including 33 of the $500 contributions) came from outside the city or
state. The class-conscious behavior of the real estate industry is
enviable.

The money was used to saturate TV and radio with 30 and 60
second spots. A dozen targeted mailings went out to computerized
lists of voters (homeowners, gays, small landlords, public housing
residents, newly registered voters, tenants, blacks, etc.) Some
households reported receiving as many as eight pieces of mail from
the No on R campaign in a single day.

The way this money was used was as significant as its
magnitude. Based on sophisticated polling techniques, the real estate
interests picked their themes and produced literature and commercials
to emphasize the winning themes, in the process totally distorting
what Prop R said. A widely shown TV commercial, designed to
capitalize on the post Proposition 13 aversion to bureaucracy, showed
a landlord and tenant carrying a carpet into the tenant's apartment, at
which point an inspector appears from behind the bushes to ask
whether the tenant has gotten approval from the government rent
control board for this and then asserts to the surprised pair that under
Prop R the board *has to approve every rent agreement, whatever the
reason.* The proposed ordinance contained no such requirement
whatsoever. Prop R backers offered a legally binding $100,000 reward
to anyone who could prove that it did (a reward no one even sought to
claim) but that didn't stop the commercial.

The specter of the Bronxification of San Francisco was harped
on constantly. Probably the most damaging piece, sent to every renter
three days before the election, was dramatically headed *Your rent is*

*about to go up!,* claiming that Prop R would lead to 9% rent increases. A widely distributed anti-R leaflet was designed to look exactly like the pro-R leaflet. When the rent control proponents publicly complained of this tactic, the chairman of the No on R group told the papers they just don't have a sense of humor. The result was a totally misled and confused electorate.

San Franciscans for Affordable Housing, the Yes on R coalition, managed to raise $54,000, a respectable figure, considering that many traditional sources of liberal money were unavailable on this issue, since lots of liberals are also property owners. The relative scarcity of funds meant little access to the most effective means of reaching voters — direct mail, television and radio.

The pro-R campaign placed principal reliance on leaflets — over 300,000 were distributed, to nearly every household in the city. As with the campaign generally, the literature was competently and professionally done, but it was difficult to get access to most large apartment buildings and literature merely left in the entranceway was bound to be disposed of by the building manager.

Tenants were reluctant to place Yes on R signs in their windows for fear of landlord reprisal. Owners of apartment buildings, construction sites, parking lots, and realty offices (of which there are 2500 in the San Francisco yellow pages, for the most part located on well-travelled streets) would plaster No on R signs saying "Build Housing, Not Bureaucracy" all over their properties.

One of the most difficult hurdles the campaign faced was the fact that the Board of Supervisors — clearly as a way of heading off the initiative — in June had unanimously passed both rent control and condominium conversion control ordinances. Although the city rent control law is probably the weakest in the country, the appeal of the "let's give the new law a chance" argument was hard to fight. The city's law permits 7% annual rent increases over and above increases needed to cover the repairs and improvements; permits landlords to raise rents at will in between tenancies (which predictably led to a big increase in evictions); and expires next September. Under Prop R rent increases could be obtained only for documented cost increases or to achieve a fair rate of return on investment; new as well as existing tenants were covered; arbitrary evictions were effectively controlled; and the ordinance would have stayed in effect so long as the housing crisis persisted.

Some of the questions and lessons from the Prop R campaign:

• *How to get renters to register and to vote is still the major problem; the big renter majority in the city's population as a whole probably drops to a minority among actual voters. Sixty-five percent of the voters in Quentin Kopp's largely white homeowner District 10 turned out on Nov. 6, in the black Fillmore District 4 and the Latino Mission District 6 the turnout figures were 40% and 44%. Combined with the higher proportion of persons over 18 and persons who actually register in the more middle-class areas of the city, the imbalance among districts is striking. Although each of the city's 11 districts has about the same population, the votes against Prop R in Kopp's district almost equalled the combined Yes on R votes in Districts 4 and 6 (where R won) and the largely black District 7 (where R got 49.2% of the vote).*

• *A related problem is how to get homeowners (who in effect were exempted from the ordinance) to side with renters, as housing consumers, rather than to see themselves as allied with those who rent out housing for a profit.*

• *There clearly is a need to do basic organizing work in communities, in order to counter the effects of expensive and dishonest media blitzes. Such prior base-building also avoids the aura Prop R had of liberal and radical outsiders pushing panaceas, which limited the campaign's access to the city's third world communities.*

• *There needs to be some effective and rapid means — whether by legislation or litigation — of preventing the dissemination of damaging factual misstatements as parts of a political campaign.*

• *The comprehensiveness of the 8500-word ordinance — intended not only to provide meaningful solutions to the city's housing crisis but to counter the standard anti-rent control arguments (that it will end new construction, lead to condominium conversions, etc.) — may have given the other side more opportunities to attack the law. When confused or overwhelmed, people may tend to vote for the status quo. Many winning voter initiatives — Proposition 13, for example — were quite short and unidimensional.*

The SFAH coalition will be staying together. One immediate task is how to relate to the five Supervisorial run-off races. In four of these districts, there is a run-off candidate who supported Prop R. If these four win, they would join two pro-rent control Supervisors who were not up for reelection, giving a pro-tenant majority on the 11-person Board. The Board then would be in a good position to strengthen the existing rent control and condo control ordinances and pass elements of the Affordable Housing package. Another immediate leverage point is the mayoral run-off; where the swing vote may rest with David Scott, a gay realtor who got 10% of the vote and who, surprisingly, supported all four progressive ballot measures. And down the pike a bit is the June, 1980 primary election, where housing activists across the state will probably be faced with a real estate industry sponsored initiative that would virtually eliminate any meaningful local rent control measures. (In recent years the right wing has tended to use the state initiative process in California, while in San Francisco the left has been the group to use it on a city level.)

San Francisco probably has the tightest housing market in the nation — virtually no vacancies, skyrocketing rents and housing prices. It may be that the gentrification process, well along its way here, has already so changed the city's demographics that the people the SFAH coalition came together to protect — the elderly, minorities, low and moderate-income families — are already too few in number to protect their own future. If so, San Francisco may become the nation's first totally middle-class city. On the other hand, the housing problem is filtering up, so that even people with good incomes are finding it increasingly difficult to buy or rent in San Francisco. Although meaningful controls on the housing market were rejected on Nov. 6, it is inconceivable that the issue will go away.

*Reprinted from SHELTERFORCE, Fall, 1979*

# Organizing a Rent Control Campaign

## EMILY PARADISE ACHTENBERG

### WHAT THE CAMPAIGN'S ABOUT

*A Strong Rent Control Law.*

Obviously, an important goal of any rent control campaign is to get a strong rent control law adopted. Don't settle for anything less, if you can help it--such as weaker rent control law, a rent grievance board without legal powers, or a rent control "study committee." Local politicians pushing for these alternatives usually want to create the illusion that they're doing something about high rents, while actually doing very little that's of use to tenants.

*An Organized Tenant Campaign.*

The rent control campaign should be a public one, with lots of visible tenant pressure on the city politicians. You can be sure that lots of pressure against rent control will be coming from the landlords. It's important to keep reminding the politicians that there are more tenants than landlords in the city, and that tenants working together can be a strong economic and political force. Also, since one of the major goals of the rent control campaign is to organize tenants, there's no point in running your campaign behind closed doors.

A visible tenant campaign also lets you take credit for the victory when rent control is finally passed. A clear tenant victory on rent control is a good way to strengthen your tenant group, and to show people that organizing makes sense.

### POLITICAL EDUCATION

During a rent control campaign, there's usually a running debate in the press, at hearings, and on the streets about the housing crisis and what can be done to solve it. Most people know that rents are rising and conditions getting worse, but they aren't sure just why this is happening. This is a good time to get out information on the housing crisis and to explain how banks' and landlords' profits contribute to it. Be sure that tenants are well informed about rent control, so they can answer the landlords' anti-rent control propaganda and be prepared to fight for strong enforcement of the law in the future.

## BUILDING A PERMANENT TENANT ORGANIZATION

During the rent control campaign, you should be looking forward to the time after rent control passes. The struggle won't end after rent control is voted in. Landlords will do everything they can to sabotage the law: by ignoring it, getting their "cronies" appointed to "administer" the law, going to court, and trying to get exemptions. They may even try to get the state legislature to weaken the law. Every one of these ploys has been tried by landlords in Cambridge, Somerville, Brookline, Lynn, and Boston.

In other words, the mere passage of rent control won't help much, unless there is an organized political force of tenants to take advantage of the law's potential benefits. If no such group exists, there's little chance that rent control will make much difference for tenants. Don't count on the courts or local politicians to do it for you.

This means that there should be a group of dedicated tenants who are willing and able to staff an office with a telephone, and who can hand out leaflets, go to building meetings and public hearings, and help tenants enforce the law themselves. This group should be able to inform tenants of their rights under rent control, help them take advantage of rent control benefits, and organize them to resist any landlord abuses of the law. If the rent control campaign is being run by a strong tenants group or groups, use it to expand and strengthen organizing efforts already underway. Try to make contacts with as many other groups who share your views of the housing situation as possible - such as labor unions, welfare groups, etc., as well as with individual tenants.

## CARRYING OUT THE CAMPAIGN
## MOBILIZING SUPPORT

Besides a core group of organizers, you'll need lots of people to help with the campaign - to write and hand out leaflets, come to meetings, public hearings, and demonstrations, and to collect signatures if you're running a petition campaign. To recruit people and spread the word about rent control, you may want to organize tenant meetings in different buildings or parts of the city. You can also send representatives to talk at meetings of other groups, such as unions, welfare groups, student groups, etc.

It's important to be able to tell each group you meet with why rent control is important for them. For instance, in talking to public housing tenants, you should explain that rent control will make it easier for them to move out of public housing if they want to. Also, since more tenants will be able to afford private housing under rent control, it will be a little easier for the people who really need public housing to get in.

You may want to make a special effort to talk to groups of small homeowners and landlords, even though they may seem to be the most outspoken opponents of rent control. Lots of the anti-control propaganda produced by large real estate interests is aimed at this group, especially about property values and taxes. Even though many small homeowners and landlords are exempt from rent control, they are definitely affected by the issue.

Actually, many small homeowners and landlords have more in common with tenants than they do with large real estate interests. They're often working people who were recently tenants themselves, and who bought their houses for long term security rather than profit. Many maintain their houses well and charge relatively low rents. You can at least try to "neutralize" this group, by explaining that rent control won't hurt owners who aren't making exorbitant profits, that rent control will cause only a slight increase in the tax rate, and that rent control can help stop speculation and neighborhood blight.

Other ways of recruiting support include radio and TV talk shows, "kitchen conferences" in the homes of active or sympathetic tenants, and door-to-door canvassing. Even if you're not running a formal initiative petition campaign, you may want to gather signatures as a way of talking to people about rent control and showing support for your campaign. Somerville tenants found that this was a useful method of organizing around rent control.

Your group should probably hold regular meetings, to plan strategy and train new members. These meetings should be open and well publicized, so that new people can find out what you're doing.

Many tenants are afraid to join an organizing campaign because they fear retaliation from their landlords. You can talk to them about the new retaliatory eviction law, which makes it illegal for a landlord to try to evict you for filing any kind of housing complaint or for joining a tenant organization. But it's also important to have people in your group who are willing to assist anyone who does run into trouble -- including legal help and help blocking evictions, if needed.

There are many ways to get out information about the rent control campaign and the housing crisis, and you'll probably want to try all of them. Leaflets, posters, radio spots, slide shows, video tapes, and talk shows can all be useful. Tenants in Lynn and Somerville got lots of publicity by writing articles in their own community newspapers. In Cambridge, tenants started a newsletter and developed a city-wide mailing list. Rent control bumper stickers were also used in Lynn.

The fall 1972 rent control campaign in Lynn shows how many of these tactics can be used to mobilize support for rent control. The campaign was organized around the November referendum, which the city council required when it passed rent control the previous February. The rent control campaign committee worked hard to build a broad alliance of tenants and small homeowners. Weekly public meetings were held. Different leaflets were prepared for different types of groups, including small homeowners. 30,000 were distributed door-to-door 2 weeks before the election. A special rent control issue of Lynn's community newspaper was published dealing with landlords' arguments against rent control. Progressive elected officials, including the mayor, publicly endorsed rent control and taped radio spots. Support was won from many groups, including union locals, mental health organizations, elderly groups, public housing tenant associations, Lynn Welfare Rights, anti-poverty agencies, and the model cities agency, which contributed $1000 to the campaign. The referendum won 22,000 to 15,000.

Tenants with rent control organizing experience in other cities can be especially useful in lending support and in helping you build your campaign. Be sure to keep in touch with the groups listed at the end of this handbook.

## ORGANIZED TENANT ACTIONS

The most important thing you can do during a rent control campaign is to create lots of organized tenant pressure that politicians will be forced to respond to. A good way to do this is through organized tenant actions.

Turning out a large crowd for any public hearings on rent control is essential. Cambridge tenants have done this consistently, especially at hearings when the council was about to pass rent control (or repeal it). Lynn tenants packed the city council hearing on rent control with nearly 1000 tenants, even though the newly elected council was already pledged to pass the law.The papier-mache rat head brought by Somerville tenants to their hearings gained lots of publicity for rent control advocates.

Different kinds of demonstrations, marches, etc. can be used throughout the campaign to build up momentum and pressure. Somerville tenants picketed the homes of Aldermen and large landlords, and demonstrated regularly at Aldermen meetings. Lynn tenants held a "tent-in" in front of city hall, to dramatize the housing crisis and announce their initiative petition campaign. The first time rent control was defeated by the Cambridge City Council, in 1969, tenants organized a vigil outside city hall which attracted lots of publicity. When the lame-duck city council repealed rent control in 1971, Cambridge tenants widely publicized their threat of a city-wide rent strike to bring rent control back.

You can probably think of many other ways to organize tenant action around rent control that make sense in your city.

## DEMANDING A PRO-TENANT RENT CONTROL SYSTEM

During the campaign, it's a good idea to work out some of the things you'll what to demand from the city after rent control passes. You'll want tenants to understand that getting rent control passed is only the first step; what's really important is the way rent control is set up and administered later.

Tenants in Lynn made specific demands for rent control enforcement during their rent control campaign. They demanded a rent control board with at least 50% low and moderate income tenants and 25% homeowners. They also proposed a specific formula for determining a landlord's "fair net operating income" (see Ch. 4). Since they were trying to get rent control through an initiative petition campaign, two petitions were circulated: one demanding passage of the state rent control law, and the other containing the specific demands for how rent control should be implemented. Tenants saw this mainly as an educational device to prepare tenants for the fight after rent control was passed.

You may feel that making very specific demands before rent control is passed could confuse the issue and weaken support for rent

control. Instead, you could organize around a few general principles –
e.g., rent decreases for substandard housing, making landlords share
property tax expenses.

## EXPOSING "NON-SOLUTIONS"

If you end up with a weaker rent control law, a rent grievance board,
or a "study committee," don't give up. By exposing the
ineffectiveness of these official bodies as much as possible, you can
make the arguments for rent control even stronger the next time
around.

### INITIATIVE PETITION CAMPAIGNS

If the politicians won't pass rent control, you can try to go around
them through an initiative petition campaign.

An initiative petition for rent control must be signed by at least
8% of the registered voters. (A few special charter cities like Lynn
require more signatures.) Then the issue goes before the local
legislative body, which must vote it up or down without amendment.
If they fail to pass it, rent control automatically goes on the ballot at
the next regular municipal election. If it is approved in this election by
at least ⅓ of all registered voters in the city, and by a majority of
people who actually vote on the measure, rent control will be enacted
into law.

If the initiative petition is signed by at least 15% of the
registered voters, the city must either pass it or hold a special election
to vote on it. (Check the municipal initiative petition law, Ch. 43 of the
Mass. General Laws, Sections 37-41, for further details.)

Initiative petition campaigns for rent control have been tried in
Cambridge and in Lynn. Both efforts were unsuccessful, but the main
problems involved were special ones which shouldn't affect
campaigns in other cities. The Cambridge petition in 1969 was barred
from the ballot by the City Solicitor and the Election Commission,
before the state rent control enabling law was enacted. At that time,
cities had no legal power to enact rent control legislation. The initiative
petition campaign organized by Lynn tenants in 1971 failed to get
enough signatures. But the Lynn city charter requires an unusually
high number of signatures, more than you need in other cities and
towns.

Despite these initial failures, both cities did pass rent control
eventually, and the petition convassing done by tenants probably laid

much of the groundwork. Also, the petition campaigns resulted in city-wide tenant organizations which are now leading the fight for strong rent control in both places. In Berkeley, California, tenants recently won rent control though an initiative petition campaign when the city council refused to enact it.

## PREPARING FOR THE CAMPAIGN

The initiative petition method has some obvious advantages. It allows people to act on their own, bypassing the politicians. Canvassing for signatures can be a good way to talk to tenants about the housing crisis and the need for rent control. It can also help recruit members for your tenants group.

But there are also disadvantages. Running a successful petition campaign takes time, planning, and lots of people who are willing to work hard. Your group will need to make a careful estimate of the amount of time and people you have to gather the necessary signatures. If it looks like a pretty futile effort, you can probably think of better organizing tactics to keep the rent control issue alive — and avoid the demoralization that could come from an unsuccessful effort.

Also, since the initiative is a way of going over the heads of local politicians and city bureaucrats, be prepared for their attempts to sabotage your petition. Because the politicians will look for any excuse to keep rent control off the ballot, it's necessary to take extra care so that everything is done exactly right.

If you decide to try a petition campaign, you'll probably want to use the 8% method — that is, getting the signatures of 8% of the registered voters and aiming for the next regular municipal election. If you're in a hurry and don't want to wait for the next regular municipal election (usually every two years), you can try the 15% method -- getting signatures from 15% of the registered voters. This way, the city council is forced to call a special election, or it can put the initiative on the ballot in any upcoming regular or special election.

But this method has serious problems. Remember that ⅓ of all registered voters in the city must approve an initiative (in addition to a majority of those actually voting on the measure). Since not many people vote in special elections, the initiative could fail even though it received an overwhelming majority of the votes cast. Voter turnout is also light in many regularly scheduled elections, especially mid-year primaries. All things considered, then, it's probably best to use the 8% method and wait till the next municipal election.

## RUNNING THE CAMPAIGN

The petitions you circulate are supposed to contain the exact wording that you want on the ballot. Check with a lawyer before sending your petition to the printer, to avoid any technical pitfalls. You might try to get the city council (or other local legislative body) to act on your petition before you go to all the trouble of collecting signatures, if you think there's a chance they might pass it. If they refuse, or vote it down, you can start the signature campaign.

**Getting Information.** It's a good idea to check your city charter right away with a lawyer, to see if there any special local initiative petition requirements. You'll also want to get the official list of registered voters from the local registrar of voters or election commission. This contains the names of all registered voters in the city, arranged by address and street number. From this list, you can calculate the number of signatures you need.

**Gathering Signatures.** There are three main ways to get lots of signatures. First, you can have tables or standing signature collectors in places where many people usually walk, such as outside a major shopping center or in front of the city hall. Second, you can send signature collectors to gatherings or meetings, such as church and social events, public hearings and demonstrations, tenant meetings, etc. Third, you can canvass door-to-door with the official voting list.

You'll probably want to use a combination of all three methods, but the door-to-door one is probably the best. It's the only way you can really be sure you're getting only the signatures of registered voters. Of course, this method also takes the most time.

Collecting signatures for an initiative petition can be just a mechanical task, or it can also be a way to strengthen your tenants group. Canvassers should hand out leaflets and other literature explaining what the rent control fight is about and what your group can do to help. Try spending some time talking with each person you ask for a signature. This may slow things down a little, but the long-term benefits to your tenants group are more important.

As the petitions come in, or near the end of the campaign, you may want to check them yourself against the voter registration list to see how many are invalid and how many more you need. It's usually a good idea to get about twice as many signatures as you need, because many will be invalid.

The amount of time it takes to collect the signatures will vary, depending on the popularity of your proposal, the community's familiarity with it, how much time you spend talking to people, and the number of people and hours per day you can devote to canvassing. To be safe, give yourself at least 4-6 months to collect signatures. You should actually begin the petition campaign at least 6-8 months before the election, because extra time is also needed after the signatures are turned in.

**Turning in the Petitions.** Plan on turning in all your signatures to the city at least two months before the election. This gives the city council time to accept or reject the proposal, and enough time for it to be printed on the ballot if the city council rejects it.

**Legal Help.** Make sure you have mapped out legal tactics to combat any sabotage efforts by the city, and a friendly lawyer or legal services office to help you. Be prepared for a legal fight, because it will probably be necessary.

*Reprinted from "Less Rent More Control: A Tenant's Guide to Rent Control in Massachusetts," Urban Planning Aids, Inc., Cambridge, Mass. 1973*

# SECTION VI

# BEYOND RENT CONTROL: INNOVATIVE HOUSING STRATEGIES

# Steps Toward a Solution of the "Housing Problem"

## RICHARD P. APPELBAUM
## AND JOHN INGRAM GILDERBLOOM

Our findings do not support the notion that new construction will have a simple and straightforward beneficial effect on the availability of low-rent housing. On the contrary, we believe that the data show that new construction may well have the opposite: newer, more expensive apartments may be replacing the low and moderate income housing stock. This results in prices going up in an area which could also have a "price leading effect" on the existing housing stock. At the very least, there is no evidence to indicate that increased supply and a reduction in scarcity will drive down rents. This was true in 1970, and we believe the conclusion holds with greater force today, when the cost of building is even higher relative to average income than it was ten years ago.

### Rent Control

Moderate rent control serves primarily to rationalize the housing market: to eliminate the excesses of rent gouging, while providing landlords and renters with annual indices of allowable rent increases. So long as inflation and speculation are not rampant, that index can be pegged to an amount which is fair and reasonable to both tenants and landlords — customarily around one-half the consumer price index, reflecting the fact that the landlord's variable costs generally amount to half or less of his/her total costs (mortgage payments generally being fixed). But when prices and interest rates are high and rising, the income-producing potential of rental property is substantially reduced. Landlords respond by both raising rents and treating their holdings as speculative investments. This creates a vicious cycle of rapidly rising rents and sales prices. Landlords respond by searching for other, more secure forms of real estate investment; tenants by pushing for strong rent control laws which limit the ability of landlords to speculate. One result is the threat of capital flight from the construction of new rental housing — a threat which is all the more serious given the national slump in rental housing construction.

Government subsidies will not solve the problem — they both fail to address the causes, and they are far too limited in scope to effectively deal with the symptoms. Nor will more construction help. New apartments will be aimed at the more profitable upper income markets; in the absence of substantial governmental subsidies, lower income rental housing simply will not be built on any scale. Nor will more expensive housing result in "filtering" to lower income renters — at least according to our evidence.

The conclusion to us appears inescapable: as we enter the eighties, the marketplace will become increasingly incapable of providing affordable housing. When one considers the increased demand that will result from the combination of demographics, the trend towards smaller household size, and continuing economic stagnation and inflation, the prognosis is serious indeed. In all this, the task of low income housers seems to us clear: we must work to forge a unified national force for affordable housing. We feel this will best be achieved if the following proposals are realized:

**1. Build a broad-based movement of subsidized and unsubsidized renters.** We must recognize that an increasingly broad segment of the American population will be denied affordable housing, and that as a result a broad housing constituency can and should be built. "Subsidized housing" is a misnomer that divides our movement. Virtually all Americans receive one form of housing assistance or another, from the federal government tax shelters, mortgage insurance, direct subsidies -- all of these are a part of the history of a housing delivery system oriented towards private profit. We strongly believe that a natural alliance already exists between recipients of Section 8 subsidies, low income tenants eligible for but unable to receive such assistance, and low-to-moderate income tenants whose income is too great to permit qualification for Section 8, yet too low to afford adequate housing. The ranks of renters will be swollen in the eighties. Many will be young families with stable, moderate incomes, who will be forced to confront the prospect of a lifetime of renting. This situation will prove fertile ground for the creation of a unified, national tenants' movement.

**2. Demand housing at prices all can afford.** We see two proposals in this regard as especially pressing:

**(a) Rejection of the outmoded "25% affordability" criterion.** Pressures will build for such rejection in the wrong direction from the real estate industry, which, already on the defensive, has argued that estimating affordability shortfalls on the basis of 25% of income overstates the extent of the housing crisis. We must push in the direction argued by Chester Hartman and Michael Stone (1980) — for the adoption of a formula which takes into account actual ability to pay. Such a formula would be based on BLS estimates of minimal requirements for food, clothing, health care, and other necessities in a particular area. The difference between this minimal non-housing budget and available household income would then constitute the estimate of needed assistance. For a four-person family earning $8500 in 1975, Hartman and Stone (1978) estimate that only $53 per month — less than 8% of household income — would be available for housing; the remainder should be made up by subsidies. Hartman and Stone claim that by this standard, some 9.5-million renter households and 11.3 million homeowner households, were overpaying in 1975 (210).

**(b) Push for strong rent control ordinances that discourage speculation by excluding refinancing costs from fair return determination.** So long as landlords are permitted to pass along the costs of refinancing at inflated values and interest rates, rent control will be powerless to deal with one of the principal causes of rising rents. We harbor no illusions concerning the effect this will have on the profitability of rental housing. For properties in overheated markets, which have been purchased or refinanced in the past year or two, this will impose a considerable burden on landlords. For other properties, it will severely curb appreciation potential by discouraging buyers. As a result, rental property will be seen as profitable largely in terms of its income generating potential. Such rent control ordinances must be coupled with anti-demolition and condominium conversion provisions, to discourage these forms of capital flight.

**3. Demand non-market solutions to the housing crisis.**

214

We must recognize that the marketplace can no longer provide affordable housing, and look to other means for providing lower income individuals and families with adequate shelter. Cooperative housing is one such possibility. This may provide a particularly attractive option when rent control or other regulations reduce the desirability of rental housing to landlords and other investors. Another option, which deserves to be given serious consideration, is the proposal by Hartman and Stone (1978) to greatly increase the quantity of publicly financed, developed, and operated housing. It is especially important that housing no longer be treated as a commodity, something to be bought and sold for profit. It is equally important that the financing of housing be removed from a private mortgaging system which indentures the future while making the construction and ownership of housing subject to the vagaries of the financial markets. Hartman and Stone convincingly demonstrate that public housing need not consist of depressing cell-block like structures in which the poor and racial minorities are consigned to a ghettoized existence. For reasons of energy and evironmental considerations as well as cost, the detached single-family suburban homestead will be less and less viable for housing Americans during the remainder of this century. Attractive urban and suburban townhouses can be built and operated with public funds, creating a viable alternative to private development and ownership for those who desire such an alternative. The costs of a full-fledged program are considerable. Hartman and Stone (1978:243-4) estimate initial costs of $58-billion annually, or around 3% of GNP. Of this amount, they estimate that $10 billion would go into direct construction grants for some 250,000 new and rehabilitated units, generating one half million jobs; $30 billion would be for operating subsidies; and $17-billion for special subsidies and acquisition of private rental housing. An additional $1 billion might be required for administration.

These costs are large, but not impossible. They are, for example, less than half of the military budget, and comparable to the increased revenues the energy companies will receive as a result of deregulation. The windfall profits tax, in fact, could be principal source of start-up capital for such a program. The resources are there — what is required is a major shift in national priorities. Sweden, among other countries, has succeeded in adequately sheltering its entire population through similar programs.

We have no illusions concerning the present feasibility of this or

**215**

our other proposals. In today's political and fiscal climate, they represent radical and possibly unpopular suggestions. But they must be raised, and they must be put on the agenda now if they are to inform discussion during the coming decade. This program may appear to many of us as extreme, but we finally believe that the day will come when a radical departure from "business as usual" will be seen as the only alternative to ever-widening hardship. It is the task of a national housing movement to create a national consciousness about housing issues, and to begin to move its constituents to press for genuine solutions to America's housing problems.

**Essay written April 1980**

# National Program to Fight Housing Inflation

## CONSUMERS OPPOSED TO INFLATION IN THE NECESSITIES

*Inflation is a national and international economic problem requiring a strong national movement that will force Washington politicians to act to counter rising housing prices. The following are some practical proposals put forth by Coin that could be implemented by the President and U.S. Congress.*

### SHORT TERM SOLUTIONS
### LOWER MORTGAGE RATES FOR NECESSITY HOUSING AND
### HIGHER MORTGAGE RATES FOR LUXURY HOUSING

Interest rates on mortgage loans to purchase existing homes have risen to a record in many localities. A rise in mortgage rates from 9% to 11% (a 22% increase) results in a 20% increase in monthly mortgage payments. For most homeowners monthly payments represent from 60-70% of the cost of home ownership.

The President should take immediate action to reduce housing inflation by directing the Federal Home Loan Bank Board (FHLBB) to establish a system of reserve requirements for mortgage loans that would lower mortgage rates for necessity housing and raise mortgage rates for luxury housing. The Credit Control Act of 1969 provides authority for the FHLBB, upon authorization from the President and the Federal Reserve Board, to require all institutional mortgage lenders to maintain special reserves for mortgage loans. Such mortgage reserves would be entirely separate from the demand and savings deposit reserves that commercial banks maintain with the Federal

Reserve Board. By paying interest on necessity mortgage reserves and no interest on luxury mortgage reserves or by imposing mortgage reserve requirements only on luxury mortgages and giving lenders a reserve credit for necessity mortgages, the FHLBB can shift relative yield to lenders of necessity and luxury mortgages. This yield shift will lower the market interest rate for necessity mortgages and raise the rate for luxury mortgages. The FHLBB should use the mortgage reserve system to lower the necessity mortgage rate by 1% (100 basic points) and raise the luxury mortgage rate by 1% (100 basic points). The FHLBB should reinvest the mortgage reserve balances in necessity mortgage loans in order to avoid any decline in the overall supply of mortgage credit.

Necessity housing should be defined as single family homes priced at $75,000 or less and low, moderate, and middle income cooperative housing. The $75,000 standard can be adjusted upward in the several SMSA's where home prices are far above the national average. Luxury housing should be defined as single second homes. The reserve requirements would not apply to multi-family housing, other than low, moderate, and middle income cooperative housing. In 1978, 80% of existing homes sold and 70% of new home purchasers would benefit from lower mortgage rates. A 1% reduction in the mortgage rate for necessity housing will lower the CPI by 0.73%.

Aside from lower mortgage payments for most home buyers and the beneficial impact on the CPI, lowering the necessity rate by 1% and raising the luxury rate by 1% will expand housing production and, thereby, moderate the housing supply shortage. Due to the mortgage interest tax deduction and less budget constraints, upper income persons are less sensitive to high mortgage rates than moderate income persons. Thus, the demand for necessity mortgage rates should result in the production of roughly an additional 130,000 homes per year, while raising the luxury mortgage rate should only reduce luxury production by roughly 30,000 units. This would be a net gain of 100,000 units per year.

Introduction of a necessity—luxury mortgage rate spread will also reduce inflation in the housing sector by shifting the distribution of new production toward necessity housing. In recent years a major cause of housing inflation has been increasing orientation of new home production toward luxury homes.

Raising the mortgage rate for luxury housing will by itself have an important anti-inflation effect. The higher rate will moderate the demand for luxury housing. A powerful demand for luxury housing has fueled inflation in many housing markets as escalating prices for luxury homes have spilled and exerted upward pressure on necessity housing prices.

Although mortgage reserve requirements are authorized by the Credit Control Act of 1969, they should be distinguished from selective credit controls. Selective credit controls are curbs on credit users imposed to avoid escalation of interest rates and a housing downturn during cyclical booms of the economy. By contrast, use of mortgage reserve requirements to establish a necessity — luxury mortgage rate spread is a useful tool to fight inflation in the housing sector under any macroeconomic condition — i.e. stagflation or recession, as well as boom. A mortgage reserve system is a cross subsidy within the mortgage sector that runs from luxury home purchasers to necessity home purchasers. It is not a program to insulate the mortgage sector as a whole from the adverse effects of a credit crunch.

## LONGER-TERM SOLUTIONS

### Selective Credit Controls

In recent years monetary policy has been the primary tool by which government has sought to curb aggregate demand when the economy has become overheated. In such circumstances the Federal Reserve Board has attempted to curb credit extensions, which stimulate aggregate demand, by raising interest rates. Selective credit controls provide an alternative method for curbing credit extension during cyclical booms of the economy. They involve the imposition of restrictive loan terms — high down payment and short maturity requirements — on certain extensions and imposition of borrowing ceilings for certain types of borrowers. Selective credit rates limit credit extensions directly, rather than relying on higher interest rates to dampen credit. Because interest cost is a key determinant of housing costs, the cost-push of restrictive monetary policy is born primarily by the housing sector. During 1978, raising interest rates added 1.7% to the CPI with 1.3% of this resulting from high rates on mortgage loans and residential construction loans.

Use of selective credit controls and less reliance on restrictive monetary policy can eliminate the extreme cyclical fluctuations in housing production: stabilizing housing production could lower the cost of housing by as much as 15% to 20%. Selective credit controls would facilitate housing stabilization by curbing credit extensions in all major economic sectors—business, consumer durables, housing—rather than in just the housing sector. In contrast, the high interest rates associated with restrictive monetary policy primarily affect the housing sector.

Aside from lowering housing production costs, stabilizing the housing sector will increase the supply of housing. Short cyclical downturns in housing output, such as occurred in 1974-75, result in a production shortfall that is difficult to make up in later years. Also, when it is necessary to limit aggregate demand, selective credit controls provide a means to curb non-essential residential production—high priced luxury homes and second homes. High interest rates for the most part curb the production of more essential moderately priced housing since the housing demand of moderate income persons is more sensitive to high interest rates than that of upper income persons.

During cyclical booms of the economy, the President should have invoked the authority conferred by the Credit Control Act of 1969 and direct the Federal Reserve Board to impose selective credit controls. When authorizing **selective** credit controls, the President should establish a housing production target for the next 12 months and direct the Federal Reserve Board to implement the credit controls in a manner that will facilitate reaching the target. Investment by large corporations and construction of luxury housing should include the following credit controls:

• Borrowing by each of the 500 largest corporations should be limited to a fixed percentage of the corporation's borrowing in the previous year. In applying the borrowing ceilings, all types of credit should be included—i.e. bank loans, commercial paper, corporate bonds. To provide flexibility, large corporations subject to the controls should be able to purchase additional borrowing rights from other large corporations which have not used their full borrowing authority under the the ceilings.

• Restrictive downpayment and maturity requirements should be imposed on mortgage loans for the purchase of luxury housing—high priced homes and second homes.

• Restrictive maturity periods should be imposed on consumer installment loans and maximum lines of credit cards should be limited.

## GOVERNMENT PROGRAMS TO EXPAND
## THE SUPPLY OF MODERATE PRICED HOUSING

Increased government action to expand the supply of moderate priced housing is necessary because the private housing market is not generating enough housing units for lower and moderate income persons. Aside from the general housing shortage, several other factors add to the severity of the shortages in the moderate priced home market. First, new residential construction has become increasingly luxury oriented and the units produced are not easily filtered down to middle income persons. Second, production of new rental housing is very limited. In 1978 the nation's rental housing stock actually declined as rental unit losses exceeded rental unit production by roughly 20,000 units. Among income groups low and moderate income persons are the most dependent on rental housing — roughly 45% of low and moderate income families are renters versus only 15% for upper income families.

Government housing subsidies for new rental units expand the supply of moderate priced housing. Rehabilitation — whether substantial or moderate — has the same supply expanding effects as new construction whenever it restores abandoned units or prevents impending abandonment.

Certain strategies will increase the supply expanding effect on government housing subsidies. Moderate rehabilitation requires less subsidy per unit than substantial rehabilitation, while new construction involves the greatest subsidy. Thus, the supply expanding effect of subsidies can be maximized by giving moderate rehabilitation units facing likely abandonment priority over substantial rehabilitation and substantial rehabilitation priority over new construction.

The primary federal housing subsidy problem — Sec. 8 rental assistance — provides rent subsidies for existing units requiring no rehabilitation, as well as rehabilitated units and new units. Although subsidies are smaller for existing units which do not require rehabilitation and are not in danger of abandonment, they do not expand the supply of housing. Thus, where rental markets are tight, subsidies should be concentrated on rehabilitation or new construction. On the other hand, high cost subsidies for new construction should not be used in a housing market where a short supply is not an underlying problem. Federal housing subsidies will have the greatest impact on supply if the higher cost supply — expanding subsidies are channeled to tight housing markets and the low cost subsidies with no supply effect are channeled to relatively loose housing markets.

Rehabilitation costs in subsidy programs can be significantly reduced by encouraging home purchasers or co-operative members to undertake some of the rehabilitation. Self-rehabilitation, known as sweat equity, can be particularly cost effective. It can lower the cost of rehabilitating multi-family building by as much as 50%.

Abandonment losses can be minimized and self-rehabilitation opportunities vastly increased by a large scale expansion of Urban Homesteading Programs. Under such programs abandoned housing owned by HUD or local governments is sold at a nominal price to low and moderate income persons who participate in the rehabilitation process. Although the amount of HUD owned housing suitable for homesteading is modest—less than 28,000 single family homes and less than 46,000 multi-family units—the volume of abandoned housing units which local governments could acquire by tax foreclosure is substantial, as many as 3 million units. New York City predicts that by 1981 it will own 250,000 multi-family units.

• The Federal subsidy for Sec. 8 and public housing should be expanded by establishing an annual target of 400,000 supply expansion units (rehabilitation and construction) for each of the next five years. In FY 1979 the Sec. 8 and public housing subsidy provided for 230,000 rehabilitation and new construction units and 130,000 existing units.

• In allocating Sec. 8 and public housing, priority should be given to lower cost subsidies—i.e. in order of priority: existing units without rehabilitation, moderate rehabilitation, substantial rehabilitation, new construction.

• In allocating Sec. 8 and other public subsidies, the higher cost subsidies that expand supply (rehabilitation and new construction) should be concentrated on tight rental markets.

• A national homesteading plan should be adopted with a goal of homesteading 100,000 abandoned units every year and employing self-rehabilitation to the greatest extent possible. Key elements of the plan would be: (1) federal monitoring of the number and condition of the abandoned units; (2) federal encouragement for local governments to aggressively take title to abandoned units and devise and expand homesteading programs; (3) homesteading of both single family and multi-family units; (4) increased federal funds to cover the cost of acquiring abandoned homes for homesteading, to provide technical assistance to homesteaders, and to finance rehabilitation at low interest rates. Overall, homesteading programs should be directed toward low and moderate income persons.

## FEDERAL INCOME TAX DEDUCTION
## FOR MORTGAGE INTEREST
## AND PROPERTY TAXES

Federal income tax provides a $12 billion tax subsidy to homeowners by allowing them to take a federal income tax deduction for mortgage interest payments and state and local property taxes. Almost all of it goes to upper income persons because, relative to moderate and lower income persons, they are more likely to be homeowners, more likely to hold mortgage debt in larger amounts, and receive a greater tax savings from the deduction due to their higher tax brackets. Taxpayers in the upper third of the income distribution receive more than 90% of the tax subsidy.

This tax break has a strong inflationary impact on home prices. Most of the tax savings are capitalized in the form of higher home prices. This inflationary effect can be seen in the much higher market value for condominium units than for comparable rental units, which reflects the fact that renters do not receive the tax break. Elimination of the tax deduction would most likely lower home prices by 10% to 15% and at the same time greatly strengthen the private rental market.

The tax subsidy provides only modest real benefit to homeowners, because most of the tax savings is lost due to the induced increase in home prices. Even worse, what little benefit is conferred does not extend to moderate income homeowners. Moderate income homeowners generally do not itemize deductions and thus do not use the mortgage interest and property tax deduction. About ⅓ of all homeowners with mortgage debt take the standard deduction rather than itemize deductions and this group is predominantly moderate or lower middle income homeowners. IRS data shows that very few taxpayers with incomes below $18,000 itemize deductions. Thus, even if the tax deduction does confer some real benefit, it does not expand home ownership opportunities because it does not reach moderate income home buyers.

The subsidy is also in large measure responsible for the rash of conversion of multi-family buildings from rental to condominium tenure, contributing to growing shortages in rental markets. Due to tax subsidy, multi-family buildings have higher market value as condominiums than as rentals. Landlords can capture this capital gain by converting. Aside from triggering conversions, the tax subsidy has more generally contributed to the depressed state of non-subsidized rental housing production.

A $12 billion federal tax subsidy that greatly inflates home prices, depresses the rental housing market, fails to expand home ownership opportunities, and primarily benefits upper income persons should be eliminated. Unlike the Federal subsidies for low and moderate income housing—about $7 billion for fiscal year 1980—which stimulates production of housing units that would otherwise not be built, the $12 billion mortgage interests and property tax subsidy does not expand supply and has a major inflationary impact.

## COOPERATIVE HOUSING

Cooperative housing provides a vehicle for low cost, good quality housing. Cooperative and other non-profit organizations can construct or rehabilitate housing units at lower costs than private developers. Cost savings result from elimination of developer profit and lower priced professional fees. Long term maintenance and operating costs are also lower for cooperative housing, because cooperative developers unlike private developers, have an incentive to construct buildings that are energy efficient and require minimium maintenance. For example, Cooperative Services of Detroit, a large cooperative housing organization that undertakes its own construction, has constructed and now manages housing units that cost 25% less to build and now rent for 33% less than comparable private developer units.

The cost savings of cooperative housing are even greater when self-help rehabilitation is involved. As indicated in the section on homesteading in New York City abandoned multi-family buildings have been rehabilitated by cooperative organizations for only 50% of the cost of comparable rehabilitation by private developers. Cooperative tenure is a prerequisite to homesteading and self rehabilitation of multi-family building. Housing cooperatives can be organized along one of several alternative ownership structures. In non-equity co-ops an incoming family pays a fixed sum, possibly $300, to become a residential member. When the family leaves the cooperative this sum is returned, but there is no equity build up. In full-equity co-ops, resident members purchase and sell their units at market rates and thus there is equity build up just as with condominium units. Limited equity co-ops allow for a limited build up of equity. Non-equity or limited-equity co-ops represent a highly desirable, low cost alternative to rental housing for low, moderate, and some middle income persons. Such co-ops insulate their resident members from the rent increases and displacement that result when real estate prices begin to escalate in the local housing market. Additionally, cooperatives provide a strong incentive for proper building maintenance--an incentive that is sadly lacking in many rental projects. At least three proposals would relieve this problem:

- Pursue large scale expansion of federal, state, and local technical assistance for cooperative housing. Such technical assistance should include financing, and legal matters and cooperative management training. Housing and Community Development Act Sec. 106 (b), Sec. 810, and Community Development Block Grant funds should be used to support technical assistance.
- Establish as a target for the Sec. 8 subsidy program that, within five years, 30% of the additional Sec. 8 housing units each must be in cooperative or other non-profit projects.
- Establish within HUD an Office of Assistant Secretary for Cooperative Housing and require GAO to identify the administrative changes that must be made in HUD local offices to facilitate greater HUD staff support for tenant and community organizations seeking to establish cooperative housing.

## BROKERAGE AND SETTLEMENT FEES

Brokerage-commissions range from 5% to 7% of the price while attorney's fees range from 3% to 5%. As home prices escalate, so have these fees which are paid on a percentage basis. The fees vastly exceed the value of the services provided. There are alternatives:

- Local governments should establish low cost brokerage services or provide technical assistance to non-profit organizations seeking to provide such services. Low cost services could reduce brokerage commissions by as much as 50%.

●HUD should prepare and disseminate educational pamphlets for homeowners on "How to Sell Your Home Without a Broker."

●The Real Estate Settlement Producers Act should be amended to require mortgage lenders to bear settlement costs–i.e. title insurance and legal fees--and to prohibit lenders from requiring borrowers to use an attorney to conduct settlement. Since there is considerable competition in the mortgage market, absorbing settlement costs into mortgage would encourage mortgage lenders to shop for low rate title insurance and to eliminate unnecessary and high priced attorneys from the settlement process. In cases where borrowers desired to be represented by an attorney, they would arrange for and pay the attorney themselves.

●Variable rate mortgages. With variable rate mortgages (VRM), the size of a homeowner's monthly mortgage payment fluctuates according to changes in money market interest rates. If VRMs become widespread, the great majority of homeowners will face higher monthly mortgage payments whenever interest rates rise. With the standard fixed rate mortgage, the monthly mortgage payment of homeowners remain constant. A shift from fixed rate mortgages to VRMs would result in much faster cost of living increases during periods of rising inflation and severely aggravate the cyclical instability of the economy. The Federal Home Loan Bank Board recently committed a grave error in authorizing VRMs for federal S&L's in all states. Federal and state savings and loans and savings banks should be prohibited from offering VRMs.

*Excerpt reprinted from: Consumers Opposed to Inflation in the Necessities, 1979, "There are Alternatives: A Program for Controlling Inflation in the Necessities of Life," Washington, D.C.*

# State and Local Program to Fight Housing Inflation

## JOHN ATLAS

*Building a national movement to counter inflation will take some time. In the meantime coalitions on the state and local level can push for legislation to fight rising housing prices.*

### STRENGTHENING TENANT AND NEIGHBORHOOD ORGANIZATIONS

The cornerstone of any anti-inflation stategy is the building of strong city wide tenants and neighborhood preservation groups. Without strong political organizations no useful reforms will be passed. Tenant organizations can:

- Produce and distribute educational material to help educate tenants as to rights which if exercised could reduce costs — i.e. rent striking when the landlord refuses to make needed repairs; the right to do self help repairs and deduct the cost from rent; return of security deposits with interest.
- Represent tenants on administrative and judical proceedings.
- Assist in obtaining federal and state and private foundation funds to rehabilitate rental housing and to organize cooperatives.
- Seek local and state laws that expand tenants rights and preserve neighborhoods.

In order to provide all these services citywide tenant organizations must have a large and stable supply of funds. Funds could be raised by:

- Tenants Resource and Advocacy Center (TRAC) Local governments should enact legislation that would establish a mechanism for collecting tenant membership contributions to a

TRAC. The contributions would be collected by landlords, turned over to the city government and then passed on to the TRAC. TRAC would be governed by a Board of Directors, elected by tenants. Depending on the type of legislation enacted, tenant contributions to TRAC could either be voluntary — allowing a rebate for tenants who do not wish to contribute — or mandatory — in essence, a rental excise tax. In either case economic benefits received by tenants would be far greater than the cost of their contributions. TRAC could also raise funds by doing the following:

- Membership dues
- Door to door canvassing and solicitation
- Community Development Block grants and other state and federal programs
- Establishing a repair service for home improvements.

In addition, certain laws can help build tenant oganizations. A comprehensive Renter's Rights Bill would include laws prohibiting retalitory and arbitrary evictions.

New Jersey has two unique and valuable tenant reforms. One requires the landlord to inform each tenant in writing who their owner, superintendent and mortgage holder are. This helps tenants who are organizing to find their enemies.

The second is the Truth in Renting Act. This law requires landlords to inform their tenants of all tenant rights existing under state law. It also prohibits landlords from using leases which contain provisions violating state law.

The concept of truth in renting has been borrowed from the consumer movement which has made full disclosure in consumer transactions a right which the public has come to expect.

The truth in renting law requires landlords to distribute a *statement* of tenant rights to every existing tenant. A copy of the *statement* must also be posted in at least one prominent location which is *"accessible to all tenants."* The agency actually writes and publishes the statement of tenants' rights. The statement is then made available to landlords and the public at a nominal fee and updated every year.

**RENT CONTROL**

The short supply of rental units and the growth of landlord cartels and other real estate political organizations (see Shelterforce

Vol. 3, No. 3) have provided landlords with economic power to raise rents far in excess of increases in operating costs. For example, in March, 1979, a large San Francisco landlord who owned 1,100 rental units announced rent increases for all his apartments ranging from 20 to 60%. The resulting tenant outrage was so great that by June it had triggered enactment of a city rent control law.

Rent control is the best stop gap law for fighting rental inflation and curbing the eviction of tenants forced out of their homes by high rent hikes. As a local effective and winnable remedy it is beginning to sweep the country. (See Shelterforce Vol. 4, No. 3).

Rent control works best when administered on a local or neighborhood level by an elected or appointed rent control board. In order to avoid a real estate oriented board, tenant activists must attempt to control its administration.

Most rent control laws regulate rent increases allowing landlords to increase rent by an annual fixed percentage ranging from a low of 2½% (some cities in new Jersey) to a percentage equal to the rise in the consumer price index. This percentage increase is supposed to cover the landlord's increased operating costs (maintenance, utilities, etc.)

Most rent controls also require landlords to maintain their buildings and prevent arbitrary evictions.

New Jersey and California courts have held that rent controls must guarantee landlords a *fair profit.* So most rent control laws have landlord *hardship* provisions to ensure their profits. Recent court rulings in Massachusetts and New Jersey declared hardship formulas that guaranteed landlords a certain rate of return on the *fair market value* of apartments to be invalid. The courts reasoned that a guarantee on *market value* protects landlords but not tenants from inflation in violation of the purpose of rent control. Local controls should avoid the fair market value system.

In order to avoid undermining efforts to expand supply, rent controls should exempt newly constructed or substantially rehabilitated rental units.

## RENT ARBITRATION AND MEDIATION

If you can't win rent control, fight for arbitration or mediation boards. These laws establish a procedure to set fair rents where tenants protest a rent increase. Arbitration laws would compel landlords to submit to an arbitrator's final decision. Mediation schemes should be avoided since landlords cannot be compelled to use mediation, nor would they be bound by the board's decisions. Mediation cases tend to involve evictions and return of security deposits rather than the level of rents.

If all you can get is mediation, it should be looked upon as a stepping stone toward rent control. The biggest danger with mediation is that it forces tenants to become involved in relatively ineffective procedure and ends up either taking the edge off tenant frustrations or increasing their cynicism and blunting political demands for stronger measures like rent control.

## RENTAL REGULATION BOARD

In Madison, Wisconsin, a new rental regulations board requires landlords to negotiate with tenants when a majority have organized a tenants union.

## OPPOSE THE LIFTING OF MORTGAGE INTEREST RATES CEILINGS (USURY LAWS)

Mortgage bankers and saving institutions are lobbying state legislators across the country to lift state ceilings on mortgage interest rates. Tenants and homeowner groups should coalesce to oppose this attempt.

## LINK DEPOSITS SYSTEMS

State and local government can establish an investment program that provides for the deposit of government funds in banks that make low interest loans to service community needs.

Government deposits have been used in Massachusetts, Illinois, Colorado and Washington, D.C. to foster social goals. For example banks that have the highest percentage of urban home improvement loans would receive government deposits.

## STATE BANKS

A state owned cooperative bank should be created to provide loans for socially useful purposes like housing.

The Bank of North Dakota, the nation's only state-owned bank, highlights in its 1977 annual report the "best year in the Bank's fifty-year history." The Bank's resources for 1977 peaked at more than $534 million. Net income was $11 million up 13% from 1976, and the Bank transferred $8 milliion of that to the state's general fund.

Progressive legislators from around the nation have used the North Dakota model as a base for other state bank proposals.

## PROPERTY INSURANCE REDLINING

HUD has found that homeowners in many older neighborhoods are forced to pay homeowner property and liability insurance premiums that are as much as 10 times greater than rates paid in other neighborhoods. Only a small portion of these higher rates are justified. State governments should enact legislation that prohibits insurance redlining and requires insurance companies to justify higher premiums with data documenting higher loss rates.

## ELIMINATION OF OVERLY RESTRICTIVE LAND USE CONTROLS, SITE DEVELOPMENT AND BUILDING CODES

Major factors limiting the supply of developable land are failure to expend sewage treatment capacity and restrictive zoning. Removal of these artificial restraints will moderate escalating land costs in many communities. The General Accounting Office estimates that unnecessarily expensive site development requirements — i.e. requirements for streets, sidewalks, driveways, storm and sanitary sewers, and water systems— have increased the cost of homes on the average by $1,300 and in some communities by as much as $2,655. Similarly, in many jurisdictions building codes require unnecessarily expensive material and techniques.

Unfortunately communities that enact these controls do so in order to avoid the construction of new housing. Efforts to knock down these barriers will probably be limited to litigation. (See Shelterforce Vol. 1, No. 2).

## ANTI-SPECULATION LAWS

The buying and selling of property for speculative investment is a major cause of the rapid increase in housing costs. Speculation prompts the frequent resale of homes and contributes to: an escalation in prices that is driving the average middle-income family out of the buying market; higher assessed valuation on homes due to higher sale prices of nearby property; and higher rents resulting from rising property taxes, and high refinancing costs being passed on to renters by property owners.

Enacting a stiff capital gains tax on short term purchase and sale of homes would reduce excess profits that power speculative investment.

Such a law should exempt homes owned for at least two years, elderly homeowners and families that must sell their homes quickly because of illness, a new baby, or job transfer.

## RENT CONTROL

The first step toward cracking down on rental inflation is the imposition of national rent and eviction control, designed to prevent rent gouging and profiteering. Such a program should include the following principles, which should be set forth in federal legislation authorizing such economic controls.

**UNIVERSAL COVERAGE.** The national rent control program should have universal coverage. Its protections should extend to all tenants, whether in private, public, subsidized, insured, city-owned, migrant, mobile, or any other kind of rental housing.

**EVICTION CONTROLS.** Historically, all serious attempts to control rents have also included controls on evictions, for a very important reason. Rent controls can easily be evaded and undermined by unscrupulous landlords if tenants can be evicted for any reason or no reason at all, which is the law in most states. In this situation, there is nothing to prevent unscrupulous landlords from simply evicting any tenants who insist upon lawful rent levels.

Therefore, an effective national program to fight rental inflation must limit justifiable reasons for evictions to a few specifically described ones, such as improper nonpayment of rent and willfull destruction of property.

**LOCAL PROTECTIONS.** The right of local areas to adopt and enforce measures giving tenants more protection than the federal program should be respected fully. Tenants should clearly be allowed to enjoy the full protections of the federal and any local programs to combat rental inflation.

**RENT CONTROLS.** The program should protect tenants against arbitrary and unreasonable rent increases, rent-gouging, and rent-profiteering. To do this it should include the following provisions:

**A. Rent Freeze.** Rents must be frozen in all rental housing from the date this legislation is made public. This freeze should continue for at least six months, while plans are made to replace it with an effective and comprehensive system of rent control.

**B. Rent Adjustments.** Following the initial rent freeze, landlords who claim their increased costs require higher rents could submit a petition for an increase to the federal agency administering the rent control system. Tenants would have the right to protest these increases. The landlord would have to prove that increased costs have so cut his profit that he is making less than a minimally reasonable profit and that his building is being adequately maintained.

If any tenant or group of tenants believe that their rent is too high, they can petition the federal agency for a rent decrease, based upon decreases in services, substantial deterioration, failure to perform ordinary repair, replacement or maintenance, or that the landlord is making more than a minimally reasonable profit.

**C. Registration.** Within 30 days of the effective date of the rent control program, all owners and managers of rental housing must register on forms provided by the federal agency including the address of the rental units, the name and address of the owner, managing agent, and mortgages (if any), rents charged for each unit as of the freeze date, the landlords cash investment in the building, and the profits made during the landlord's most recent accounting year.

Tenants in any rental housing which has not been properly registered by this deadline should be entitled to a 20% reduction in rent until the housing has been properly registered.

However, no tenant should be evictable for nonpayment in a good faith dispute about the amount due, and the tenant does pay the amount determined to be due by any final judgment within 30 days of such judgment.

There should also be protections against tenants being evicted through coop or condominium conversion.

**D. No Vacancy Decontrol.** Tenants should have effective civil remedies for any landlord violations or attempted violations of this program, including rent overcharges, harassment, retaliation or false registration. The remedy should include the tenant's right to recover three times the monthly rent (or the overcharge, whichever is greater), plus costs and reasonable attorney's fees (where applicable). Tenants should be entitled to deduct this amount from rent owed by written notice of the landlord.

The second step to crack down on rental inflation involves maintenance and enhancing the available supply of rental housing. This should include restrictions on coop and condominium conversion, a moratorium on federally-financed demolition of sound rental units and increased direct grants of federal funds for rehabilitation and new construction of low and moderate income housing.

The third step to crack down on rental inflation is to control and limit key factors contributing to skyrocketing housing costs. This should include interest rates, fuel oil, cost and natural gas prices, lumber prices and local property taxes.

Finally, wage controls should be opposed because they have historically been used in a way very detrimental to working people.

*Reprinted from SHELTERFORCE, Summer 1979*

# Reducing Housing Costs: A South Coast Comprehensive Housing Program

## SOUTH COAST INFORMATION PROJECT· HOUSING TASK FORCE

### INTRODUCTION

A successful local housing program will require a fundamental commitment on the part of all residents of the South coast: *A commitment to make the local housing market serve the interest of our community.* Through a combination of local control and market incentives, we can direct our local market towards the goal of preserving and supplying affordable housing.

In this brief paper we offer the outline of a three part housing program. First, the runaway rental housing market must be brought under local control. Second, the existing housing stock must be protected against demolition, conversion, and decay. Finally, the housing market must be guided towards forms of home ownership and rentals that will assure long-run affordability without requiring massive intervention by state or federal agencies.

Before turning to specific policies, however, we note two preconditions which must be met before any serious attempt to alleviate the local housing crisis can truly hope to succeed.

First, it must be recognized that our housing problem is a regional one. Policies adopted in one jurisdiction will impact all others. Therefore it is essential that the various communities of the South Coast plan, fund, and implement a comprehensive area wide housing program. The important thing is that the local governments delegate sufficient power to permit effective areawide planning and implementation.

Second, local population growth must be kept in balance with growth in the local housing supply. Housing growth is currently restricted on the South Coast through water moratorium outside Santa Barbara City, and through the city's 85,000 population ceiling. The county is presently considering a growth-limitation ordinance that would restrict the annual increase in the number of dwelling units to 1.2%. These measures, intentionally or unintentionally, seek to curb growth through a restriction in the housing supply. *Such an approach to growth-management in the long run can only contribute to the escalation of housing prices.* As the 1975 Impacts of Growth study said, "...restriction of residential construction does not stop population growth; it only stops housing growth. The results thus tend to be undesirable for the living standards of residents."

Growth management is more effectively brought about by planning for orderly industrial and commercial expansion in keeping with the capacity of the housing supply. The county is presently studying the relationship between economic expansion, population growth, and housing costs. We urge the eventual adoption of regionwide policies that would regulate growth in keeping with the findings of that study. Expansion in the housing supply will then reflect the needs of local residents, without fear that massive population growth will result.

## 1. REGAINING CONTROL OVER THE RENTAL HOUSING MARKET

Control over rents is currently in the hands of investors. This has resulted in a speculative price spiral with tenants paying the bill for speculation. In order to stop rent gouging and bring speculation under control we recommend:

• *The South Coast communities enact uniform areawide Rent Control ordinances.*

These ordinances must guarantee fair return to property owners consistent with other investments of similar risk. The ordinance should also restrict annual rent increases to one half the rate of the Consumer Price Index (C.P.I.). This is because only half of a landlord's costs rise with inflation; the other half is the mortgage payment which is usually fixed. The ordinances should also exempt all new construction, have a provision to discourage speculation, and provide protection against arbitrary evictions and poor maintenance.

Similar moderate rent control ordinances are now in effect in over 120 cities across the country, and over half of all California residents are now covered by rent control.

## 2. PRESERVING THE EXISTING SUPPLY OF HOUSING

There are approximately 65,000 housing units on the South Coast. It is extremely important to protect this existing stock against market forces that would tend to remove it.

### Condominium Conversions

One particularly profitable alternative \ investment is the conversion of rental units into condominiums, which typically sell for triple the value of an apartment. This takes units previously affordable to low and moderate income households and turns them into investment opportunities for the wealthy. The city of Santa Barbara has already recognized the threat of condominium conversion, and passed an ordinance which restricts the number of conversions allowable each year. That ordinance is a helpful step but does not go far enough. It fails to assure that the newly converted units will be owner-occupied, thereby permitting apartments to be sold at inflated prices and then returned to the market at higher rent levels. We recommend:

• *The City's condominium conversion ordinance be strengthened and adopted throughout the South Coast.*

This ordinance should limit the annual number of conversions to a number consistent with the rental housing needs of the area. It should contain protections against displacement of current renters in units that are converted. It should require that the majority of units converted be affordable to the majority of homebuyers in the area. Also, limited-equity cooperative conversions, made available to existing tenants, should be exempt from any ordinance.

### Demolitions and Commercial Conversion

Another profitable alternative investment is the conversion of residences into office or commercial uses. Sometimes the structure is demolished; other times it is remodeled and adapted to the new use. In either case valuable housing stock is lost to the marketplace. There exists substantial office space in the region, especially downtown Santa Barbara, and therefore conversions should be discouraged.

The City of Santa Barbara recognized this problem in its 1980 *Housing and Commercial Assessment Study,* which identified many neighborhoods in which current zoning and market forces are combining to create irreversible large-scale transitions from residential to commercial use. The study estimates that some 4,000 housing units could potentially be converted. We recommend:

• *Demolitions and commercial conversions on the South Coast be regulated with a high priority given to preserving the existing housing stock.*

Neither demolitions nor conversions should be allowed unless affordable replacement housing is provided. One possibility is to require mixed use commercial/residential construction, whereby residential space is incorporated within the design of the commercial structure — for example apartments above stores or offices.

Additionally, the city is overzoned for commercial use, although much commercial land has housing on it. The potential for commercial expansion is both growth inducing and threatens our housing. We recommend:

• *Existing commercially zoned but residentially used land in the city be reviewed for possible rezoning to permanent residential use.*

## Rehabilitation

According to a 1977 County survey of local housing, half of all the housing on the South Coast is in need of repair and nearly 10% is seriously deteriorated. These units comprise a good part of our rental housing supply. While there is serious danger that many of these units may deteriorate beyond repair if left unattended, current market conditions provide little incentive for investors to rehabilitate them. Several rehabilitation programs presently exist on the South Coast; however they are limited in scope.

The longest running program is operated by Santa Barbara City. Begun in 1977, it targets low-income homeowners. To date that program has successfully rehabilitated 100 homes. The city has recently begun another program in conjunction with Santa Barbara Savings and Loan to try to reach some of the rental units in need of rehabilitation. The county has begun a homeowner rehabilitation program in Summerland. These programs are a modest beginning. We recommend:

• *A substantially augmented program to rehabilitate the area's housing stock be pursued throughout the South Coast.*

## 3. REDIRECTING THE MARKET TO PROVIDE AFFORDABLE HOUSING

The current housing market has proven incapable of providing affordable housing for local residents. It is possible, however, for local governments — acting through a regionwide entity — to create incentives for the marketplace to provide needed affordable housing. This can be done through land use planning, by carefully allocating scarce resources like land and water and by encouraging limited-equity cooperative housing.

## LAND USE PLANNING

The right of local communities to decide how their land is used is a long established responsibility of local government. This determination expresses itself in zoning law, which allocates to each parcel of land a designation (residential, commercial, industrial etc.) and a density (how many units can be built per acre.)

There are three major land use programs that can be used to encourage affordable housing; inclusionary zoning, bonus density, and mixed use.

### Inclusionary Housing

Under an inclusionary housing program, development is only permitted if a designated percentage of units are set aside for low and moderate income households. These units are financed from developer profit and not from the other market level units. This approach is in effect in a number of areas, including Orange County and Palo Alto, and is currently operating in the California Coastal Zone. We recommend:

• *New housing developments be required to set aside a specified percentage of their units at prices affordable to low and moderate income residents of the South Coast.*

### Bonus Density

Bonus Density is the granting of higher density than is otherwise permitted under existing zoning for developments that satisfy certain conditions. Such conditions can include environmental and aesthetic considerations, as well as requirements that some percentage of resulting housing be affordable to the majority of residents. Rents or prices could be required to fall within a certain range with guarantees that they would remain affordable.

Higher densities both permit economies of scale in construction and spread the high cost of land over a larger number of dwellings. Unfortunately, this issue has been clouded locally by conflict between developers who oppose existing low density regulations, and environmentalists who believe that unwanted population growth and unsightly boxlike apartments will immediately follow any relaxation of density standards.

We believe that this conflict is a false one. Greater density can be allowed without the danger of sacrificing the community's character or widespread desire to control growth. We recommend:

• *Carefully planned density bonuses for affordable units be granted consistent with population limits and environmental protection.*

Any planning for greater density must be carefully done on a community-wide basis rather than project by project. It is essential that overall environmental effects, desired areawide population ceilings and the availability of water and land be coordinated. Santa Barbara City is currently identifying areas where density can be increased while remaining within the voter mandated 85,000 population ceiling. This effort should be encouraged throughout the South Coast.

**Mixed-Use Zoning**

Zoning ordinances can be revised to require that affordable housing be provided as part of an overall package with other more profitable forms of development. We have already mentioned one approach — the development of a new zoning designation that requires the intermingling of residential and commercial uses. We recommend:

• *Mixed-use zones replace commercial zones where appropriate, to encourage the construction and conversion of commercial structures to include affordable residential uses.*

## LIMITED EQUITY COOPERATIVE HOUSING

The goal of this housing program is to return control over housing to the people who live in it. The best way to accomplish this is to expand opportunities for homeownership, particularly among the low and moderate income residents who are now stranded in the rental market.

Limited equity cooperatives provide the best way in the long run to accomplish this, because limited equity cooperatives combine the benefits of home ownership with the advantages of affordability.

Limited equity coop housing is operated through a non-profit corporation which holds a single mortgage on the property. The corporation is democratically run with an elected board of directors.

Under typical arrangements, each new owner of a coop purchases a share for a minimal down payment. Monthly payments include each owner's share of the common mortgage plus a fee for maintenance and operating expenses. When an owner wishes to move, s/he sells the share back to the coop which then resells it to a new owner. Since the whole process takes place within the coop's corporation, no new financing or real estate fees are involved.

The cooperative is called "limited equity" because the appreciation in the value of each members share is limited by common agreement to a low level. According to California state law, that limit is an annual 10% on the downpayment or approved improvements only. Coop members can not sell their units for whatever the market will bring. In this way the price of coop units quickly falls below the market value for similar housing.

While a typical condominium or home nowadays is sold and refinanced at ever inflating prices many times over its lifespan, a limited equity cooperative is never sold. The original mortgage is retained until it is fully paid, at which time the monthly payments of coop owners decrease to the amount necessary to operate and maintain the units. The principle difference between coop ownership and private homeownership is that within coops owners may change many times without the coop itself-changing ownership. Owners share the full privileges and rights of private ownership, including the tax benefits. These are benefits that are not available to tenants in rental housing.

Santa Barbara City has indicated support for limited equity coops by providing financial assistance for several pilot projects. We recommend:

• *The present cooperative effort on the South Coast be expanded, by giving top priority to the allocation of public funds for this purpose.*


## PRIORITY ALLOCATION OF LAND AND WATER

Development of new housing on the South Coast is limited not only by the community's desire to limit population, but also by a shortage of developable land and available water. Since the need for affordable housing is greater than for other kinds of development, these limited resources should be preserved and allocated to maximize

# COMPARISON OF COST BETWEEN LIMITED EQUITY COOP AND RENTAL PROPERTY

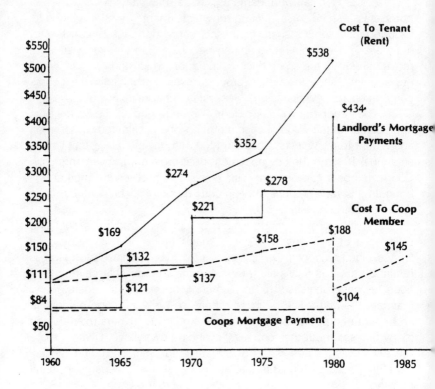

## ASSUMPTION

Total Construction Cost:
$174,193.00

**Rental Property Mortgages**

| 1960 | 6.25% | $139,354 |
| 1965 | 6.5% | $212,515 |
| 1970 | 9.5% | $285,677 |
| 1975 | 9.5% | $358,838 |
| 1980 | 13.5% | $432,000 |

**Coop Mortgage:**

1960   6.25%   $139,354

12 Unit building built in 1960
(3 bedroom apartments)

the building of affordable housing. We recommend:

• *Local water resources be combined on a South Coast wide basis and new water permits be granted based on a system that favors the construction of affordable housing.*

By coordinating the water supplies of all South Coast communities, the additional water required to allow new housing development could be made available, and this water should be restricted primarily to affordable housing construction. Similarly, because of the high cost of land on the South Coast, it is necessary that land be made available in order to bring the prices down to levels affordable by low and moderate income residents. We recommend:

• *Local governments acquire and make available developable land with long term minimal payment lease agreements, for the construction of cooperative housing.*

The public should set aside land from several sources: unused school sites, underutilized parkland, transfers of state and federally owned local land, and land purchased on the open market are some options. Requiring developers of market housing to contribute a designated amount of land is another. Requiring major industrial firms doing commercial expansion to set aside sufficient land to house their additional employees is still another.

The City of Santa Barbara currently has one such program, called "landbanking". It should be expanded and adopted by the other South Coast communities.

## WHERE DOES THE MONEY COME FROM?

Most of the actions suggested above do not require any significant expenditures. They do, however, require changes in attitude by local government towards the housing market. Two programs also do involve significant amounts of money: the expanded broad housing rehabilitation program, and the aggressive program to finance housing cooperatives. These are vitally important in the long run if we are to solve the problem of affordable housing.

Funding for the housing program should be pooled in one large South Coast wide capital fund. This would allow administrative consolidation and the greatest possible flexibility in matching state and federal monies.

On the next page are seven methods for raising money for the housing capital fund. Although each method has advantages and disadvantages, each could contribute to a well financed housing program capable of making progress towards assuring that housing on the South Coast remains affordable to the people who live here.

**Federal and State Funds:** Both the Federal and State governments operate numerous programs designed to promote affordable housing. The available money for these programs, however, is limited and must be applied for on a competitive basis. With the centralization of all South Coast housing programs, we would be able to maximize the amount of federal and state housing money received.

Additionally, all South Coast communities currently receive Federal Block Grant Funds which are primarily designed for housing-related projects. While these funds cannot be pooled, they can be considered as part of the overall capital fund.

**Tax-Exempt Revenue Bonds:** Municipalities have the authority to issue tax-exempt revenue bonds and use the money to provide low interest housing loans. The bonds are an attractive investment because they provide tax-exempt income. Because of this, the bonds can sell for a lower interest rate than corporate bonds, and the community is able to tap a substantial source of low interest capital. The bonds are paid back through revenue generated.

**Municipal Borrowing:** Local governments can borrow money from local financial institutions at interest rates two to three points lower than current market rates. This is because the interest income received by banks is tax-exempt. These funds can then be reloaned as part of the housing program for the same below market interest rate. This kind of program is currently operating in San Francisco and other communities.

**Local Housing Bonds:** If support for the local housing program is strong enough, an issue of small denomination housing bonds (based on the model of U.S. Savings Bonds), might prove a successful way to raise additional money for the capital fund. Since small denomination bonds would reach moderate income people who are not able to participate in the more expensive municipal bond market, it could provide a double service, by increasing the capital available to the local housing program, and by allowing moderate income residents to earn tax-exempt income.

**Pension Funds:** Millions of dollars locally which are traditionally invested in low yield corporate bonds. These funds usually end up leaving the community and being invested by large mutual investment corporations. Pension funds could be redirected into the local capital housing fund with no reduction in either rate of return or the long term security of the investment, but with a potentially sizable effect on the supply of affordable housing. Such a program would benefit local employees and employers who pay into these pension funds by helping to control the prices of housing and by redirecting large amounts of local money back into the local economy.

**Redevelopment Tax-Increment Funding:** In portions of the community designated as redevelopment areas, this form of funding can make significant contributions to the supply of affordable housing. Once an area is designated a redevelopment area, the property tax base is "fixed" at the base year. Local government continues to receive the same amount of property taxes from that area in succeeding years, while any increases in the taxes paid due to appreciation go into the redevelopment tax increment fund and may be used to provide affordable housing.

**Use of Private Financial Institutions:** Local financial institutions should have a strong interest in an areawide housing program. With active cooperation between the administrators of the housing fund and these private institutions, the amount of funding available for the promotion of affordable housing programs could be expanded.

*Essay written June 1980*

# California Housing Action and Information Network Housing Conference

## CHESTER HARTMAN

What kind of legislation should housing activists be pushing?

What laws will best protect tenants against evictions, rising rents, and deteriorating conditions? What laws can protect all housing consumers against speculation and "gentrification" (the uprooting of lower income and ethnic neighborhoods for the benefit of higher income families?)

These were the issues discussed at the second annual meeting of the California Housing Information and Action Network (CHAIN) co-sponsored by the San Francisco Housing Coalition. I hope the following report will help stimulate ideas for new legislation in states across the country.

Nearly 200 housing activists from all over the state met in San Francisco on January 14, under the auspices of CHAIN. The group's second annual meeting drew people from neighborhood groups, elderly organizations, staffs of local and state elected officials, tenant unions, and labor organizations. Most were from the Bay area, but significant delegations showed up from L.A., Sacramento, Santa Cruz and San Jose. The day was enlivened by good guerilla theater by the Santa Cruz Housing Action Committee and by the announcement that the California Housing Council's Sacramento lobbyist was the central figure in an FBI investigation into suspected vote-buying. One topic of interest in that investigation was the bill banning local rent control ordinances, which the Legislature passed in 1977 under heavy pressure from landlord groups but which Governor Brown vetoed.

## UNWORKABLE STATE LAWS

The focus of the meeting was largely on state legislation. Richard Blumberg, an attorney with Berkeley's National Housing Law Project, offered an overview of California's landlord-tenant law, concluding, "In a word, it stinks!" Blumberg said that although the state has many nominally useful laws to protect tenants, most of the laws have intentionally been devised to be unworkable.

Although "repair and deduct" is a potentially effective tenant self-help remedy, the state statute allows a deduction equal to only one month's rent, once a year. But seriously unsafe conditions that landlords refuse to repair are more costly than a month's rent.

The state law prohibiting "retaliatory action" as an increasing rent, threatening eviction or decreasing services to tenants who lawfully complain to code officials, lasts a mere two months. Most other states offer six months to a year of protection. Surely, protection against retaliation should be without time limitations, and protected activities should be extended to included tenants' oral complaints to landlords and tenants' joining tenant unions.

## PROGRESSIVE LAWS PROPOSED

Senate Majority Leader David Roberti (D-Hollywood), one of the few progressive state legislators in the housing field, outlined some important bills coming up in the current session. These include:

• A Just Cause Eviction bill, modeled after New Jersey legislation, will be introduced by Assemblyman Alan Sieroty (D-Los Angeles). The bill prohibits eviction except for statutorily defined "just cause" such as failure to pay rent; extreme disorderly conduct or substantial property damage; breach of major rules and regulations of the property; the building is being vacated or the unit is being closed down, remodeled, or coverted to a cooperative or condominium; the owner is moving into the unit; or the tenant is an employee whose employment is terminated. Now, in California, like in most states, any tenant without a lease can be evicted on 30 days' notice from the landlord. The Sieroty bill would offer tenant security against arbitrary ousters by landlords.

• A bill to control speculation in land and housing by imposing steep taxes on the profits from property held for short periods. Tax rates would go up, the shorter the period of the holding. Such a tax already exists in Vermont.

• Reform of the Marks-Foran Residential Rehabilitation Program. Marks-Foran provides less than market (6-7%) interest rates on rehabilitation loans, in conjunction with area-wide code enforcement (a less good version of the older Section 312 Federal program, known as Federally Assisted Code Enforcement or FACE, which is just being revived and offers 3% loans). The program has been used primarily in San Francisco, known as RAP or Rehabilitation Assistance Program, here it has become a tool for "gentrification." With "gentrification," middle and upper income people, ably assisted by real estate speculators, buy into low-income neighborhoods and force poor people out by raising rents and effecting posh renovation jobs.

Among the reforms being pushed are neighborhood control of the program, controls on speculation and resale, relocation assistance for people displaced, rent subsidies to prevent displacement, and use of less costly rehabilitation codes. More meaningful rent controls are also being proposed, since presently minimal controls are afforded to only those building in a rehabilitation area using Marks-Foran loans.

In addition to the state legislation mentioned by Senator Roberti, several other cities besides San Francisco, notably Los Angeles and Santa Cruz, are preparing anti-speculation laws. Rent controls, closely related to anti-speculation ordinances, are a live issue in cities such as Santa Monica and Santa Barbara, where a rent control initiative is on the upcoming June ballot.

## CONTROL RAMPANT SPECULATION

The San Francisco Housing Coalition, representing some 20 city and neighborhood groups, is focusing on a city ordinance to control rampant housing speculation. The ordinance taxes profits from residential real estate held less than one year at an 80% rate, 60% on property sold in the second year of ownership, 30% in the third and fourth years, and 15% in the fifth year. After five years, there is no taxation on the sale. Tax revenues generated by those who nonetheless buy and sell quickly will go into a special housing rehabilitation fund.

The proposed ordinance exempts new construction and non-income property owned and lived in by persons over 62. Additionally, certain expenses would be deductible from the taxable amount, such

248

as code required repairs. An appeal process is available to persons who are forced to sell within five years due to circumstances beyond their control, such as job transfer or change in family composition.

## CHANGE DEMOLITION TO REHABILITATION

The S.F. Housing Coalition described other elements of its legislative packet: reform of the Marks-Foran RAP program along the lines outlined above; control over displacement and demolition by private developers; modification of the city's "repair and demolish" law which permits the city to act directly to repair and then place a lien on a seriously substandard building, where the landlord has ignored orders to repair. To date, the city has used its power under the "repair and demolish" law and the revolving fund established thereunder, solely to tear down buildings. The Bureau of Building Inspection (BBI), like most code enforcement agencies, takes the easier route of tearing down rather than repairing buildings.

The Housing Coalition hopes to make the "repair and demolish" law into a renovation housing program, instead of a housing demolition program. Its proposed amendment requires the BBI to renovate where the cost to remedy the hazardous violations averages less than $20,000 per unit ($10,000 per unit in hotels) and it forbids rent increses for five years following repairs. The amendment also requires that property that the city acquires through foreclosure under the repair and demolition program be sold, on a priority basis, to tenant cooperatives, community development corporations and non-profits, or any other means by which the property will be maintained as low-income housing.

The Coalition's introduction of legislation regulating the activities of private entrepreneurs, who redevelop without government aids, is brand new ground and is sure to cause anguished outcry among the property rights *ueber alles* advocates.

## PUSHING RELOCATION BENEFITS

Where housing is demolished or tenants are displaced under government-sponsored programs, fairly good (although far from perfect) laws exist to guarantee decent relocation housing at affordable rents, and replacement of torn down units. The SF Housing Coalition is attempting to expand such protections to purely private activity, since the city has the responsibility to protect its housing stock and its residents from arbitrary displacement.

**249**

The draft ordinance provides that persons so displaced be offered decent relocation housing in socially and ethnically comparable areas, at rents not to exceed 10% over what the tenant had been paying. It requires that where the rental vacancy rate is less than 3%, equivalent one-for-one replacement housing units must be provided, either within the building being constructed on the site (if the displacement/demolition is for residential re-use), or elsewhere (if the displacement/demolition is for non-residential re-use).

## CONTROLLING DEMOLITION PERMITS

The city's instrument to effect compliance is through its control over issuance of demolition permits. No permit will be granted until adequate relocation has been carried out. Replacement housing must *first* be constructed before a demolition permit will be granted for non-residential re-use. Where residential re-use is intended, there must first be a guarantee, signed under penalty or perjury, to make units available (equivalent in number to those units being torn down) to lower income tenants at rents they can afford through federal Section 8 subsidies or any other means.

*Reprinted from SHELTERFORCE, Spring 1978*

# Toward an Economic Democracy Housing Program

## MARK SIEGEL

*California is a garden of Eden*
*A paradise to have and to see*
*But believe it or not*
*You won't like it so hot*
*If you don't have the do-re-mi.*
*...Woody Guthrie "DO-RE-MI"*

### INTRODUCTION

The importance of housing production in California is quickly replacing tax reform as the preeminent political issue in the State. Emigrants have historically been attracted to the "golden bear" state to escape from economic and political problems around the world. Both the climate and the economy have been factors that account for one hundred years of constant growth in California. Yet, the State has been unable to meet the constantly growing demand for affordable housing. Our population is one of the fastest growing in the country and housing starts are at all time lows. State and local governments are just beginning to react to the crisis, as industries announce that they will not build new plants because there is no place to house their work force. Reports of overcrowding and "hotbedding" (families sleeping in shifts) make the need for affordable housing even clearer. The initial reaction by most local governments is to simply conserve what existing affordable housing remains. Rent control, eviction protections and bans on condominium conversions are techniques used by localities to protect housing consumers and conserve the rental stock. In turn, landlords and property interests have counter-attacked with Proposition 10 and other local efforts to undo gains made by tenant organizations.

As this battle rages over what to do about existing housing, it is also increasingly clear that housing activists must examine the structural make-up of the housing industry that brought us to this crisis. The only way out of the present housing crisis is to build up the housing supply. Consumers and housing activists should prepare themselves to participate in this debate if we have any expectation of influencing the future quality of life in our state.

A major point of recognition in the development of any housing production strategy is that there is no single cause of the shortage of housing in California; and therefore, no single solution to the problem.

Because inflation has hit all aspects of housing production, it will take a variety of approaches to increase the housing supply, focusing on all the individual elements of the housing production pipeline — *capital, land use and zoning, fees and permits, alternative technologies, conservation and consumer rights.* According to figures supplied by the Building Industry Association, since 1975 the cost of capital for housing has increased over four times, land costs have tripled and labor costs have doubled. Fees paid by developers for government services and processing of permits have skyrocketed since Proposition 13, and new efforts by the Public Utilities Commission to charge developers the full cost of gas line hook-ups could drive development costs up even more.

It would be foolish to believe that all we have to do is "get government off the backs of the developers" to solve the housing shortage. The legitimate interests of housing consumers and local residents must be protected. Those who have to live in the "new communities" must have some mechanism for participating in the decision making process that will ultimately effect their quality of life. Thus, approaches and solutions outlined in this paper have been developed around a common philosphy: that the principles of economic democracy must be applied as we attempt to solve the problems of cost and supply of housing.

## CAPITAL

The rising cost of construction capital is a major cause of increased housing prices. While labor costs have doubled since 1975,

252

the cost of capital has gone up 400%. In 1949, financing costs accounted for only 5% of the total construction cost of a project. Today it is well over 10%.

The most obvious way in which the cost of capital adds to the cost of housing is through the high interest rates. As the federal government uses high interest rates to slow down inflation, it becomes increasingly more expensive to obtain construction loans. The result is that housing construction becomes the first victim in the war against inflation.

This situation is further exacerbated by the way in which financial institutions choose to lend their money. A prominent executive of a major savings and loan commented that financial institutions have made a mistake in devoting a disproportionate share of money in the 1970s to buying and selling existing buildings, and failed to provide adequate amounts of capital for construction. This phenomenon is a result of the savings and loans riding the tiger of inflation. As the shortage becomes more acute, demand starts to drive up the price. As inflation spirals upward, investment goes into real property. The ¼ acre single-family unit in the San Fernando Valley or Orange County is one of the best hedges on inflation and has attracted many speculators and small investors to "hop on the tiger." Housing construction, with its bureaucratic delays and susceptibility to political in-fighting, is seen as a risky investment. Savings and loans, like all corporations, have a committment to obtain the best rate of return for its investors. Therefore, their money inevitably goes to the safest and most secure investment — existing housing — at the expense of new construction. Consequently, a community's need for new housing is rarely reflected on the balance sheet.

In the past, CED has proposed ways to provide capital at interest below market rates. They include:

1) **The Establishment of a State Bank or Municipal Finance Agency,** which would provide public sector funds for socially and financially responsible investment. Public treasuries are currently invested in stocks and bonds with no regard to keeping the money in California or directing it toward specific state needs. By chartering a public financial institution, public money could be directed toward economic needs in California, particularly housing. Besides making a profit for the investor (the state), it would both produce jobs and housing, in addition to increasing the tax base.

2) **The Development of a Link Deposit Program,** where

government would deposit their idle reserves in banks and lending institutions that have the best track record for housing construction. Further, the participating government could insist on devoting a certain percentage of their money for new construction. This would set up a system where lending institutions would compete to land the public account, thus further stimulating construction opportunities.

3) **Public Control of Pension Funds.** Currently, the multi-million dollar pension fund capital pool is invested into stocks and bonds with the rate of return and risk the only investment criteria. There is a growing consensus among all participants in the housing debate that pension funds can be a new source of construction and mortgage capital. The political debate yet to come is over who will control these funds. In California alone, state and local retirement funds amount to nearly $30 billion, while private pension plans amount to another $30 billion. At present, less that 20% of the monies in these funds are invested in the State of California. It is imperative that the employees who pay into these pension funds have a "greater democratic control over decisions to invest their retirement savings."

4) **Low Interest Bonds** issued by either the State or local, governments. Because the profits on these bonds are tax-exempt, market investors will be attracted to them even it they do not pay the same rate of return as non-tax exempt investments. The government could then turn around and lend the money raised, from the sale of the bonds, at below market rates. For example, a bond issued at 7% would be viable at the current market rate. The money raised could be devoted towards mortgages for affordable units at 8%. The significance to the purchaser of a $50,000 home at 8% would mean a relatively modest $386 for their monthly payment over the $564 payment on a current mortgage rate of 13%. A difference of $178 per month.

## LAND USE AND ZONING

Land is the largest cost component of a construction project. As land prices rise, a result of supply and demand, they change the nature of construction. A developer feels that a cheap structure built on expensive land will have a high price anyway, but will have little demand. Thus, developers will build only if the cost of the structure is more than 45% to 50% of the total project cost. If it lies below that percentage, the structure will not be built. The result of course, because of the high price in land, is that expensive housing is the only housing being built.

The supply of vacant land in built-up urban areas is very limited, which makes in-fill very difficult. According to the Los Angeles City Housing Element, an acre of privately owned vacant land, zoned for single family residential use, costs an average of $100,000 to $200,000. An acre of multiple family zoned land costs between $500,000 and $1 million. However, in Los Angeles, there are less than 5000 acres of such land available. It is also interesting to note that only half of that is privately owned, the rest is owned by government agencies of all levels.

Economic Democrats should support the following proposals to reduce land costs:

1) **Land Banking** - The government would turn over, trade or "writedown" the land it owns to developers for low and moderate income housing projects. Long term leasing of this land is another approach where the government could keep tighter restrictions on the use of the land parcel. In order to ensure that affordable housing is what the land will be used for, and to ensure long term affordability, the government could give priority to bids submitted by non-profit community development corporations or similiar quasi-public agencies.

2) **Better Land Utilization.** By encouraging mixed used zoning (similar to that found in eastern cities and in older parts of Los Angeles), and by encouraging higher density when appropriate we can make more efficient use of an increasingly diminishing resource. Density bonuses to builders is one way to reduce "per unit" costs. The zoning commission would allow a builder to exceed zoning requirements if the additional units are affordable. The recent trend, however, has been to "roll back" zoning and decrease permissable density. These pressures usually come from the local property owners trying to protect remaining open space. A major contradiction remains to be reconciled as those in need of housing are pitted against those who have housing and want to draw up the bridge to their communities.

3) **Inclusionary Zoning** which would prescribe the amount of low income housing to be built in particular tracts and communities is now being used with a degree of success in Orange County.

4) **Relax Parking and Set-Back Requirements** for multiple units for senior citizens and others who do not own cars, and in communities conducive to use of public transportation.

## FEES AND PERMITS

Local cities and counties have jurisdiction over land use decisions. In an effort to provide reasonable and controlled growth while, at the same time, protecting open spaces and the quality of life for its residents, these localities over the past 40 years have overlayed a complicated permit and regulatory review process which drives up the cost of housing. The permits range from building and safety to environmental review, from zoning to tract map approval. Though all the areas of regulation are important and should not be eliminated, the bureaucratic procedure for processing these permits can be streamlined considerably.

The cost and delays of government processing affect housing in two ways. First, delays in the permit process always increases the financing and overhead costs. Due to recent rapid inflation in the cost of building materials, increases in the price of the final product can amount to one or two percent each month of delay. Secondly, in times of inflation, the builder will seek to hedge his bets and invest in projects that can absorb abrupt changes in market conditions. This usually means the builder will only build high priced housing projects.

State and local governments should work towards minimizing the time delays in the permit process whenever possible, without sacrificing the quality of housing construction. Such streamlining efforts should keep in mind that community input should not be reduced. With these principles in mind, the following proposals are ways of cutting the permit red tape:

1) **Consolidation of Various Permits,** such as plumbing, electric zoning, etc, into one permit. The permit office must be adequately staffed to advise developers of procedures and deficiencies in the builder's file. Case workers should be assigned to monitor the individual projects from start to finish. This system is already employed in San Diego and has helped that city to process permits in one third the time it takes Los Angeles. Permit expediters are not new to Los Angeles though — the city continually uses them to make life easier for film producers who want to use the city's streets for location shots.

2) **Priority Processing** should be given to projects that conform to the policy goals set forth in the city's housing element. Specifically, low and moderate income rental housing should be given "cuts in line" over expensive tracts and office buildings. The local governments could perhaps go further by reducing the time it takes to

process permits for low and moderate income housing by self imposing time deadlines. Failure to reach these deadlines would result in automatic approval if no local appeal has been filed.

3) **Relax Environmental Impact Report (EIR)** requirements for urban infill projects which conform to the city's housing element and local plans. Each city is mandated to develop general plans that outline their proposed growth plan. Part of these plans are housing elements which are detailed housing objectives and goals. These could function as Master Environmental Impact Reports. The EIR process is both time consuming and expensive for the small builder, adding to the total cost of the building. A cost that is ultimately passed on to the consumer. While environmental quality standards should not be compromised, nothing is discovered or accomplished by subjecting the developer to repetitive EIR submissions in urban areas. Since localities need flexibility to deal with local environmental concerns, the need for EIR should be left to local options.

4) **A Fee Deferment Program** for small builders who are constructing low and moderate income housing. Since Proposition 13 in 1978, fees have increased signficantly as localities try to make up for lost revenues by charging developers the full cost of processing. Builders must pay these fees when they file for a permit, tying up capital at a time when they have yet to receive construction or long term financing.

While government red tape is a favorite topic for industry spokespersons, the truth is that bureaucratic elimination or significant reduction will not build more housing. The real barriers remain land availability and financing costs. However, the reduction of red tape will certainly help matters.

## ALTERNATIVE TECHNOLOGIES

New technologies in housing construction can reduce construction costs and deliver the product faster than traditional construction or "on-site" methods. The State of California's projection of 600,000 new units by 1995 is staggering to the mind. One housing expert has projected that the only way to meet this goal is to have trucks driving down streets and dropping off houses. In fact, that is what manufactured housing is all about. New technologies, including concrete, aluminum or using traditional construction materials, can be produced by an assembly line and shipped to the housing site and assembled.

The cost savings can be significant. According to the Manufactured Housing Institute, site built homes cost about $22 a square foot, while a manufactured home costs only $10 or $15 per square foot, excluding land costs. According to the Federal Trade Commission, manufactured housing represents 90% of all housing under $30,000 built in the western United States.

One of the problems of manufactured housing, similar to that of the solar energy industry, is that of community acceptance. Most cities, including Los Angeles, prohibit manufactured homes in residential R-1 zones because of the public views such housing as "trailers" and all the negative images they conjure up. Mobile homes are thought to depreciate in value, thus subtracting from property values. Recent changes in the tax code will help things — California has moved to tax these homes as actual land improvements (that is, they add value and appreciate), instead of as motor vehicles which is how they were considered previously. This change will, hopefully, lead banks to offer more favorable loans to purchasers over longer time periods.

Another significant occurrence in regard to mobile homes is the passage of AB 2698 (Roos) which would allow the transport of 14 foot wide vehicles over the highways. The previous limit was 12 feet and was the narrowest limit in the nation. This new law will enable California manufacturers to export materials thus, helping them achieve better economies of sale.

The political and practical problems with manufactured housing are considerable. Sellers are often required to add so many luxury items, such as two car garages, trash compacters, fully developed landscaping, hatched roofs, etc. that the homes no longer are affordable. This phenomenon occurs because, not only do local agencies require it, but the developer tries to anticipate demand so increases the "attractiveness" of the unit. The industry is also predominantly non-union, which will mean resistance from the building trades who will view manufactured housing as taking away their jobs. But as unions begin to organize this sector of housing, it will surely grow in public acceptance. Certainly, we need all types of new housing if we are to meet the challenge that lies ahead.

Lastly, mobile homes are traditionally put in "parks" which are owned by landlords who charge rent for the "pad" or foundations.

Traditional landlord/tenant tensions exist. Park dwellers have organized the Golden State Mobile Homeowners League (GSMOL) to fight for tenant protections and are often more victimized and in turn more militant than their urban counterpart. Non-profit cooperative park development should be encouraged and conversion assistance be given to existing park residents when requested.

In general, Economic Democrats should support the following:

1) **AB 2740 (Mangers)** which would allow mobile homes to receive existing state housing assistance money available to other forms of housing.

2) **Model Projects** including cooperative mobile home parks and demonstrations of new technologies.

3) **Changes in Local Zoning** which would allow mobile homes into specific neighborhoods.

## HOUSING CONSERVATION

Just as the energy shortage, conservation of housing can go a long way toward relieving the crisis situation. Condominium conversions and demolition of habitable housing should be stopped immediately. Those developers who wish to demolish existing housing to make way for higher density projects should be required, where feasible, to preserve and move the existing structure to parts of the city where it is needed. Government rehabilitation programs need to become more effective in dealing with getting the money out of the administration and into the communities where it is needed. The use of development and block grant money should be prioritized for low and moderate income housing.

The affordability of the existing rental stock should be protected by localities. This housing must be saved from the speculator who adds nothing to the housing stock except tenant grief. The most effective mechanism so far developed is rent controls that prohibit the pass through of the new mortgage payment when an apartment is sold. Tenants should be afforded "collective bargaining rights" to peacefully bargain with the supplier (landlord) of their housing. This would required strong statewide "just cause eviction" protections and a prohibition on evictions when the dominant reason is to raise rents. Tenants who live in rent controlled areas that have the vacancy decontrol loophole should be able to bring up the defense of eviction to raise rents in court.

Lastly, discrimination in housing cannot be tolerated. Traditional tactics of pitting one group of tenants against another is regressive and destructive to our social fiber. Committing one group of housing consumers to second class status is obscene in modern society. Fair housing for children statewide legislation is of foremost importance if we are to house our families in the only standard the most populous and richest state in the nation should accept — quality.

*Essay completed August 1980*

# Urban Renewal Without Removal

## THOMAS R. ANGOTTI AND BRUCE DALE

Bologna, Italy has one of the most enlightened housing and renewal programs in the Western World. The original plan was introduced by a municipal government which has been dominated by the Italian Communist party since the end of World War II. It is the largest Communist party in the West and has recently obtained either majority control or participation in most of Italy's major city governments (Milan, Turin, Genoa, Florence, Naples and many smaller municipalities.

"Urban renewal" means tearing down older housing in the central city, removing the low income residents and putting up new commercial buildings or high-rent apartment houses. Bologna, however, adopted a plan that called for a moratorium on new housing construction and the rehabilitation of existing housing in the city center, with public funds. Originally the plan called for the city government to purchase housing in renewal areas or take it over by eminent domain, then fix it up and lease it to lower income residents. But that idea generated so much opposition from small property owners (and gained so little support from the Communist party, which was trying to attract votes from the middle class) that the municipal government abandoned it — and modified the plan — in 1972.

Under the new rules, only real estate owners and corporate landlords are subject to land taking through eminent domain. Small property owners who don't want to sell their properties instead sign a contract with the city, which guarantees the status of residing tenants, limits rents, and provides for low-interest loans and sometimes outright grants to cover renovation expenses so that tenants will pay no more than 12 percent of their income toward rent under the contract. The city can lease apartments that remain vacant for more than four months, has the option to buy if the property is sold, and reserves the right to take it by eminent domain "Should the owner fail to carry out any part of the agreement." Eventually the expectation is that all of the property will revert to the city.

## URBAN RENEWAL AMERICAN STYLE

The net effect of publicly financed urban renewal programs in the United States has been to break up old residential neighborhoods and displace their low-income residents. As a result of urban renewal programs, low rent, working-class housing in the central core is replaced by luxury housing, commercial or administrative building. The displaced residents are forced to accept more expensive housing, often in worse neighborhoods, with a minimum of assistance in relocation.

Working-class housing, when centrally located, is considered fair game for speculative redevelopment. And it is traditional in America and in Europe for working -class families to live in the central core — originally to be near their workplaces, then for economy and convenience.

In the process of metropolitan growth these communities are often taken over by speculators and subjected to renovation (or demolition and reconstruction) by private and public interests alike. A period of housing decay may precede renewal but is tolerated, even encouraged, as an intermediate state which will facilitate future profits by reducing acquisition costs and inviting large-scale redevelopment. Whether or not rehabilitation is directly assisted by public programs, the net effect is always the same: destruction of working-class communities in the central core.

## THE EXAMPLE OF BOLOGNA

Bologna, Italy, is the first industrial city in the Western world to have a central city renewal program that aims to preserve the historical and social character of the urban environment by not displacing low-income people from their homes. This renewal program is probably the only one of its kind in a capitalist country. Its success is due to a basic political commitment by a communist administration to reinforce the social foundations of the central core by improving the physical environment, increasing the level of services available to residents, and promoting democratic participation in decision making.

The main theoretical basis of the Bologna program is a concept of the city, including its services and buildings, as a public good. Simply stated, it means that the needs of the people — all of the people — come before profit. Within the limits of the Italian capitalist economic and legal structure the program attempts to eliminate land speculation in both the center and the periphery of the city. The main features of the plan stem from these general principles:

1. The use of public housing subsidies for conservation and renovation rather than new construction.

2. Democratic participation in the planning process at the neighborhood as well as city-wide level.

3. Adoption of a comprehensive planning approach which takes into account the role of the historic center in overall metropolitan and regional growth.

4. Conversion of historic buildings to collective use.

5. Development of a rigorous scientific system of classification of building types and strict regulation of rehabilitation.

In its original form the 1969 master plan for Bologna declared that the city had no economic or social justification for continued growth if the human quality of urban life were to be preserved. Hence a moratorium on all new construction was declared. The people, however, did have the right and need for improved housing, which was the reason for a new focus on the historic center. Improved housing had to come from the existing housing stock. It was in the historic center that public investment could fulfill the dual intention of conserving and historic heritage and providing better housing for the lower income population. Expansion and new construction had tended to produce largely luxury apartments of which Bologna already had an adequate supply. Publicly financed renovation was therefore seen as a mechanism capable of providing adequate low-income housing.

## CITIZEN PARTICIPATION

The issue of citizen participation in Bologna led in 1964 to the formation of neighborhood councils as a means of decentralizing administrative functions and facilitating direct public involvement. Representation on the councils is based on the votes received during municipal elections. These councils have been consulted repeatedly throughout the development of the plan and have been given official status and responsibilities within the plan's administration.

The first completed housing was built on a vacant city-owned lot and is being used for relocating people temporarily while their apartments are being renovated. In July 1975, the city received final approval for a proposed long-term contract which will allow it to expand renewal operations to privately owned dwelling units. Large or corporate real estate holders in the renewal area will have their properties expropriated; others will be encouraged to sell to the city. Small property owners (owners of one, two, or three apartments) who do not wish to sell are obliged to sign a long-term agreement with the city which guarantees the status of tenants, limits rents, and provides for low-interest loans to cover renovation expenses.

## HOUSING AND SOCIAL CHANGE

A major cornerstone of Bologna's original housing program, before its revision in 1972, was the principle of collective ownership and management of property. Private property within renewal parcels was to be taken by eminent domain and returned after renovation to locally organized cooperatives. This was based on the assumption that private property was the major obstacle to rational renewal. A very meticulous and innovative interpretation of the Italian 1971 housing law was the basis for the unprecedented taking of land for the renovation of old housing, rather than just for construction of new housing. The cost of expropriation was linked to a formula which basically led to payments far below market price

The initial reaction to the housing plan was quite favorable. However, small property owners, many of whom were working-class, became sharply aligned against the tenants who stood to benefit from the scheme. They argued that the expropriations were discriminatory and that they were being deprived of their small holdings while owners outside the historic center were not touched.

The right wing and center parties exploited the small owners' discontent and denounced the program, launching a national campaign to stop it, claiming that it was a threat to all private property. There was also a marked absence of support from the central committee of the Communist party, whose strategy was designed to expand the party's political base to include the middle class, and this would be hindered, the party believed, by the small non-speculative property owner's fear of the original plan. The prospect of delaying the program with legal proceedings and widening internal divisions within the left led the city council eventually to reverse itself and withdraw the expropriation clause, substituting a contract between city and owners which would guarantee the status of tenants, limit rents, and provide for low-interest loans and grants.

## EDUCATIONAL ERROR

The failure of planners and the political leadership to obtain the use of eminent domain (expropriation) was due to two major errors. The first, an error of objective analysis, considered small property owners in the same class as medium and large owners and speculators. Many small owners are in fact working-class families that use housing as a form of savings and as old age insurance. It is idealistic and unrealistic to treat all property holdings as if they were the fruits of mercenary speculation. Although private property is a major obstacle to rational planning, it is the large corporate land owners and the speculators who are the greatest violators. The elimination of property with general acceptance requires a national revolutionary change. It cannot be fully achieved at the local level independently.

The second error was the failure to discuss expropriation at all levels of the political structure. By not encouraging public debate and developing awareness of the necessity of this tool to realize equitable housing, the city officials found themselves with insufficient support. At the very least it was a case of unclear political strategy.

The renewal program must be seen as only part of a larger political struggle. Small and medium property owners may become allies of the left or may otherwise strengthen the forces of reaction. Insistence on the use of expropriation could only have served to separate the working class from its natural allies and stall the realization of an important reform.

Substituting the contract for expropriation in the program does not essentially compromise the basic principles. The use of this contract will alter significantly the relationship between landlord and tenant. The contracts are to be negotiated by the neighborhood councils with city supervision. The basic model of the contract also contains guarantees that protect tenants from high rents and eviction. Let us examine some aspects of the contract model recently approved by Bologna City Council.

The contract provides for their principal means of financing renovation: outright grants from the city, loans with subsidized interest payments, or a combination of the two. Most of the contracts will probably provide for loans rather than grants, since the latter are to be used only in cases where the owner is a resident and lacks adequate income to satisfy the loan conditions. Grants are 20-year contracts and the loans will be for 15, 20 or 25 years. Grants may cover the full costs of renovation and loans wil normally cover up to 80 percent of the costs.

Rents are fixed at established public housing rent levels. The average family will pay 12 percent of its income for rent. New tenants must meet the public housing qualifications. The city reserves the right to sublease an apartment for a tenant who does not have sufficient income to meet established rents (thus subsidizing rents) or if the tenant's income becomes too high to increase rent. The city may also lease an apartment if it is left vacant for more than four months. Under the grant agreement, the owner of the dwelling has the right to occupy an apartment for the duration of his/her lifetime. The legal heirs may occupy the unit if they reimburse the city for the cost of renovation plus inflationary increases. As most of the people in this category are of low-income families it is expected that most of the units will revert to the city for eventual conversion to cooperative housing.

## INTEREST SUBSIDIES CRITICAL

The contracts providing for interest subsidies are the most critical to the success of the program. Theoretically, property owners could take advantage of the loan subsidy and subsequent increase in the market value of their housing and, after the contract period is over, gouge on rents and make removal of low-income tenants a reality. This eventuality, however is unlikely for these reasons:

1. Italian rent control laws do limit rent increases.

2. Since profit is not included in the rent formula, owners may be encouraged to sell to the city which has the option to buy.

3. Corporate speculators are excluded from contracts and will have their holdings expropriated.

4. The city reserves the right to utilize its powers of eminent domain should the owner fail to carry out any part of the agreement.

5. The city can use every incentive and regulatory device at its disposal to promote conversion of housing units from private to cooperative ownership.

## LESSONS FOR U.S.

The Bologna municipal government has become a model of

progressive administration. But in the long run the contradiction between private property and public purpose will have to be confronted.

In the meantime, Bologna demonstrates that within the capitalist system if you have a progressive political base, renewal without removal is possible, at least on a limited scale.

To overcome the handicaps of a social system based on private ownership and profit a city in the U.S. could follow Bologna's foot steps if it used large public housing subsidies and restrained speculation.

Bologna's renewal program proved that central city housing can be rehabilitated without removing people and destroying neighborhoods. The critical lesson may be that the housing question must be first confronted as a political question.

*Adapted from SOCIAL POLICY - May/June 1976*

# Bibliography

Asterisk (*) Indicates Important Work

**Abbott, Edith,** 1936. *The Tenements of Chicago, 1908-1935.* The University of Chicago, Chicago, Illinois.

**Abrams, Charles,** 1965. *The City is the Frontier.* Harper and Row, New York.

**Achtenberg, Emily,** 1973. "The Social Utility of Rent Control", in John Pynoos, et al., eds., *Housing Urban America.* Aldine Publishing Company, Chicago.*

**Achtenberg, Emily,** 1974. "Why Rent Control is Needed" — Summary published by Urban Planning Aid.*

**Achtenberg, Emily,** 1975. "Critique of the Rental Housing Association Rent Control Study: An Analysis of the Realities of Rent Control in the Greater Boston Area," Urban Planning Aid.*

**Achtenberg, Emily,** 1976. *Evaluation of Rent Control as a Housing Policy,* from Seminar on Rent Controls sponsored by BHA's Housing and Development Reporter and the Institute for Professional and Executive Development, Inc.*

**American Federation of Labor; Congress of Industrial Organizations,** 1975. *Survey of AFL-CIO Members Housing.*

**Angotti, Thomas,** 1977. *Housing in Italy.* Praeger, New York.*

**Apartment and Office Building Association,** 1977. Fact Sheet — Deterioration and Abandonment, in *Rent Control Report* by National Association of Realtors, Second Edition, Chicago, Illinois.

**Appelbaum, Richard and John Gilderbloom,** 1980. Housing Disinvestment and Rent Control: Steps Toward a Solution of the Housing Problem, Foundation for National Progress, San Francisco.*

**Appelbaum, Richard,** 1973. *Size, Growth and U.S. Cities.* Praeger Publishers, New York.

**Baar, Kenneth K. and W. Dennis Keating,** 1975. "The Last Stand of Economic Substantive Due Process — The Housing Emergency Requirement for Rent Control." *Urban Lawyer,* Vol. 7, No. 3 (Summer 1975).*

**Beard, Charles,** 1944. *A Basic History of the United States.* Blakiston, Philadelphia.

**Blumberg, Richard E., Brian Quinn Robbins and Kenneth K. Baar,** 1974. "The Emergence of Second Generation Rent Controls." *Clearinghouse Review,* 8 (August 1974), pp. 240-249.*

**Brenner, Joel F. and Herbert M. Franklin,** 1977. *Rent Control in North America and Four European Countries.* Washington, D.C.: The Council for International Urban Liaison.*

**Bureau of the Census,** 1978. *Statistical Abstract of the United States,* U.S. Department of Commerce, Washington, D.C.

**Bureau of Labor Statistics,** 1979. *CPI Detailed Report,* May 1979, U.S. Department of Commerce, Washington, D.C.

**Burghardt, Stephen,** 1972. *Tenants and the Urban Housing Crisis,* The New Press, Dexter, Michigan.*

**California Housing Council, Inc.,** 1977. *The Case Against Rent Control.* San Mateo, California.

**CALPIRG, 1980.** *Speculation and the Housing Crisis,* University of California, San Diego.

**Campbell, Angus, Phillip Converse, Warren Miller and Donald Stokes,** 1960. *The American Voter.* Wiley, New York.

**Campbell, Angus; Gerald Gurin, and Warren Miller,** 1954. *The Voter Decides.* Row, Peterson and Co., Evanston, Illinois.

**Cantril, Hadley,** 1941. *The Psychology of Social Movements,* John Wiley and Sons, New York, 1941.

**Clavel, Pierre, John Forester, and William W. Goldsmith,** 1980. *Urban and Regional Planning in An Age of Austerity.* Pergamon Press, New York.*

**COACT,** 1979. *Residential Property Turnover Study,* Madison Wisconsin.

**Coalition for Housing,** 1977. *Rent Control and the Housing Crisis in Southern California.* Los Angeles, California.

**Cohen, Julius,** 1946. "Rent Control After World War I - Recollections", *N.Y.U. L.Q.*

*Coker, Francis W.,* 1942. *Democracy, Liberty and Property.* MacMillan, New York.

**Community Development Department,** 1978. *Report to Ad Hoc Committee on Rent Freeze,* Community Development Department, City of Los Angeles.

**Community Development Department,** 1979. *Rent Stabilization Study,* Community Divisions, Community Development Department, Los Angeles.

**Comptroller General,** 1979. *Report to the Congress of the United States: Rental Housing: A National Problem That Needs Immediate Attention.''* Washington, D.C.: U.S. General Accounting Office, Nov. 8, 1979.*

**Congressional Research Service,** 1978. *The Theory of Rent Control.* Washington, D.C. Library of Congress.

**de Jouvenel, Bertrand.** 1948. *No Vacancies,* Foundation for Economic Education, Inc., Irvinton-on-Hudson, New York.

**Department of Housing and Community Development,** 1977. *California Statewide Housing Plan, 1977. Sacramento, California.*

**Downing, A.J.,** *1850. The Architecture of Country Houses.* Appleton and Co., New York.

**Donnison, D.V.,** 1967. *The Government of Housing.* Penguin Books, London.

**Dreier, Peter, John Gilderbloom and Richard Appelbaum,** 1980. Rising Rents and Rent Control: Issues in Urban Reform in Pierre Clavel, John Forester and William W. Goldsmith, *Urban Planning in an Age of Austerity.* Pergamon Press, New York.*

**Drellich, Edith Berger and Audree Emery,** 1939. *Rent Control in War and Peace.* National Municipal League, New York.

**Eckert, Joseph,** 1977. *The Effect of Rent Controls on Assessment Policies, Differential Incidence of Taxation and Income Adjustment Mechanisms for Rental Housing Brookline, Massachusetts.* Ph.D. Thesis, Tufts University.*

**Engels, Frederick,** 1954. "How Prudhon Solves the Housing Question",1872; reprinted in *The Housing Question,* Progress Publishers, Moscow*

**Fisher, Ernest M.,** 1966. "Twenty Years of Rent Control in New York City", in *Essays in Urban Land Economics.* Berkeley, Ca.: Real Estate Research Program, University of California, pp. 31-67.

**Frankena, Mark,** 1975. "Alternative Models of Rent Control", *Urban Studies,* 12 (Fall 1975), pp. 303-308.

**Friedman, Milton, and George Stigler,** 1946. "Roofs or Ceilings? The Current Housing Problems", *Popular Essays on Current Problems,* Vol. I, No. 2, September 1946.

**Garrigon, Richard T.,** 1978. "The Case for Rising Residential Rents", *Real Estate Review,* Fall 1978, Volume 6, No. 2. The Real Estate Institute of New York University.

**Gilderbloom, John,** 1976. *Department of Housing and Community Development Report to Donald E. Burns, Secretary, Business and Transportation Agency, on the Validity of the Legislative Finding of A.B. 3788 and the Economic Impact of Rent Control,* September 7, 1976. Department of Housing and Community Development, State of California, Sacramento.

**Gilderbloom, John,** 1978. *The Impact of Moderate Rent Control in the United States: A Review and Critique of Existing Literature:* California Department of Housing and Community Development.*

**Gilderbloom, John,** 1980. *Moderate Rent Control: The Experience of U.S. Cities,* Conference on Alternative State and Local Public Policies, Washington, D.C.

**Gottlieb, Robert and Irent Wolt,** 1977, *Thinking Big.* G.P. Putnam's Sons, New York.

**Grebler, Leo,** 1952. "Implications of Rent Control in the U.S." *International Labor Review,* Vol. 65, April 1952.

**Gribetz, Judah and Frank Grad,** 1966. "Housing Code Enforcement: Sanctions and Remedies", *Columbia Law Review,* Vol. 66, 1966.

**Gruen, Claude and Nina Gruen,** 1977. *Rent Control in New Jersey: The Beginnings.* San Mateo, California: California Housing Council.

**Hartman, Chester,** 1975. *Housing and Social Policy.* Prentice-Hall, Englewood Cliffs, New Jersey.*

**Hartman, Chester,** 1978. "The Big Squeeze", *Politics Today,* (May-June).*

**Hartman, Chester and Michael Stone,** 1978. "Housing: A Socialist Alternative," from *The Federal Budget and Social Reconstruction: The People and the State,* Marcus G. Raskin, Editor; Institute for Policy Studies and Transaction Books.*

**Harvey, David,** 1973. *Social Justice and the City.* John Hopkins Press, Baltimore, Maryland.*

**Hawley, Peter K.** 1976. *Housing in the Public Domain: The Only Solution.* Metropolitan Council on Housing, New York.*

**Hayek, F.A.,** 1972. The Repercussions of Rent Restrictions in *Verdict on Rent Control,* Institute on Economic Affairs, Cormorant Press, England.

**Henry, Tony,** 1976. "Organizing for Action", *Strength Through Unity,* Report of National Conference of Public Housing Tenants, Ottawa, May 22-24, 1976.

**Heskin, Allan,** 1978. "The Warranty of Habitability Debate: A California Case Study", *California Law Review,* Vol. 66, No. 1., January, 1978.

**Indritz, Tova,** 1971. "Tenants Rights Movement", *New Mexico Law Review,* Vol. 1, January.

**Institute for Social Science Research** CWA. V. Clark, Alan Heskin and Louise Manvel, 1980. *Rental Housing in the City of Los Angeles,* Institute for Social Science Research, University of California, Los Angeles.*

**Jacob, Mike and Linda Lillow,** 1978. "Understanding Landlording", California Housing Action and Information Network, Oakland.

**Jacob, Mike,** 1979. "CPI Rent Increases: Boondoggle for Landlords, Raw Deal for Renters", California Housing Action and Information Network, Oakland.

**Jennings, Thomas,** 1972. "A Case Study of Tenant Union Legalism", *Tenants and the Urban Housing Crisis,* The New Press, Dexter Michigan.

**Johnson III, Reuben and Ronald Lawson,** 1975. *The Complex Reality of a Social Movement: Movement Organizations and the Internal Dynamics of the Tenants' Movement in New York City",* Paper presented at the Fifth Bicentennial Convention of the American Studies Association, San Antonio, Texas, November 1975.

**Katz, Stuart,** 1972. "The Organizational Structure and Staff Membership Roles of a Tenant Union", in *Tenant and the*

273

*Housing Crisis,* Burghardt, Stephen (ed.), The New Press, Dexter, Michigan.

**Keating, W. Dennis,** 1976. *Rent and Eviction Controls: An Annotated Bibliography* (Council of Planning Librarians Exchange Bibliography No. 1136 - October 1976 - 1313 E. 60th Street, Chicago, Illinois 60637)*

**Keating, Dennis with John Atlas,** 1972. "Battling over Rent Control", *Shelterforce,* Winter 1977.

**Keating, Dennis W.,** 1978. "Tenants Hound Landlords for Rebates", *In These Times,* September 6-12, 1978, p.4.

**Kristof, Frank S.,** 1976. "Housing and People in New York City: A View of the Past, Present, and Future", *City Almanac,* Vol. 10, No. 5 (February 1976).

**Lawson, Ronald; Stephen Barton, and Jenna Weissman Joselet,** 1977. *From Riches to Storefront: Women in the Tenant Movement,* Paper presented at the meeting of the American Sociological Association, Chicago, September, 1977.

**Lett, Monica,** 1976. *Rent Control: Concepts, Realities, and Mechanisms,* New Brunswick, N.J.: The Center for Urban Policy Research Rutgers University.

**Lindbeck A.,** 1978. "Rent Control as an Instrument of Housing Policy", in A.A. Nevitt (ed.), *The Economic Problems of Housing.* Macmillan, New York.

**Lipsky, Michael,** 1970. *Protest in City Politics: Rent Strikes, Housing, and The Power of the Poor.* Rand McNally and Company, Chicago.

**Lowry, Ira S.,** *et al.* 1970. Rental Housing in New York City (New York: Rand Institute 1970-1971), Vol. 1, Confronting the Crisis (1970) and Vol. 2, The Demand for Shelter.

**Marcuse, Peter,** 1975. "Residential Alienation, Home Ownership and the Limits of Shelter Policy," *Journal of Sociology and Social Welfare,* Vol. III, No. 2, November 1975, pp. 181-203

**Marcuse, Peter,** 1978. *Housing Policy and the Myth of the Benevolent State* *, in *Social Policy* Jan./Feb 1978

**Marcuse, Peter,** 1978. "The Political Economy of Rent Control: Theory and Strategy". Columbia University Division of Urban Planning, Papers in Planning, 7, New York.

**Marcuse, Peter,** 1979. *Rental Housing in the City of New York: Supply and Condition 1975-1978.* New York: City of New York.

**Martin, Phillip,** 1976. "Baylor Law Review," Vol. 28. Winter, 1976.

**Massachusetts Department of Corporations and Taxation,** 1974. In Harbridge House, *A Study of Rent and Eviction Controls in the Commonwealth of Massachusetts.* Prepared for the Joint Legislature Commitee on Local Affairs.

**Moody, Linda,** 1972. "Landlords and Tenants: Oakland Landlord/Tenant Intervention Unit", *The Police Chief,* Vol. 39, 1972, p. 32.

**Moskovitz, Myron and Peter Honigsberg,** 1970 "Tenant Union-Landlord Relations Act", *Geo Law Journal* Vol. 58, June, 1970, p. 1103.

**Moskovitz, Myron Ralph Warner, and Charles E. Sherman,** 1974. *California Tenants Handbook,* Occidental, California: Nole Press.*

**Naison, Mark,** 1972. "The Rent Strikes in New York", in *Tenants and the Urban Housing Crisis,* Stephan Burghardt (ed.), The New Press, Dexter, Michigan, 1972, pp. 19-34.

**National Advisory Commission on Civil Disorders,** 1978. *Report of the National Advisory Commission on Civil Disorders,* Bantam Books, New York.

**National Commission on Urban Problems,** 1968. *Building the American City,* Report to Congress and the President of the United States 91st Congress, 1st Session, House Document.

**National Housing Law Project,** *Housing Law Bulletin* (bimonthly) (Suite 300, 2150 Shattuck Avenue, Berkeley, CA 94704)

**Note,** 1967. "Residential Rent Control in New York City," *3 Columbia Journal of Law and Social Problems* 30-65 June 1967.

**Note,** 1968. *Yale Law Journal* Vol. 77, June, p. 1368.

**Oberschall, Anthony,** 1973. *Social Conflict and Social Movement,* Prentice Hall, pp. 118-119.

**Office of the City Clerk, City of Santa Monica,** 1978. "Transcript: Portion of Proceedings of Santa Monica City Council Meeting Held 7:30 p.m.," July 25, 1978.

**Olson, Mancur,** 1971. *The Logic of Collective Action.* Harvard University Press, Cambridge, Massachusetts.

**Paish, F.W.,** 1950. The Economics of Rent Restriction. *Lloyds Bank Review.*

**Patrick, Kathryn Lori,** 1978. "Rent Control: A Practical Guide for Tenant Organizations," *15 San Diego Law Review* 1185 (1978) (see "Sample Rent Control Legislation").

**Pennance, F.G.,** 1972. "Introduction," *Verdict on Rent Control,* Institute of Economic Affairs, Cormorant Press, England.

**Pickvance, C.G.,** 1978. "On the Study of Urban Social Movements", in *Urban Sociology,* C.G. Pickvance (ed.), Tavistock Publications, London.*

**Piven, Frances Fox and Richard Cloward,** 1967. "Rent Strike", *The New Republic,* December 2, p. 11.

**Post, Landgon,** 1938. *The Challenge of Housing,* Farrar and Rinehart, Inc., New York.

**Pynoos, Jon, Robert Schafer and Chester Hartman,** 1973. *Housing Urban America,* Aldine Publishing Company, Chicago.*

**Real Estate Research Council of Southern California,** 1978. *Real Estate and Construction Report,* Second Quarter, Los Angeles.

**Rhyne, Charles, William Asch, and Pay Wynns,** 1975. *Municipalities and Multiple Residential Housing: Condominium and Rent Control* (National Institute of Municipal Law Officers, 839-17th Street, N.W., Washington, D.C. 20006) (see "NIMLO Model Rent Control Ordinance").

**Rossiter, Clinton,** 1962. *Conservatism in America,* Knopf, New York,

**Rydenfelt, Sven,** 1949. "Rent Control Thirty Years On", in *Human Action: A Treatise on Economics.* Yale University Press, New Haven.

**Samuelson, Paul,** 1967. *Economics: An Introductory Analysis.* McGraw Hill, New York.

**Santa Monica Department of Environmental Services,** 1978. "Everything You Want to Know About Santa Monica".

Santa Monica Rent Control Board, 1979. Proposed General Adjustment, Santa Monica, California.

**Seldon, Arthur,** 1972. "Preface," *Verdict on Rent Control,*

Institute of Economic Affairs, Cormorant Press, England.

**Selesnick, Herbert L.,** 1976. Harbridge House Inc. *Rent Control.* Lexington Books.*

**Sennett, Richard,** 1970. *Families Against the City: Middle Class Homes of Industrial Chicago, 1972-1890.* Harvard University Press, Cambridge.

**Sklar, Kathryn Kish,** 1971. *Catherine Beecher.* Yale University Press, New Haven.

**Southern California Association of Governments,** 1978. *Review of Third Year Housing and Community Development Title I Block Grant Applications.*

**Starr, Roger,** 1973. *America's Housing Challenge,* Hill and Wang, New York.

**State of California,** 1973. *Statewide Housing Element, Phase II,* Department of Housing and Community Development.

**Sternberg, Arnold,** 1978."Testimony, Assembly Committee on Housing and Community Development", in *Forum,* Vol. 1, No. 3, April 5, pp. 10-12.

**Sternlieb, George,** 1974. *The Realities of Rent Control in the Greater Boston Area,* New Brunswick, New Jersey: Center for Urban Policy Research.

**Sternlieb, George,** *et al.,* 1975. "Fort Lee Rent Control," New Brunswick, New Jersey: Center for Urban Policy Research.

**Stone, Michael,** 1975. "The Housing Crisis, Mortgage Lending, and Class Struggle," *Antipode-7:2* (September): 22-30.*

**Tietz, Michael,** ed. Vol. 4, 1970. *The Impact of City Programs* Chapter II, Rent Control. New York Rand Institute.

**United States Senate,** Committee on Banking, Housing and Urban Affairs, 1976. *Report on the York City Loan Program.* 94th Congress, Second Sesson, May 17, 1976.

**Urban Planning Aid, Inc., 1975.** "Critique of the Rental Housing Association Rent Control Study: *An Analysis of the Realities of Rent Control in the Greater Boston Area.*" Cambridge, Mass., May.*

**U.S Bureau of the Census,** 1971. *Historical Statistics of the U.S.: Colonial Times to 1970, Part, 2,* Washington, D.C.: USGPO, Lines N-238-245.

**U.S Bureau of the Census,** 1974. *Annual Housing Survey: 1974, Current Housing Reports Series H-170-74-7,* U.S. Department of Housing and Urban Development, Office of Policy Development and Research, Washington, D.C.: USGPO.

**U.S Bureau of the Census,** 1976. *General History Characteristics: Current Housing Reports: 1976,* Annual Housing Survey, Series 14-150-76, Washington, D.C.: USGPO.

**U.S Bureau of the Census,** 1977. *Statistical Abstract of the United States: 1977,* Washington, D.C.: USGPO.

**U.S. Department of Commerce,** Bureau of the Census, 1978. *Current Population Reports Series p-60,* No. 113, Washington, D.C., July 1978.

**Vancouver Interdepartmental Study Team on Housing and Rents,** 1975. *Housing and Rent Control in British Columbia.* Vancouver, B.C.: Ministry of Housing, October 20, mimeo.

**Vaughan, Ted,** 1968. "The Landlord-Tenant Relationship in a Low Income Area", *Social Problems,* Vol. 16, No. 2, Fall.*

**Warner, Jr., Sam Bass,** 1972. *The Urban Wilderness,* Harper and Row, New York.

**Willis, John W.,** 1950. "Some Oddities in Law of Rent Control," *University of Pittsburgh Law Review,* 11 (Summer 1950), pp.609-623.*

**Willis, John,** 1950. "Short History of Rent Control Laws." *Cornell Law Quarterly,* 36 (Fall 1950), pp. 54-92.*

**Woods, Tighe E.,** 1950. "Administration of a Law: Federal Rent Control." *Notre Dame Lawyer,* 25(Spring 1950), pp. 411-437.

# Biography

### Emily Paradise Achtenberg

47 Halifax Street, Boston, Mass. 02130 (617) 524-3982 or 742-0820
Ms. Achtenberg has made some of the most important contributions to the rent control movement. She is a housing consultant for government and community groups. She is author or co-author of the following: *The Social Utility of Rent Control, Why Rent Control is Needed, Housing and Rent Control in British Columbia, Less Rent, More Control, Tenants First! A Research and Organizing Guide to FHA Housing and Hostage: Housing and the Massachusetts Fiscal Crisis.* She is currently involved in an evaluation of HUD management and property disposition policies for formerly subsidized multifamily projects. In addition, she has worked for the Tenants' Education Program at the Boston Community School and has also worked for Urban Planning Aid.

### Thomas R. Angotti

Division of Urban Planning, Columbia University, New York City, New York 10021. (212) 768-9890
Mr. Angotti completed a book: *Housing in Italy: Urban Development and Political Change* published by Praeger. An edited portion of it appears in this book. He has published articles on housing in the Monthly Review and Black Scholar.

### Richard P. Appelbaum

Sociology, University of California, Santa Barbara, California 93106.
He is co-author of the highly respected *Effects of Urban Growth* and author of *Size, Growth and U.S. Cities* — both published by Praeger. He recently finished a National Science Foundation Public Service Science Residency to work on the causes of the rental housing crisis. In addition, he has begun work on a book along with John Gilderbloom on housing.

**John Atlas,**

Shelterforce, 380 Main Street, East Orange, New Jersey 07018 (201) 678-6778 or 678-5353.

Mr Atlas is a founding member of Shelterforce, the New Jersey Tenant Organization and the recently formed National Tenant Union. He is currently an editor of *Shelterforce* and is a legal service attorney specializing in landlord/tenant law. He is considered an expert in rent control law.


**Peter Barnes**

The Solar Center, 1115 Indian Street, San Francisco, CA 94107. (415) 957-9660

Peter Barnes was the west coast editor of *The New Republic* magazine for six years, and also a Washington correspondent for *Newsweek*. He is the author of two books and numerous articles on economic and political issues. He also served on the staffs of former Senators Eugene McCarthy, Walter Mondale and Fred Harris. At present he is president of The Solar Center, an employee-owned solar design and installation company in San Francisco.


**Richard Blumberg,**

National Housing Law Project, 2152 Shattuck 300, Berkeley, California 94704 (415) 548-9400

Mr. Blumberg along with Dennis Keating and John Atlas is the nation's leading expert on rent control laws. He is editor of the highly acclaimed *Housing Law Bulletin* and is the author of numerous books and journal articles on landlord/tenant relations. He is currently Senior Staff Attorney at the National Housing Law Project.


**Michael Brenneman**

Mr. Brenneman is President of Brenneman Associates in Washington D.C. Brenneman began his real estate career as a broker in Washington D.C. in the early 1960's managing the Watergate Complex. Beginning in 1970, Brenneman worked in Florida with the U.S. Home Corp. the nation's largest home builder. In 1973, he founded Brenneman Associates. The company has become one of the largest developers of condominiums and co-ops in the metropolitan area. It now handles seven or eight projects at a time with gross sales this year of about $35 million. This article is reprinted with permission from November 1978 *Sojourners.*

### Bruce Dale
56 West 22, New York, New York 10010. (212) 675-3937
Mr. Dale is an architect, has collaborated on public housing and planning projects in Italy and is now Director of the Bureau of Renovation Programs, New York City. He is also co-coordinator, New York Network/Forum.

### Peter Dreier
Sociology Department, Tufts University, Medford Massachusetts 02155 (617) 628-5000
Mr. Dreier is currently on leave from the Sociology Department at Tufts and is working for Massachusetts Fair Share. He recently received a grant from the National Science Foundation Public Service Science residency to study condominium conversions. He was a co-founder of the Massachusetts Tenants Organization.

### Chester Hartman,
360 Elizabeth Street, San Francisco, Ca 94114. (415)282-1249
Mr. Hartman is an urban planner living in San Francisco. He holds a Ph.D. in city and regional planning from Harvard and has taught there, at Yale and at the University of California Berkeley. His books include *Housing and Social Policy, Yerba Buena: Land Grab and Community Resistance in San Francisco,* and *Housing Urban America* (co-edited with Jon Pynoos and Robert Schafer).

### David Harvey
505 West 34th Street, Baltimore, Maryland 21211 (310) 367-5417 or 338-7099
Mr. Harvey is currently Professor of Geography and Environmental Engineering at John Hopkins University. He is author of the highly acclaimed *Social Justice and the City* — a book that has had a major impact on the theory of cities. Mr. Harvey was a participant in the successful Baltimore rent control campaign.

### Alan Heskin
School of Architecture and Urban Planning, University of California at Los Angeles, Los Angeles, California 90024 (213) 825-4374.
Mr. Heskin is currently Assistant Professor of Architecture and Urban Planning. He is currently engaged in a study of "tenant conscious-

ness" funded by the National Institute for Mental Health. He recently co-authored a study on the impact of moderate rent control in Los Angeles and is a consultant to the City of Los Angeles on rent control. He was formerly with the National Housing Law Project, specializing in landlord/tenant law.


## Mike Jacob

CHAIN Newsletter, 3001 Galindo, Oakland, Ca 94601. (415) 444-2633
Mr. Jacob is currently editor of the *California Housing Action and Information Network News*. He has been an active leader in tenant unions around California.


## Dennis W. Keating

432 Hudson Street, Oakland, California 94618 (415)428-2169
Mr. Keating—along with Richard Blumberg and John Atlas—is recognized as one of the nation's leading experts in rent control law. He teaches courses in housing and urban planning at San Francisco State University and University of California at Berkeley. He is co-author of *The People's Guide to Urban Renewal* and has written numerous law articles on housing. He's currently working at the National Housing Law Project studying "fair return formulas" in New Jersey's rent controlled cities.


## Mary Jo Kirschman

751 East 36th Street, Baltimore Md 21218. (301)467-0261
Ms. Kirschman is a community organizer who was one of the founders and coordinators of the Baltimore Rent Control Campaign.


## Claudia Leight, Elliot Lieberman, Jerry Kurtz and Dean Pappas

c/o New American Movement, P.O. Box 7213, Baltimore, Md 21218
These people are community organizers involved with the Baltimore Rent Control Campaign and are members of the New American Movement.


## Cary Lowe

California Public Policy Center, P.O. Box 3519, Los Angeles, California

90051. (213)628-8888
Mr. Lowe is the director of the California Public Policy Center and has served on Governor Brown's task forces on housing and investment policies. He's currently teaching at the University of California, Los Angeles in the Urban Studies Department and is working on a book discussing the housing crisis.

### Peter Marcuse
Department of Urban Planning, 410 Avery Hall, Columbia University, New York City, New York 10027 (212) 280-3513 or 280-3322
Mr. Marcuse is a lawyer and Professor of Urban Planning at Columbia. He was President of Los Angeles Planning Commission and is now a member of Manhattan Community Board 9. He is author of *Rental Housing in the City of New York.*

### James O'Connor
College 8 University of California, Santa Cruz, Santa Cruz, California 95064 (408) 429-2900
Mr. O'Connor is professor of Sociology and Economics at the University of California, Santa Cruz. He is author of one of the most important books written in the past 10 years: *The Fiscal Crisis of the State;* he is also author of *The Origins of Socialism in Cuba* and *The Corporations and the State.* He is also editor of *Latin American Perspectives, Working Papers on Kapitalistate* and *Social Theory and Practice.*

### Evelyn Onwuachi
c/o Neighborhood Information Sharing Exchange, 1725 K Street N.W., Washington D.C. 20006
Ms. Onwuachi is the Housing Information Specialist at NISE. She has been a staff and a boardmember at City Wide Housing Foundation. She is a certified housing counselor and has organized and aided many tenant associations in the District. She currently participates in the Rent Control Steering Committee (of D.C.). She is an Executive Board member to the National Tenants Union.

### Chuck Ross
Mr. Ross is a freelance writer living in Santa Monica who has had articles in the *Los Angeles Times* and *New West Magazine.*

**Mark Siegel**

1612 Cerro Gordo, Los Angeles, CA 90026. (213)485-3391
Mark Siegel is a member of Governor Brown's task force on affordable housing and a deputy for Los Angeles City Council member Joel Wachs.

**Tim Siegel**

Kalorama Station, P.O. Box 21002, Washington D.C. 20009 (202) 265-1305.
Mr. Siegel is a former board member of the City Wide Housing Foundation, is editor of *Shelterforce* and is co-coordinator for the Common Capital Fund in Washington D.C. He has traveled widely around the East Coast giving seminars on the housing crisis to various government and community groups.

**South Coast Information Project Housing Task Force**

P.O. Box 1346 Santa Barbara, California 93102 (805) 966-2503
These articles were written and researched by the following persons: William Glennon, Richard Appelbaum, John Gilderblom, Jennifer Bieglow, Ruth Schwartz, Don Olsen, Craig Reinarman, Dick Flacks, Gale Trachtenberg, Neal Linson, Todd Glasser, Jon Goldhill, Julie Horvath, Janet Anderson and many others.

**Michael Stone**

College of Public and Community Service, University of Massachusetts, Boston, Mass. 02125
Mr. Stone Teaches in the Center for Community Planning, College of Public and Community Service, University of Massachusetts in Boston. He has worked with community groups in New Jersey and Massachusetts as an advocacy planner, researcher, technical assistant, trainer and organizer. He is the author of *People Before Property: A Real Estate Primer and Research Guide* and co-author of *Tenants First: A Research and Organizing Guide to FHA Housing* and *Hostage! Housing and the Massachusetts Fiscal Crisis*.

# Resources

## Important books, articles, pamphlets, films, organizations.

**Beyond URLTA: A Problem for Achieving Real Tenant Goals.** By Richard Blumberg and Brian Robbins. 11 Harvard Civil Rights Law Review 1 (Win., 1976).

This article examines the Uniform Residential Landlord-Tenant Act; discusses landlord-tenant reform going beyond the Act and tenant tactics in achieving decent housing; and proposes a system of security of tenure/just cause eviction.

**Campaign for Economic Democracy News,** California Campaign for Economic Democracy, 409 Santa Monica Blvd, 214, Santa Monica, California 90401. (213) 393-3701.

This is the newspaper of the Campaign for Economic Democracy which includes news items on housing as well as solar news, investment policy, cancer research, and left strategy. Fifteen dollar subscription also includes: invitation to CED events; workshops on community organizing skills, electoral campaigning and principles of economic democracy.

**The Center for Community Change;** 1000 Wisconsin Avenue, N.W.; Washington, D.C. 20007. (202) 338-6310.

This Center is interested in reaching groups and individuals working for social change on the community level. The Center produces a bi-monthly newsletter, MONITOR, which analyzes changes in Federal programs and Congressional actions. Subscriptions are $10/year but are provided at no charge to non-profit community organizations. The publication includes "community action guides" which have focused on Community Development Block Grants, CETA, and Revenue Sharing.

**Chainletter.** CHAIN. 2300 Foothill Blvd., Oakland, California 94601. 532-6400.

Newsletter of the California Housing Action and Information Network, a network of tenants rights and housing organizations in California. Lets you know what's happening in the housing movement in a state that's a leader in housing activism. $10, highly recommended.

**Community Design Centers;** Community Design Center Directors' Association; 380 Main Street; East Orange, New Jersey 07018. (201) 678-9720.

Provides planning, architectural and other technical assistance to nonprofit neighborhood and community organizations for housing and local development projects, particularly in depressed/disadvantaged communities. There are presently 64 Community Design Centers located in 33 states. To contact the one nearest you, write or phone the Community Design Center Directors' Association.

**Community Development Digest.** Community Development Publications; 399 National Press Building, Washington, D.C. 20045.

Federal, state and local happenings in housing and community development. Each issue has a reference section listing where to obtain copies of Congressional bills, reports on Federal agency actions and regulations, etc. Biweekly newsletter. ($117/year.)

**Cooperative Housing.** Midwest Association of Housing Cooperatives, 343 South Main, Ann Arbor, MI 48108. (313)994-4314

This 262-page book is packed with information on all phases of co-op membership and administration. It is a valuable tool for board members of housing cooperatives, especially those working with low- to middle income co-ops; but it is equally useful for co-op members and for anyone wishing to start a housing cooperative.

**Cooperative Housing Bulletin.** NAHC, 1828 L St., N.W., Suite 100, Washington, D.C., 20036.

Gives information on conferences, workshops, legislation, technical assistance available to those involved in housing cooperatives or wanting to be. Also news of other housing cooperatives, the Co-op Bank, etc.

**Disclosure,** Natinal Peoples Action, 1123 West Washington Blvd., Chicago, Illinois 60607

This is a monthly newsletter published by the Housing Training and Information Center which reports and analyzes community struggles around the country. It focuses on redlining, greenlining and FHA/HUD policies.

**Exploratory Project on Economic Alternatives,** EPEA, 2000 P Street, N.W., Suite 515, Washington, D.C., 20036.

This foundation-sponsored project has produced a series of economic policy reports on such subjects as inflation, housing, food policy, cooperatives, citizen access, and capital and community. Write for publications list.

**Fair Housing for Children,** P.O. Box 5877, Santa Monica, CA, 90405.
(213) 393-1093.

Fights against landlord policies that discriminate against people with children. Model anti-discrimination laws for cities and states available.

**Grassroots Fundraising Book,** By Joan Flanagan. The Youth Project, 1000 Wisconsin Avenue N.W., Washington, D.C. 20007.

Starting from step one and assuming that the reader is a novice, the author explores the whys and hows of raising money in one's community. All kinds of grassroots fundraising are discussed, from booksales and holiday parties to telethons and Las Vegas casino nights. Every tenant union should have this book.$4.75.

**Hostage!** By Michael Stone and Emily Achtenberg, Boston Community School; 107 South Street; Boston, MA 02111.

A new publication from The Boston Community School, which explores housing and the Massachusetts fiscal crisis. The problems in the national economy, how the banks use state subsidized housing to trigger crises, and why tenants and taxpayers pay for their reaping of profits. Its value goes beyond those in Massachusetts. Highly recommended for anyone who wants to understand the present fiscal crises and housing problems. Price: $1.25 per copy plus 25¢ postage; 10 or more, $1.00 per copy (including postage). Send checks payable to HOUSING BOOKLET.

**Housing Bibliography** by Mary Vogel. Housing Issues Task Force. 200 Josephine, Denver, Co 80206.

Annotated housing bibliography, prepared for the National Lawyers Guild Housing Task Force; it covers books, articles and publications and deals with historical as well as current works. 7 pages, $1.00.

**Housing and Development Reporter.** Bureau of National Affairs. 1231 25th Street, N.W. Washington, D.C. 20037. Biweekly. ($350/ year).

Bibliography of housing and community development activities. Covers all national and most state and local activities. Also provides complete updated review of challenges to Federal laws and regulations related to housing.

**Housing in the Public Domain** by Peter K. Hawley. Metropolitan Council on Housing. 24 West 30th Street, New York, N.Y. 10001.

The book is crammed with easily readable technical data that define a housing system based on need rather than profit. Solutions for the financing of construction, the transfer of existing units from private ownership to the public domain as well as creation of a non-bureaucratic system of tenant control are all dealt with in detail. Highly recommended. $3.60.

**Housing Resource Manual.** Pratt Institute Center for Community and Environmental Development, 275 Washington Avenue, Brooklyn, New York 11205.

1979 ($5.) Source of information on housing and community development programs. Lists and describes resources to assist neighborhood and community groups with self-help projects. Primarily focuses on New York City, but should be useful to housing groups elsewhere.

**In These Times.** 1509 North Milwaukee Avenue, Chicago, Illinois 60622.

Nonsectarian, weekly Left newspaper. Regularly reports on progressive political officials, union struggles, and Left activities abroad. A readable, nonrhetorical style distinguishes the paper from other Left publications. Essential reading for keeping up with progressive, grass roots and national Left politics in the U.S. $17.50 a year.

**Journal of Housing.** NAHRO, 2600 Virginia Ave., N.W., Wash., D.C. 20037.

The professional journal of the National Association of Housing and Redevelopment Officials, an organization composed mainly of agency people who work in the field of housing, urban re-development or community development. Liberal-reformist in its approach but keeps you in touch with what's going on.

**Metropolitan Washington Planning and Housing Association.** 1225 K Street, N.W. Washington, D.C. 20005. (202) 737-3700.

Provides technical assistance to neighborhood groups on reinvestment issues and strategies. Monthly newsletter, *The Advocate,* updates reinvestment activities. (Free to members.)

**National Association of Neighborhoods.** (NAN), 1651 Fuller Street, N.W. Washington, D.C. 20009. (202)332-7766

Works in support of neighborhood organizations by promoting local government decentralization and responsiveness to neighborhood-based development activities, also involved with displacement issues. Publishes monthly newsletter for members, *NAN Bulletin,* which contains neighborhood development information and describes NAN involvement in housing development activities across the country. ($10/year to individuals, $25 to institutions).

**National Committee Against Discrimination in Housing.** 1425 H. Street N.W. Washington, D.C. 20005. (205) 783-8150.

Works with fair housing advocacy and community development groups to ensure rights of minorities and poor persons to decent housing of their choice, Offers legal and technical assistance, field services and research and public information programs. Publishes two newsletters: *The Flash,* which is published periodically to report on important news in the housing field ($2 for 15 issues); and bimonthly, *Trends in Housing,* which updates organization activities ($5/year).

**National Housing Law Project Bulletin.** NHLP, 2150 Shattuck 300, Berkeley, Ca. 94704. (415) 548-9400.

Covers legal events that form tenant/landlord law — especially rent control laws. Also covers the Housing and Community Development Act. Highly recommended!

**National Rural Center.** 1828 L. Street, N.W., Washington, D.C. 20036.
(202) 331-0258.

Develops and advocates housing policy alternatives relating to rural needs by conducting demonstration programs, using the results of existing research, evaluating Federal programs and pursuing basic research. Monitors the writing of national legislation and program regulations. Provides information services and publications, including monthly, *Rural Community Development Newsletter.* (Free.)

**National Rural Housing Coalition Rural Housing Congressional Round-Up.** NRHC, 1016 16th Street N.W., Washington, D.C. 20036. (202)775-0046

Keeps subscribers informed of significant legislature and administrative rural housing developments and analyzes governmental actions affecting rural housing.

**National Low-Income Housing Coalition.** NLIHC, 215 Eighth St. NE., Wash., D.C. 20002.

These mailings are mainly in the form of legislative alerts regarding national legislation or regulations regarding housing. Some analysis of the impacts of various proposals is given.

**New School for Democratic Management.** 589 Howard Street, San Francisco, California 94105. (415) 543-7873.

Offers courses and workshops in financial management, marketing and accounting, with emphasis on community development. Has several regional offices and administers educational programs in a number of cities.

**People Before Property** by Urban Planning Aid. Midwest Academy. 600 W. Fullerton, Chicago, Illinois 60614.

This is a nuts and bolts information guide to help people uncover who owns what and where. It explains in detail the economics of rental housing — cash flow, tax shelter, appreciation and refinancing. Highly recommended.

**The Peoples Guide to Urban Renewal,** Berkeley Tenants Union, 2022 Blake Street, Berkeley, Ca 94704.

This is a resource tool intended for use by lawyers, community organizers and their advocates involved in redevelopment struggles. Highly recommended!

**Planners Network.** 360 Elizabeth St., San Francisco, Ca. 94114.

One of the best sources of news on what radical planners and community organizers are doing throughout the country. Dozens of conferences, papers, books, actions, etc. are announced in every issue. Highly recommended.

**The Political Economy of Rent Control: Theory and Strategy** by Peter Marcuse. Columbia University Department of Urban Planning, Papers in Planning 7 Columbia University, New York, New York 10027.

This is perhaps the best paper written on the theory of rent control from a political economy perspective. The paper addresses the pros and cons of whether rent control can be an agent for social change.

**Problems in Political Economy: An Urban Perspective** by David M. Gordon. 2nd Edition. Lexington, Mass: D.C. Heath and Co., 1977.

Ten short articles comprise the section of this book dealing with housing. Four of the articles give impressions, and definitions of the housing problem in the U.S., while six give an analysis of past actions and the need for re-direction in the future. Although the editor's own perspective is radical, he has selected articles which represent liberal and conservative views as well as radical viewpoints.

**The Public Works** COOP, 1904 Franklin, Oakland, California 94618. (415)832-8300

*The Public Works* is published quarterly by the Community Ownership Organizing Project (COOP). The newsletter focuses on effecting structural change at the community level through community ownership of real estate, utilities and economic enterprises. It reflects COOP's experiences with community ownership and explores new ideas and strategies.

**Pushed Out for Profit.** Optic Nerve, 141 Tenth Street, San Francisco, California, 94103.

This film is an excellent half-hour color documentary on the impact of speculation and what people are doing to save their homes and communities. It was designed for television broadcast and use in both the classroom and organizing meetings. The documentary is currently available in videotape formats for a sliding scale rental or purchase fee.

**Redevelopment**, San Francisco Newsreal, 630 Natona, San Francisco, California 94103.

This is the best film every made on the housing struggle. The film provides a careful examination of the renewal process and social and political implications of a number of major projects. The film carries the message that people can fight city hall.

**Rent and Eviction Controls: An Annotated Bibliography** by Dennis W. Keating. Council of Planning Librarians Exchange Bibliography No. 1136 - October 1976 - 1313 E. 60th Street, Chicago, Illinois 60637.

Lists almost every book or article ever written on rent control, with a brief synopsis of each article. Highly recommended.

**Rental Housing: A National Problem That Needs Immediate Attention** by the Comptroller General. U.S. General Accounting Office, Distribution Section, Room 1518, 441 G Street, N.W., Washington, D.C. 20548.

This important report discusses the crisis situation existing in the Nation's rental housing market and the particularly bleak prospects facing lower income renters. This has the most up to date statistics on the nations housing crisis.

**The Rights of Tenants** by Richard E. Blumberg and James R. Grow. Avon Books, Mail order Department, 250 West 55th Street, New York, N.Y. 10019.

Provides valuable information on truth in renting, discrimination, leases, rent control, taking your landlord to court and much more. $2.20. Highly recommended

**ROOF**. Shelter, 157 Waterloo Rd., London SE 1 8 UU.

News, analyses and editorials on what's happening in housing in Great Britain and on the continent.

**Rural America, Inc.** 1346 Connecticut Avenue, N.W. Washington, D.C. 20005 (202) 679-2800.

Represents rural interests by providing information and technical assistance on rural housing and other programs. Assists groups in identifying funding sources for housing rehabilitation. Publishes many publications, including monthly newspaper, *Rural America* ($10/year); and monthly newsletter, *RHA (Rural Housing Alliance) Reporter* (free to members).

**Saving Neighborhoods** by Cary D. Lowe. California Public Policy Center, P.O. Box 3519, Los Angeles, California 90051.

The pamphlet discusses many of the issues involved in the task of upgrading neighborhoods. Oriented primarily toward government planning agencies, community groups should also find it helpful. 64 pages: $2.00.

**Shelterforce.** 380 Main St., East Orange, N.J. 07018.

"Analyzes housing problems from the people's point of view". News, analysis, book reviews, how-to articles, etc. by radical activists around the U.S. $5.00 for 6 issues. Highly recommended.

**Tenants and the Urban Housing Crisis**. edited by Stephen Burhadt. The New Press, 9200 Island Lake Road, Dexter, Michigan, 48130.

This volume is a series of essays discussing the recent history of the tenants movement, inlcuding the 1964 Harlem and 1968-69 Ann Arbor rent strikes. It also includes specific chapters on tenant organizing strategies and tactics.

**Understanding Landlording** by Mike Jacob and Linda Lillow, California Housing Action and Information Network. 132 A East 12th Street, Oakland, California 94609. (415) 444-2633.

A small pamphlet on costs and profits-depreciation, appreciation — involved in landlording. A must for any tenant activist. $1.00.

**Urban and Regional Planning in an Age of Austerity,** edited by Pierre Clavel, John F. Forester, and William W. Goldsmith.

Pergamon Press, Inc. Maxwell House, Fairview Park, Elmsford, New York 10523.

Analyzes the development of austerity policies at all levels of government in the Untied States. Alternative planning strategies and roles are presented to deal with budget and program cutbacks. Includes three articles on the housing crisis. Highly recommended. 300 pages long, $5.95.

**Ways & Means**. Conference on Alternative State and Local Policies. 1901 Q Street, N.W. Washington, D.C. 20009.

The newsletter of the national conference is published six times a year. Regular information on progressive legislation and programs at the state and local level. Best source of information on alternative policies for state and local government. $10.00 a year.

**Winning Rent Control In A Working Class City** by Baltimore Rent Control Campaign. 2319 Maryland Avenue, Baltimore, Maryland 21218 (301) 243-5815.

This is a xerox book containing reprints of pro and con rent control literature used in the successful Baltimore rent control campaign; includes press clippings of the rent control campaign and attorney's request that a T.V. station comply with the "Fairness Doctrine". Highly recommended. 70- pages, $3.00.

# Tenant Unions

## A partial listing of United States tenant groups
*Listed addresses and phone numbers subject to change.

Albany United Tenants
77 Columbia Street
Albany, New York 12210

Ann Arbor Tenants Union
530 South State Street
Ann Arbor, Michigan 48109

Back Bay/Beacon Hill Tenant Union
P.O. Box 86 - Aster Station
Boston, Mass 02123

Baltimore City Tenants Association
2319 Maryland Ave.
Baltimore, MD 21218
(301) 889-7803

Belleville-Joralemon Gardens
Tenants Association
476 Joralemon Street
Apartment G-6
Belleville, New Jersey 07109

Berkeley Tenants Union
2022 Blake Street
Berkeley, CA 94704

Boston Peoples Organization
431 Columbus Avenue
Boston, MA 02118
(617) 267-3759

Burbank Tenants Union
P.O. Box 856
Burbank, CA 91503

California Housing Action and Information Network
2300 Foothill Blvd.
Oakland, California 94601

Cambridge Tenants' Organization
634 Mass. Ave.
Cambridge MA 02139

Cape Cod and Islands Tenants Council
Box 195
Hyannis, Massachusetts 02601
(617) 775-1070

Champaign-Urbana Tenant Union
298 Illini Union
Urbana, Illinois 61801
(217) 333-0112

City Wide Housing Coalition
1470 Irving N.W.
Washington D.C. 20010
(202) 737-3703

Cleveland Tenants Organization
Colonial Arcade, Suite 215
530 Euclid Avenue
Cleveland, Ohio 44114
(216) 621-0540

Coalition for Economic Survival
5520 W. Pico Blvd.
Los Angeles, California 90019
(213) 938-6241

Columbus Tenants Union
5 W. Northwood Ave.
Columbus, Ohio 43201
(614) 294-6834

Community Congress of San Diego
1172 Morena Blvd.
San Diego, California 92110

Cotati Citizens Alliance
8196 El Rancho
Cotati, California 94928

Dayton Tenants Organization
1352 W. Riverview Ave.
Dayton, Ohio
(513) 274-2137

Denver Tenants Organization
1284 Columbine Street Apt. 3
Denver, Colo. 80206
(303) 355-5305

Detroit Tenants Union
3535 Cadillac Power
Detroit, MI 48226

Detroit United Community Housing Coalition
47 E. Adams 2nd floor
Detroit, Michigan 48226

El Monte Citizens For Fair Housing
P.O. Box 5586
El Monte, CA 91734

Evanston Tenants Organization
611 Wesley Avenue
Evanston, Illinois 60202
(312) 453-6955

Indiana Housing Coalition
P.O. Box 44329
Indianapolis, Indiana 46244

Ingram County Tenants Union
631 N. Magnolia
Lansing, Michigan 48912

Knoxville Tenants Organization
1216 Daylily Drive 170
Knoxville, Tenn. 37920

Long Beach Housing Action Association
2625 East 3rd Street
Long Beach, California 90814
(213) 438-4110

Louisville Tenants Union
425 W. Mohammad Ali Blvd.
Louisville, Kentucky 40208
(502) 587-0287

Madison Tenants Union
1045 E. Dayton Street
Madison, Wisconsin 53703
(608) 257-0143

Massachusetts Tenants Organization
150 Lincoln Street
Boston, MA 02111
(212)598-4900

Metropolitan Council on Housing
24 West 30th Street

New York, New York 10001
(212) 725-4800


Miami Beach Tenants Association
924 Lincoln Road
Miami Beach, Florida 33140
(305) 532-1774

Michigan Tenants Rights Coalition
855 Grove
East Lansing, Michigan 48923
(517) 487-6001

Midwest Academy
600 West Fullerton Avenue
Chicago, Illinois 60614
(312) 975-3670

Minneapolis Coalition for Affordable Housing
118 East 26th Street, South
Minneapolis, MN 55404

Minnesota Tenants Union
1513 East Franklin Ave. South
Minnesota, MN 55404
(612) 871-2701

Montclair Tenants Organization
73 Grove Street 3
Montclair, New Jersey 07042

National Association of Neighborhoods
1612 20th Street N.W.
Washington, D.C. 20009
(202) 332-7766

National Tenants Union
c/o Shelterforce
380 Main Street

East Orange, New Jersey 07018
(201) 678-6778

Network
P.O. Box 1346
Santa Barbara, California 93102

New Jersey Tenants Organization
389 Main Street
Hackensack, New Jersey 07601

New Orleans City Wide Housing Coalition
1802 Orleans Street
New Orleans, LA 70116

New York State Tenant and Neighborhood Council
198 Broadway, Room 1100
New York, New York 10038
(212) 964-7200

Oakland Tenants Union
2300 Foothill Blvd.
Oakland, California 94601

Oregon State Tenants
P.O. Box 7224
Salem, Oregon 97301

Park West Village Tenants Association
400 Central Park West
New York, New York 10025

Pasadena Tenants Union
P.O. Box 3586
Pasadena, CA 91103

Peoples Housing Network

198 Broadway
New York, New York 10010

People's Action for Change
206 West 4th Street
Duluth, Minnesota 55806
(218) 722-7720

Philadelphia Tenant Action Group
1411 Walnut Street
Suite 826
Philadelphia, Pennsylvania 19102
(215) 563-5402

Renters Rights Organization
6529 Trigo, No. 8
Isla Vista, California

Rogers Park Tenants Committee
1122 Lunt Ave.
Chicago, Illinois 60626
(313) 937-7888

San Diego Tenants Union
2220 Broadway
San Diego, California 92101
(714) 239-3297

San Francisco Tenants Union
558 Capp Street
San Francisco, California 94110

Santa Barbara Tenants Union
331 N. Milpas, C
Santa Barbara, California 93120
(805) 962-3660

Santa Cruz Housing Action Committee
1004 Ocean Street
Santa Cruz, California 95060

Santa Monicans for Renters Rights
740 Raymond Ave.
Santa Monica, California 90405

Seattle Tenants Union
1133 23rd Ave.
Seattle, Washington
(206) 323-0706

Somerville Tenant's Union
38 Union Square
Somerville, MA 02143
(617) 666-2400

St. Louis Tenants Union
8 North Euclid
St. Louis, Missouri 63156

St. Paul Tenants Union
500 Laurel Avenue
St. Paul, Minnesota 55102

Symphony Tenants Organization
P.O. Box 577
Boston, Mass 02123

Tenants for Fair Housing
c/o Getker
2317 Ashton Street
Columbia, South Carolina 29204

Texas Tenant Union
P.O. Box 221
Forth Worth, Texas 76101

# RENT CONTROL LAW OF SANTA MONICA

Article XVIII is enacted as follows:

## ARTICLE XVIII. RENT CONTROL

**Section 1800. Statement of Purpose.** A growing shortage of housing units resulting in a low vacancy rate and rapidly rising rents exploiting this shortage constitute a serious housing problem affecting the lives of a substantial portion of those Santa Monica residents who reside in residential housing. In addition, speculation in the purchase and sale of existing residential housing units results in further rent increases. These conditions endanger the public health and welfare of Santa Monica tenants, especially the poor, minorities, students, young families, and senior citiznes. The purpose of this Article, therefore, is to alleviate the hardship caused by this serious housing shortage by establishing a Rent Control Board empowered to regulate rentals in the City of Santa Monica so that rents will not be increased unreasonably and so that landlords will receive no more than a fair return on their investment.

In order to accomplish this purpose, this Article provides for an elected rent control board to ensure that rents are at a fair level by requiring landlords to justify any rents in excess of the rents in effect one year prior to the adoption of this Article. Tenants may seek rent reductions from the rent in effect one year prior to the adoption of this Article by establishing that those rents are excessive. In addition to giving tenants an opportunity to contest any rent increase, this Article attempts to provide reasonable protection to tenants by controlling removal of controlled rental units from the housing market and by requiring just cause for any eviction from a controlled rental unit.

**Section 1801. Definitions.** The following words or phrases as used in this Article shall have the following meanings:

(a) BOARD: The term "Board" refers to the elected rent control board established by this Article.

(b) COMMISSIONERS: The members of the Board and Interim Board are denominated Commissioners.

(c) CONTROLLED RENTAL UNITS: All residential rental units in the City of Santa Monica, including mobile home spaces and trailers and trailer spaces, except:

(1) Rental units in hotels, motels, inns, tourist homes and rooming and boarding houses which are rented primarily to transient guests for a period of less than fourteen (14) days.

(2) Rental units in any hospital, convent, monastery, extended medical care facility, asylum, non-profit home for the aged, or dormitory owned and operated by an institution of higher education.

(3) Rental units which a government unit, agency or authority owns, operates, manages or in which governmentally-subsidized tenants reside only if applicable Federal or State low or administrative regulation specifically exempt such units from municipal rent control.

(4) Rental units in owner occupied dwellings with no more than three (3) units.

(5) Rental units and dwellings constructed after the adoption of this Article; this exemption does not apply to units created as a result of conversion as opposed to new construction.

(d) HOUSING SERVICE: Housing services include but are not limited to repairs, maintenance, painting, providing light, hot and cold water, elevator sevice, window shades and screens, storage, kitchen, bath and laundry facilities and privileges, janitor services, refuse removal, furnishings, telephone, parking and any other benefit, privilege or facility connected with the use or occupancy of any rental unit. Services to a rental unit shall include a proportionate part of services provided to common facilities of the building in which the rental unit is contained.

(e) LANDLORD: An owner, lessor, sublessor or any other person entitled to receive rent for the use and occupancy of any rental unit, or an agent, representative or successor of any of the foregoing.

(f) RENT: All periodic payments and all nonmonetary consideration including but not limited to, the fair market value of goods or services rendered to or for the benefit of the landlord under an agreement concerning the use or occupancy of a rental unit and premises, including all payment and consideration demanded or paid for parking, pets, furniture, subletting and security deposits for damages and cleaning.

(g) RENTAL HOUSING AGREEMENT: An agreement, oral,

written or implied, between a landlord and tenant for use or occupancy of a rental unit and for housing services.

(h) RENTAL UNITS: Any building, structure, or part thereof, or land appertenant thereto, or any other rental property rented or offered for rent for living or dwelling house units, and other real properties used for living or dwelling purposes, together with all housing services connected with use or occupancy of such property such as common areas and recreational facilities held out for use by the tenant.

(i) TENANT: A tenant, subtenant, lessee, sublessee or any other person entitled under the terms of a rental housing agreement to the use or occupancy of any rental unit.

(j) RECOGNIZED TENANT ORGANIZATION: Any group of tenants, residing in controlled rental units in the same building or in different buildings operated by the same management company, agent or landlord, who requests to be so designated.

(k) RENT CEILING: Rent ceiling refers to the limit on the maximum allowable rent which a landlord may charge on any controlled rental unit.

(l) BASE RENT CEILING: The maximum allowable rent established in Section 1804 (b).

## Section 1802. Interim Rent Control Board:

No later than thirty (30) days after the adoption of this Article, the City Council of the City of Santa Monica shall appoint a five-member Interim Rent Control Board. No person shall be appointed to the Interim Rent Control Board unless he or she is a duly qualified elector of the City of Santa Monica. The Interim Board shall exercise the following powers and duties until the Permanent Board is elected in accordance with the provisions of Section 1803 (d) and assumes office;

(1) Require registration of all controlled rental units under Section 1803 (q).

(2) Seek criminal penalties under Section 1810.

(3) Seek injunctive relief under Section 1811.

## Section 1803. Permanent Rent Control Board:

(a) COMPOSITION: There shall be in the City of Santa Monica a Rent Control Board. The Board shall consist of five elected Commissioners. The Board shall elect annually as chairperson one of its members to serve in that capacity.

(b) ELIGIBILITY: Duly qualified electors of the City of Santa Monica are eligible to serve as Commissioners of the Board.

(c) FULL DISCLOSURE OF HOLDINGS: Candidates for the position of Commissioner shall submit a verified statement listing all of their interests and dealings in real property, including but not limited to its ownership, sale or management, during the previous three (3) years.

(d) ELECTION OF COMMISSIONERS: Commissioners shall be elected at general municipal elections in the same manner as set forth in Article XIV of the Santa Monica City Charter, except that the first Commissioners shall be elected at a special municipal election held within ninety (90) days of the adoption of this Article. The elected Commissioners shall take office on the first Tuesday following their election.

(e) TERM OF OFFICE: Commissioners shall be elected to serve terms of four years, beginning on the first Tuesday following their election, except that of the first five Commissioners elected in accordance with Section 1803 (d), the two Commissioners receiving the most votes shall serve until April 15, 1985 and the remaining three Commissioners shall serve until April 18, 1983. commissioners shall serve a maximum of two full terms.

(f) POWERS AND DUTIES: The Board shall have the following powers and duties:

(1) Set the rent ceilings for all controlled rental units.

(2) Require registration of all controlled rental units under Section 1803 (q).

(3) Establish a base ceiling on rents under Section 1804 (b).

(4) To make adjustments in the rent ceiling in accordance with Section 1805.

(5) Set rents at fair and equitable levels in order to achieve the intent of this Article.

(6) Hire and pay necessary staff, including hearing examiners and personnel to issue orders, rules and regulations, conduct hearings and charge fees as set forth below.

(7) Make such studies, surveys and investigations, conduct such hearings, and obtain such information as is necessary to carry out its powers and duties.

(8) Report annually to the City Council of the City of Santa Monica on the status of controlled rental housing.

(9) Remove rent controls under Section 1803 (r).

(10) Issue permits for removal of controlled rental units from

rental housing market under Section 1803 (t).

(11) Administer oaths and affirmations and subpoena witnesses.

(12) Establish rules and regulations for deducting penalties and settling civil claims under Section 1809.

(13) Seek criminal penalties under Section 1810.

(14) Seek injunctive relief under Section 1811.

(g) RULES AND REGULATIONS: The Board shall issue and follow such rules and regulations, including those which are contained in this Article, as will further the purposes of the Article. The Board shall publicize its rules and regulations prior to promulgation in at least one newspaper of general circulation in the City of Santa Monica. The Board shall hold at least one (1) public hearing to consider the views of interested parties prior to the adoption of general adjustments of the ceilings for maximum allowable rents under Section 1805 and any decision to decontrol or re-impose control for any class of rental units under Section 1803 (r). All rules and regulations, internal staff memoranda, and written correspondence explaining the decisions, orders, and policies of the Board shall be kept in the Board's office and shall be available to the public for inspection and copying. The Board shall publicize this Article so that all residents of Santa Monica will have the opportunity to become informed about their legal rights and duties under rent control in Santa Monica. The brochure will be available to the public, and each tenant of a controlled rental unit shall receive a copy of the brochure from his or her landlord.

(h) MEETINGS: The Board shall hold at least forty-eight (48) regularly scheduled meetings per year. Special meetings shall be called at the request of at least three Commissioners of the Board. The Board shall hold its initial meeting no later than 15 days after taking office.

(i) QUORUM: Three Commissioners shall constitute a quorum for the Board.

(j) VOTING: The affirmative vote of three Commissioners of the Board is required for a decision, including all motions, regulations, and orders of the Board.

(k) COMPENSATION: Each Commissioner shall receive for every meeting attended seventy-five ($75.00), but in no event shall any Commissioner receive in any twelve month period more than forty-seven hundred and fifty dollars ($4,750) for services rendered.

(l) DOCKETS: The Board shall maintain and keep in its office all hearing dockets

(m) VACANCIES: If a vacancy shall occur on the Board, the Board shall within thirty (30) days appoint a qualified person to fill such a vacancy until the following municipal election when a qualified person shall be elected to serve for the remainder of the term.

(n) FINANCING: The Board shall finance its reasonable and necessary expenses by charging landlords annual registration fees in amounts deemed reasonable by the Board. The first annual registration fee shall be set by the Board within thirty days after assuming office. The Board is also empowered to request and receive funding when and if necessary, from any available source for its reasonable and necessary expenses. Notwithstanding the preceding provisions of this paragraph, the City Council of the City of Santa Monica shall appropriate sufficient funds for the reasonable and necessary expenses of the Interim Board and Board during the six month period following adoption of this Article.

(o) RECALL: Commissioners may be recalled in accordance with the provisions of Article XIV of Santa Monica City Charter.

(p) STAFF: The Board shall employ and pay such staff, including hearing examiners and inspectors, as may be necessary to perform its functions efficiently in order to fulfill the purposes of this Article.

(q) REGISTRATION: Within sixty (60) days after the adoption of the Article, the Board shall require the registration of all appropriate units. The initial registration shall include the rent in effect at the time on the date of the adoption of this Article, base rent ceiling, the address of the rental unit, the name and address of the landlord, the housing services provided to the unit, a statement indicating all operating cost increases since the base rent ceiling date, and any other information deemed relevant by the Board. The Board shall require the landlord to report vacancies in the controlled rental units and shall make a list of vacant controlled rental units available to the public. If the Board, after the landlord has proper notice and after a hearing, determines that a landlord has willfully and knowingly failed to register a controlled rental unit, the Board may authorize the tenant of such a nonregistered controlled rental unit to withhold all or any portion of the rent for the unit until such a time as the rental unit is properly registered. After a rental unit is properly registered, the Board shall determine what portion, if any, of the withheld rent is owed to the landlord for the period in which the rental unit was not properly registered. Whether or not the Board allows such withholding, no landlord who has failed to register properly shall at any time increase rents for a controlled rental unit until such units are properly registered.

(r) DECONTROL: If the average annual vacancy rate in any category, classification, or area of controlled rental units exceeds five (5) percent, the Board is empowered, at its discretion and in order to achieve the objectives of this Article, to remove rent controls from such category, classification or area. The Board may determine such categories, classifications, or areas for purposes of decontrol consistent with the objectives of this Article. In determining the vacancy rate for any category, classification or area of controlled rental units, the Board shall consider all available data and shall conduct its own survey. If units are decontrolled pursuant to this subsection, controls shall be reimposed if the Board finds that the average annual vacancy rate has thereafter fallen below five (5) percent for such category, classification or area.

(s) SECURITY DEPOSITS: Any payment of deposit of money the primary function of which is to secure the performance of a rental agreement or any part of such agreement, including an advance payment of rent, shall be placed in an interest bearing account at an institution whose accounts are insured by the Federal Savings and Loan Insurance Corporation until such time as it is returned to the tenant or entitled to be used by the landlord. The interest on said account shall be used by the landlord to offset operating expenses and shall be a factor in making individual rent adjustments under Section 1805. In lieu of complying with this requirement, the landlord may pay interest directly to the tenant in accordance with the requirements of any state law.

(t) REMOVAL OF CONTROLLED RENTAL UNIT FROM RENTAL HOUSING MARKET: Any landlord who desires to remove a controlled rental unit from the rental housing market by demolition, conversion or other means is required to obtain a permit from the Board prior to such removal from the rental housing market in accordance with rules and regulations promulgated by the Board. In order to approve such a permit, the Board is required to make each of the following findings;

(1) That the controlled rental unit is not occupied by a person or family of very low income, low income or moderate income.

(2) That the rent of the controlled rental unit is not at a level affordable by a person of family of very low income, low income, or moderate income.

(3) That the removal of the controlled rental unit will not adversely affect the supply of housing in the City of Santa Monica.

(4) That the landlord cannot make a fair return on investment by retaining the controlled rental unit.

Notwithstanding the foregoing provisions of this subsection, the Board may approve such a permit:

(1) If the Board finds that the controlled rental unit is uninhabitable and is incapable of being made habitable in an economically feasible manner, or

(2) If the permit is being sought so that the property may be developed with multifamily dwelling units and the permit applicant agrees as a condition of approval that the units will not be exempt from the provisions of the Article pursuant to Section 1801 (c) and that at least fifteen (15) per cent of the controlled rental units to be built on the site will be at rents affordable by persons of low income.

## Section 1804. Maximum Allowable Rents.

(a) TEMPORARY FREEZE: Rents shall not be increased during the one hundred-twenty (120) day period following the date of adoption of this Article.

(b) ESTABLISHMENT OF BASE RENT CEILING: Beginning one-hundred-twenty (120) days after the adoption of this Article, no landlord shall charge rent for any controlled rental units in an amount greater than the rent in effect on the date one year prior to the adoption of this Article. The rent in effect on that date is the base rent ceiling and is a reference point from which fair rents shall be adjusted upward or downward in accordance with Section 1805. If there was no rent in effect on the date one year prior to the adoption of this Article, the base rent ceiling shall be the rent that was charged on the first date that rent was charged following the date one year prior to the adoption of this Article.

(c) POSTING: As soon as the landlord is aware of the maximum allowable rent, the landlord shall post it for each unit in a prominent place in or about the affected controlled rent units. The Board may require that other information it deems relevant also be posted.

## Section 1805. Individual and General Adjustment of Ceilings on Allowable Rents.

(a) The Board may, after holding those public hearings prescribed by Section 1803 (g), set and adjust upward and downward

310

the rent ceiling for all controlled rental units in general and/or for particular categories of controlled rental units deemed appropriate by the Board. Such an adjustment, however, need not take effect immediately, and the Board may decide that new rent ceilings shall not take effect until some reasonable date after the above-stated time periods.

(b) Each year the Board shall generally adjust rents as follows:

(1) Adjust rents upward by granting landlords a utility and tax increase adjustment for actual increases in the City of Santa Monica for taxes and utilities.

(2) Adjust rents upward by granting landlords a maintenance increase adjustment for actual increases in the City of Santa Monica for maintenance expenses.

(3) Adjust rents downward by requiring landlords to decrease rents for any actual decreases in the City of Santa Monica for taxes.

In adjusting rents under this subsection, the Board shall adopt a formula of general application. This formula will be based upon a survey of landlords of the increases or decreases in the expenses set forth in this subsection.

(c) PETITIONS: Upon receipt of a petition by a landlord and/or a tenant, the maximum rent of individual controlled rental units may be adjusted upward or downward in accordance with the procedures set forth elsewhere in this Section. The petition shall be on the form provided by the Board. Notwithstanding any other provision of the Section, the Board or hearing examiner may refuse to hold a hearing and/or grant a rent adjustment if an individual hearing has been held and decision made with regard to maximum rent within the previous six months.

(d) HEARING PROCEDURE: The Board shall enact rules and regulations governing hearings and appeals of individual adjustment of ceilings on allowable rents which shall include the following:

(1) Hearing Examiner: A hearing examiner appointed by the Board shall conduct a hearing to act upon the petition for individual adjustment of ceilings on allowable rents and shall have the power to administer oaths and affirmations.

(2) Notice: The Board shall notify the landlord if the petition was filed by the tenant, or the tenant, if the petition was filed by the landlord, of the receipt of such a petition and a copy thereof.

(3) Time of Hearing: The hearing officer shall notify all parties as to the time, date and place of the hearing.

(4) Records: The hearing examiner may require either party to a rent adjustment hearing to provide it with any books, records and papers deemed pertinent in addition to that information contained in registration statements. The hearing examiner shall conduct a current building inspection and/or request the City to conduct a current building inspection if the hearing examiner finds good cause to believe the Board's current information does not reflect the current condition of the controlled rental unit. The tenant may request the hearing examiner to order such an inspection prior to the date of the hearing. All documents required under this Section shall be made available to the parties involved prior to the hearing at the office of the Board. In cases where information filed in a petition for rent ceiling adjustment or in additional submissions filed at the request of the hearing examiner is inadequate or false, no action shall be taken on said petition until the deficiency is remedied.

(5) OPEN HEARINGS: All rent ceiling adjustment hearings shall be open to the public.

(6) RIGHT OF ASSISTANCE: All parties to a hearing may have assistance in presenting evidence and developing their position from attorneys, legal workers, recognized tenant organization representatives or any other persons designated by said parties.

(7) HEARING RECORDS: The Board shall make available for inspection and copying by any person an official record which shall constitute the exclusive record for decision on the issues at the hearing. The record of the hearing, or any part of one, shall be obtainable for the cost of copying. The record of the hearing shall include: all exhibits, papers and documents required to be filed or accepted into evidence during the proceedings; a list of participants present; a summary of all testimony accepted in the proceedings; a statement of all materials officially noticed; all recommended decisions; orders and/or rulings; all final decisions, orders and/or rulings, and the reasons for each final decision, order and/or ruling. Any party may have the proceeding tape recorded or otherwise transcribed at his or her own expense.

(8) QUANTUM OF PROOF AND NOTICE OF DECISION: No individual adjustment shall be granted unless supported by the preponderance of the evidence submitted at the hearing. All parties to a hearing shall be sent a notice of the decision and a copy of the findings of fact and law upon which said decision is based. At the same time, parties to the proceeding shall also be notified of their right

to any appeal allowed by the Board and/or to judicial review of the decision pursuant to this Section and Section 1808 of this Article.

(9) CONSOLIDATION: All landlord petitions pertaining to tenants in the same building will be consolidated for hearing, and all petitions filed by tenants occupying the same building shall be consolidated for hearing unless there is a showing of good cause not to consolidate such petitions.

(10) APPEAL: Any person aggrieved by the decision of the hearing examiner may appeal to the Board. On appeal, the Board shall affirm, reverse or modify the decision of the hearing examiner. The Board may conduct a de novo hearing or may act on the basis of the record before the hearing examiner without holding a hearing.

(11) FINALITY OF DECISION: The decision of the hearing examiner shall be the final decision of the Board in the event of no appeal to the Board. The decision of the hearing examiner shall not be stayed pending appeal; however, in the event that the Board on appeal reverses or modifies the decision of the hearing examiner, the landlord, in the case of a upward adjustment in rent, or the tenant, in the case of a downward adjustment of rent, shall be ordered to make retroactive payments to restore the parties to the position they would have occupied had the hearing examiner's decision been the same as that of the Board's.

(12) TIME FOR DECISION: The rules and regulations adopted by the Board shall provide for final board action on any individual rent adjustment petition within one-hundred and twenty (120) days following the date of filing of the individual rent adjustment petition.

(13) BOARD ACTION IN LIEU OF REFERENCE TO HEARING EXAMINER: The Board, on its own motion or on the request of any landlord or tenant, may hold a hearing on an individual petition for rent adjustment without the petition first being heard by a hearing examiner.

(e) In making individual and general adjustments of the rent ceiling, the Board shall consider the purposes of this Article and shall specifically consider all relevant factors including but not limited to increases or decreases in property taxes, unavoidable increases or decreases in operating and maintenance expenses, capital improvement of the controlled rental unit as distinguished from normal repair, replacement and maintenance, increases or decreases in living space, furniture, furnishings or equipment, substantial deterioration of the controlled rental unit other than as a result of ordinary wear and tear, failure on the part of the landlord to provide adequate housing services or to comply substantially with applicable housing, health and safety codes, federal and state income tax benefits, the speculative nature of the investment, whether or not the property was acquired or is held as a long term of short term investment, and the landlords rate of return on investment. It is the intent of this Article that upward adjustments in rent be made only when demonstrated necessary to the landlord making a fair return on investment.

(f) No rent increase shall be authorized by this Article because a landlord has a negative cash flow as the result of refinancing the controlled rental unit if at the time the landlord refinanced, the landlord could reasonably have foreseen a negative cash flow based on the rent schedule then in existence within the one year period following refinancing. This paragraph shall only apply to that portion of the negative cash flow reasonably forseeable within the one year period following refinancing of the controlled rental unit and shall only apply to controlled rental units refinanced after the date of adoption of this Article.

(g) No rent increase shall be authorized by this Article because a landlord has a negative cash flow if at the time the landlord acquired the controlled rental unit, the landlord could reasonably have foreseen a negative cash flow based on the rent schedule then in existence within one year period following acquisition. This paragraph shall only apply to that portion of the negative cash flow reasonably foreseeable within the one year period following acquisition of a controlled rental unit and shall only apply to controlled rental units acquired after the date of adoption of this Article.

(h) No landlord shall increase rent under this Section if the landlord:

(1) Has failed to comply with any provision of this Article and/or regulations issued thereunder by the Board, or

(2) Has failed to comply substantially with any applicable state or local housing, health or safety law.

## Section 1806. Eviction:

No landlord shall bring any action to recover possession or be granted recovery of possession of a controlled rental unit unless:

(a) The tenant has failed to pay the rent to which the landlord is entitled under the rental housing agreement and this Article.

(b) The tenant has violated an obligation or covenant of his or her tenancy other than the obligation to surrender possession upon proper notice and has failed to cure such violation after having received written notice therof from the landlord in the manner required by law.

(c) The tenant is committing or expressly permitting a nuisance in, or is causing substantial damage to, the controlled rental unit, or is creating a substantial interference with the comfort, safety, or enjoyment of the landlord or other occupants or neighbors of the same.

(d) The tenant is convicted of using or expressly permitting a controlled rental unit to be used for any illegal purpose.

(e) The tenant, who had a rental housing agreement which has terminated, has refused, after written request or demand by the landlord, to execute a written extension or renewal thereof for a further term of like duration and in such terms as are not inconsistent with or violative of any provisions of this Article and are materially the same as in the previous agreement.

(f) The tenant has refused the landlord reasonable access to the controlled rental unit for the purpose of making necessary repairs improvements required by the laws of the United States, the State of California or any subdivision thereof, or for the purpose of showing the rental housing unit to any prospective purchaser or mortgager.

(g) The tenant holding at the end of the term of the rental housing agreement is a sub-tenant not approved by the landlord.

(h) The landlord seeks to recover possession in good faith for use and occupancy of herself or himself, or her or his children, parents, brother, sister, father-in-law, mother-in-law, son-in-law, or daughter-in-law.

(i) The landlord seeks to recover possession to demolish or otherwise remove the controlled rental unit from rental residential housing use after having obtained all proper permits from the City of Santa Monica.

Notwithstanding the above provisions, possessions shall not be granted if it is determined that the eviction is in retaliation for the tenant reporting violations of this Article, for exercising rights granted under this Article, including the right to withhold rent upon authorization of the Board under Section 1803 (q) or Section 1809 or for organizing other tenants. In any action brought to recover possession of a controlled rental unit, the landlord shall allege and prove compliance with this Section.

**Section 1807:** Non-waiverability: Any provision, whether oral or written in or pertaining to a rental housing agreement whereby any provision of this Article for the benefit of the tenant is waived, shall be deemed to be against public policy and shall be void.

**Section 1808. Judicial Review:** A landlord or tenant aggrieved by any action or decision of the Board may seek judicial review by appealing to the appropriate court within the jurisdiction.

**Section 1809. Civil Remedies:**

(a) Any landlord who demands, accepts, recieves, or retains any payment of rent in excess of the maximum lawful rent, in violation of the provisions of this Article or any rule, regulation or order hereunder promulgated, shall be liable as hereinafter provided to the tenant from whom such payments are demanded, accepted, received or retained, for reasonable attorney's fees and costs as determined by the court, plus damages in an amount of five hundred dollars ($500) or three (3) times the amount by which the payment or payments demanded, accepted, received or retained exceeds the maximum lawful rent, whichever is the greater.

(b) In lieu of filing a civil action as provided for in Section 1809 (a), the Board shall establish by rule and regulation a hearing procedure similar to that set forth in Section 1805 (d) for determination of the amount of the penalty the tenant is entitled to pursuant to Section 1809 (a). After said determination, the tenant may deduct the penalty from future rent payments in the manner provided by the Board.

(c) If the tenant from whom such excessive payment is demanded, accepted, received or retained in violation of the foregoing provisions of this Article or any rule or regulation or order hereunder promulgated fails to bring a civil or administrative action as provided for in Section 1809 (a) and 1809 (b) within one-hundred and twenty (120) days from the date of occurrence of the violation, the Board may settle the claim arising out of the violation or bring such action. Thereafter, the tenant on whose behalf the Board acted is barred from also bringing an action against the landlord in regard to the same violation for which the Board has made a settlement or brought an action. In the event the Board settles said claim, it shall be entitled to retain the costs it incurred in settlement thereof, and the tenant against whom the violation has been committed shall be entitled to the remainder.

316

(d) The appropriate court in the jurisdiction in which the controlled rental unit affected is located shall have jurisdiction over all actions brought under this Section.

**Section 1810. CRIMINAL REMEDIES.** Any landlord violating this Article shall be guilty of a misdemeanor. Any landlord convicted of a misdemeanor under the provisions of this Article shall be punished by a fine of not more than five hundred dollars ($500) or by imprisonment in the county jail for a period not exceeding six months, or by both such fine and imprisonment.

**Section 1811. INJUNCTIVE RELIEF.** The Board, and tenants and landlords of controlled units, may seek relief from the appropriate court within the jurisdiction within which the affected controlled rental unit is located to restrain or enjoin any violation of this Article and of the rules, regulations, orders and decisions of the Board.

**Section 1812. PARTIAL INVALIDITY.** If any provision of this Article or application thereof to any person or circumstances is held invalid, this invalidity shall not affect other provisions or applications of this Article which can be given effect without the invalid provision of application, and to this end the provisions of this Article are declared to be severable. This Article shall be liberally construed to achieve the purposes of this Article and to preserve its validity.

# About the Editor

John Gilderbloom
Sociology Department, University of California, Santa Barbara, CA
93106

Mr. Gilderbloom teaches Sociology at the University of California, Santa Barbara; he expects to get his Ph.D. in Sociology there in 1982. He is currently an Associate Fellow at the Foundation for National Progress in San Francisco. He is also Chair of the California Housing and Action Information Network Committee on Affordable Housing. He was formerly a staff person with the California Department of Housing and Community Development where he authored a major study on rent control. Mr. Gilderbloom has published a number of articles on rent control and the housing crisis. He now works as a consultant on rent control to numerous government and community groups.

# Notes